Computer Science Workbench

Editor: Tosiyasu L. Kunii

Nadia Magnenat-Thalmann
Daniel Thalmann

Computer Animation

Theory and Practice

With 156 Figures
54 of them in Color

Springer-Verlag
Tokyo Berlin Heidelberg New York

Prof. Dr. Nadia Magnenat-Thalmann
Hautes Etudes Commerciales
Université de Montréal
Montréal H3C 3J7 Canada

Prof. Dr. Daniel Thalmann
Département d'Informatique
et de Recherche Opérationnelle
Université de Montréal
Montréal H3C 3J7 Canada

ISBN 4-431-70005-6 Springer-Verlag Tokyo Berlin Heidelberg New York
ISBN 3-540-70005-6 Springer-Verlag Berlin Heidelberg New York Tokyo
ISBN 0-387-70005-6 Springer-Verlag New York Heidelberg Berlin Tokyo

Library of Congress Cataloging in Publication Data
Magnenat-Thalmann, Nadia, 1946–
Computer animation.
(Computer science workbench)
Bibliography: p.
1. Computer animation. I. Thalmann, Daniel.
II. Title. III. Series.
TR897.5.M33 1985   778.5′347′02854   85-9755
ISBN 0-387-70005-6 (U.S.)

© Springer-Verlag Tokyo 1985

Printed in Japan

Typesetting: Asco Trade Typesetting Ltd., Hong Kong
Printing and Binding: Sanshodo Printing, Tokyo

Series Preface

Computer Science Workbench is a monograph series which will provide you with an in-depth working knowledge of current developments in computer technology. Every volume in this series will deal with a topic of importance in computer science and elaborate on how you yourself can build systems related to the main theme. You will be able to develop a variety of systems, including computer software tools, computer graphics, computer animation, database management systems, and computer-aided design and manufacturing systems. Computer Science Workbench represents an important new contribution in the field of practical computer technology.

Tosiyasu L. Kunii

Preface

Computer Animation: Theory and Practice is the first book to attempt to present all aspects of computer animation. As various subjects are treated in this book, it is intended to be an introduction for designers and animators, a reference book for professionals in computer graphics as well as a manual for university teachers in computer graphics and computer animation. As stated in the title, both theoretical and practical aspects are presented in detail. Computer animation is treated using concepts familiar to those working in traditional animation. These people will read about techniques involved in computer-assisted animation such as keyframe interpolation and coloring and painting techniques. The reader will also find a great deal of information concerning the state-of-the-art in computer animation and complete history of animation systems and languages. The book also includes a complete list of computer-generated films from 1961 to 1984.

Emphasis is also placed on three-dimensional computer animation. This is generally viewed as having four major steps: object modeling, object motion, virtual camera motion and image rendering. Image synthesis will be the subject of a future book entitled *Image Synthesis: Theory and Practice*, two chapters of the present book are also devoted to this essential topic for computer animation. Basic algorithms are described for hidden-surface removal, light reflection, shading, texture, transparency and shadows. The latest techniques are also presented including ray tracing, fractals and particle systems. As object and camera motions are important steps in three-dimensional computer animation, this book explains the different approaches to the design of these motions with many examples. Several languages and systems are presented including the extensible director-oriented system MIRANIM. Practical examples and case studies are described. A complete case study, the design of the computer-generated film *Dream Flight* is explained from story-board to image production. There is also a chapter dedicated to human modeling and animation.

Finally, this book provides not only extensive information on techniques and tools, but also includes a large collection of the most impressive computer-generated images.

N. Magnenat-Thalmann
D. Thalmann

Acknowledgements

The authors are very grateful to Professor Tosiyasu L. Kunii who strongly encouraged the publication of this book. They would also like to thank all the individuals and organizations who provided illustrative material and/or comments and suggestions:

Norman Badler, University of Pennsylvania
Loren Carpenter, Lucasfilm Ltd.
Edwin Catmull, Lucasfilm Ltd.
Robert Cook, Lucasfilm Ltd.
Franklin Crow, Ohio State University
Charles Csuri, Cranston-Csuri Productions
Tom DeFanti, University of Illinois
William Fetter, SIROCO, Bellevue, Washington
Alain Fournier, University of Toronto
Copper Giloth, Real Time Design Inc.
Donald Greenberg, Cornell University
Pat Hanrahan, New York Institute of Technology
Don Herbison Evans, University of Sidney
Pat Lehman, Community College of Denver
Nelson Max, Lawrence Livermore Laboratory
Xavier Nicolas, Sogitec Audiovisuel, France
Alan Norton, IBM
Frederic I. Parke, New York Institute of Technology
J.C. Pennie, Omnibus Computer Graphics Inc., Toronto
C. Sleichter, Computer Image Corp.
Jane Veeder, Real Time Design Inc.
Marceli Wein, National Research Council of Canada
Mayumi Yoshinari, NHK Tokyo
David Zeltzer, Ohio State University
Association for Computing Machinery
IEEE Computer Society

The authors are also indebted to the students and research assistants who have produced images with the MIRA system: Philippe Bergeron, Nicolas Chourot, Mario Fortin, Marc Feeley, François Gagnon, Serge Lafrance, Louis Langlois,

François Marceau, Daniel Ouimet and Christian Roy. They also would like to thank Ann Laporte who revised the English text.

The authors express their gratitude to the "Service de la Recherche des Hautes Etudes Commerciales de Montréal," which partly sponsored the production of the illustrations.

Finally, the authors are very thankful to Evelyn Kohl of the University of Geneva (Switzerland), who has produced the manuscript of this book.

Table of Contents

1. Introduction

If there is one area where the advent of the computer is hotly contended, it is art. How can that symbol of logic and reason, the computer, play a role in artistic creation, where freedom and intuition hold sway? There is, of course, a natural self-defense mechanism operating here: Stage actors for years disdained the cinema while many a film actor is still reluctant to appear on television. A new medium, a new mode of expression, evokes skepticism—even outright rejection.

Nevertheless, no sooner was the computer born—about thirty years ago— than some "artists," such as Ken Knowlton of Bell Laboratories, began using these machines to create drawings and even animate them. Computer art competitions such as the Annual Art Contest in the United States have been organized, although they have yet to win recognition from the artistic community.

Today computers are widely used in painting, sculpture, architecture and music. One yardstick for evaluating the success of this new medium in the art world is the extent to which "works" produced by computer are accepted for exhibitions, contests and other traditional public showings. Computer paintings have yet to be hung in major museums, and computer-composed symphonies are still not included in the world's great music festivals. But there is one area of art where the computer is beginning to make a breakthrough: the animated film. As early as 1974, the Hungarian Peter Foldes won the *Prix du Jury* at the Cannes Film Festival with his computer-aided film, *La Faim*.

This film is based primarily on the so-called "interpolation" technique which involves supplying the computer (a National Research Council of Canada machine) with two drawings and commanding it to compose as many intermediate images as required. This is a boon to animated-film makers, since the essence of animation lies in producing a rapid series of drawings, each slightly different from its predecessor, to create the impression of movement or change in shape. If the computer is given two images, a man and a bird, for example, it will produce all the intermediate drawings that will show the gradual metamorphosis of man to bird.

The computer is also finding increasing use in the enormous task of filling in colors. This, of course, plays a very important role in animation, as filling in each drawing with paint is both time-consuming and tedious by hand. Computers now exist which allow the artist to select the color, specify the areas he wants filled in, and have the machine do the work.

Animation modeled by computer is particularly fascinating, for here the machine plays a fundamental role in the creation of a three-dimensional world. Furthermore, with computers it becomes possible to produce all the tens of thousands of drawings needed for an animated film.

Current experiments in computer-aided three-dimensional animation are to be found mainly in North America and Japan. In the United States, about 15 minutes of Walt Disney's science-fiction film *TRON* were computer-animated by the U.S. companies Information International and MAGI-Synthavision, while the titles and opening scenes were also done by computer by two other U.S. corporations, Digital Effects and Robert Abel. Another film containing scenes produced by computer is *Return of Jedi*, in which the special effects were by Lucasfilm.

As for Canadian experiments in computer animation, a film entitled *Dream Flight* was recently made in Montreal using the graphic language MIRA developed by the authors. That film won first prize at the Computer Film Festival in London in November 1982, despite stiff U.S. competition. Even more significantly, perhaps, this was the only computer-aided film among the 80 selected from a total of 440 films at that bastion of tradition, the 1983 Annecy Festival.

This book is the first to attempt to present all aspects of computer animation. It offers the basic principles of conventional animation, then discusses the role of the computer. It briefly describes the development of the medium in various organizations, from the early systems at Bell Labs to the production of *TRON* and *Star Trek II*. Computer-assisted animation is presented and key-frame and paint systems are emphasized. The steps in modeled animation are then introduced. The best techniques in image rendering are described in detail: hidden surfaces, light reflection, shading, ray tracing, transparency, texture, shadows, fractals, particle systems, anti-aliasing and motion blur. Human modeling and animation is then discussed. The impact of new concepts in programming languages is also treated and the role of actor systems is emphasized. Various case studies made jointly at the Business School and the Computer Science Department of the University of Montreal are shown and the way that *Dream Flight* was produced is explained in detail. Appendices provide exhaustive information about computer animation organizations, computer animation systems and computer-generated films.

2. Conventional Animation

2.1 Basic Principles of Conventional Animation

Animation can be defined in different ways. For John Halas [1968], one of the world's most famous animators, "movement is the essence of animation." A similar approach defines animation as "art in movement." Some more precise definitions are given below:

1. Animation is a technique in which the illusion of movement is created by photographing a series of individual drawings on successive frames of film. The illusion is produced by projecting the film at a certain rate (typically 24 frames/second).

2. Animation refers to the process of dynamically generating a series of frames of a set of objects, in which each frame is an alteration of the previous frame.

Although these definitions describe the principle of animation as it was conceived 75 years ago, they are still valid today in many cases. Conventional animation is generally based on a frame-by-frame technique. Computer animation is often carried out using a similar strategy. However, in the case of real-time animation, the definitions (especially the first one) are inaccurate. For example, video games are quite different from the products of conventional animation. Moreover, it is quite limitative to state that animation is similar to movement, because animation can exist without movement, for example:

- in metamorphosis, where one object is transformed into another
- in color changes (e.g., the hero turns red with emotion)
- in changes of light intensity (e.g., the sun disappears behind the mountains).

Conventional animation is oriented mainly towards the production of two-dimensional cartoons. Every frame is a flat picture and is purely hand-drawn. These cartoons are complex to produce and may involve large teams like Walt Disney or Hannah-Barbera productions.

2.2 How Are Cartoon Animated Films Made?

Cartoon animated films are produced in studios, which differ in their production methodologies. However, a brief description of the major common steps can be given:

1. **The story**
   As in an ordinary film, the animated film generally tells a story. To describe this story, three "documents" are required, each refining of the previous one:
   – **The synopsis** is a summary of the story in a few lines (one page maximum).
   – **The scenario** is a detailed text that describes the complete story without any cinematographic references.
   – **The storyboard** is a film in outline form. It consists of a number of illustrations arranged in comic-strip fashion with appropriate captions. The number of individual illustrations within a storyboard will vary widely. What is important is that they represent the film's key moments. It is also important to note that a film is composed of **sequences** that define specific actions. Each sequence consists of a series of **scenes** that are generally defined by a certain location and set of characters. Scenes are divided into **shots** that are considered as picture units. Fig. 2.1 shows the organization of a film.

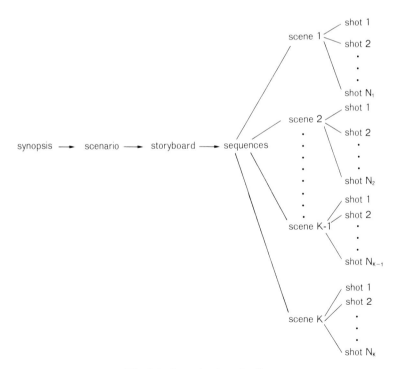

Fig. 2.1. Organization of a film

2. **Layout**

   This step consists mainly of the design of the characters to be animated and action plotting. Based on the storyboard, the relationship between shapes and forms in the background and foreground is decided.

   The layout department in an animation studio has to finish drawings of the settings and sketch background layouts. The artists must have knowledge of the physical characteristics of the camera that will be used to photograph the frames.

3. **Sound track**

   In conventional animation, sound track recording has to precede the animation process, since the motion must match the dialog and/or music.

4. **Animation**

   The animation process is carried out by animators who draw key frames. Often an animator is responsible for one specific character.

5. **In-betweening**

   "In-betweens" are defined as drawings which are placed between two key positions, or frames. Assistant animators draw some in-betweens and in-betweeners draw the remaining figures. The work of the assistant animators requires more artistry than that of in-betweeners, whose task is almost automatic.

6. **Xeroxing and inking**

   Sketches are usually drawn in pencil. They then have to be transferred to acetate cels, using modified Xerox cameras. Lines must be inked in by hand.

7. **Painting**

   As cartoon animated films are usually in color, they must go through a painting stage. This work requires patience and accuracy. Cels must have the right degree of opacity and static backgrounds also have to be painted.

8. **Checking**

   Animators need to check the action in their scenes before shooting.

9. **Cameras**

   The final photography of composite animation is usually done on color films or videotapes.

10. **Editing**

    This last step is considered part of the postproduction stage.

2.3 Multiplane and Shooting Phase

The shooting phase in film production is not a trivial operation. Movements can be simulated at this stage by moving certain cels in relation to others. To facilite this process, producers use complex machines called **multiplanes**. As shown in Fig. 2.2, a multiplane is a machine 3.50 meters high, with a camera at the top. The animation board has a plate glass base. A number of glass layers are placed beneath the camera lens at varying distances. Note that during simulated camera motion, the motion speed of the different decors must be inversely proportional to the distance between the decor and the camera.

Multiplanes allow the operator to produce special effects which we will define in the next section.

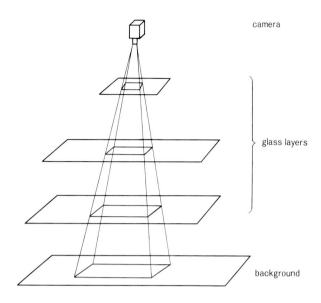

Fig. 2.2. Multiplane

2.4 Some Techniques and Special Camera Effects

Special camera effects are used in conventional animation, but they can be difficult to produce and sometimes very expensive. As they can be easily simulated using a computer, the most important techniques will be defined here.

Pan	A pan (contraction of panorama) is an effect in which the camera is moved horizontally from one point to another.
Tilt	A tilt is an effect in which the camera is moved vertically from one point to another.
Zoom	A zoom is an effect which makes a subject appear larger or smaller. In a two-dimensional cartoon, the effect can be obtained by moving the camera closer to or further away from the subject. This technique of moving the camera is quite impossible in three dimensions, because of the perspective effect; however, excellent zoom lenses can be used in the camera to get the three dimensional effect. A zoom can be continuous.
Spin	A spin is an effect produced by rotating the camera.
Fade-in	A fade-in is an effect used at the beginning of a scene: The scene gradually appears from black.
Fade-out	A fade-out is an effect used at the end of a scene: The scene gradually darkens to black.

Cross-dissolve   A cross-dissolve is an effect that is very often used for the transition between scenes. It corresponds to a fade-out of one scene and a fade-in of the next scene over the same length of film.

Wipe   With the wipe effect, one scene appears to slide over the preceding scene. Fig. 2.3 shows different possible forms for the dividing lines between the scenes.

For other special effects like superimpositions or multiple-image effects, an **optical printer** is essential to conventional animation. This is a movie camera which is focussed on the gate of a lensless movie projector to duplicate one piece of film onto another. Fig. 2.4 shows the principle of a simple optical printer.

Optical printers can be used:

- to make positive and negative prints
- to convert from one format to another (16 mm, 35 mm)
- to modifiy the speed of an action
- to improve the quality of a film
- to reprint several cycles of a repeated motion
- to superimpose titles and logos
- to provide fade and wipe effects.

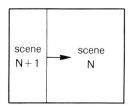 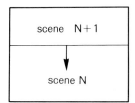 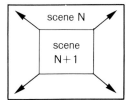

Fig. 2.3. Wipes

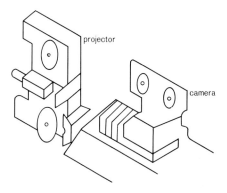

Fig. 2.4. Principle of a simple optical printer

SCENE	TITLE	ANIMATOR	FOOTAGE	SEQUENCE

ACTION	DIAL						DIAL	CAMERA INSTRUCTIONS
	1						1	
	2						2	
	3						3	
	4						4	
	5						5	
	6						6	
	7						7	
	8						8	
	9						9	
	0						0	
	1						1	
	2						2	
	3						3	
	4						4	
	5						5	
	6						6	
	7						7	
	8						8	
	9						9	
	0						0	
	1						1	
	2						2	
	3						3	
	4						4	
	5						5	
	6						6	
	7						7	
	8						8	
	9						9	
	0						0	
	1						1	
	2						2	
	3						3	
	4						4	
	5						5	
	6						6	
	7						7	
	8						8	
	9						9	
	0						0	
	1						1	
	2						2	
	3						3	
	4						4	
	5						5	
	6						6	
	7						7	
	8						8	
	9						9	
	0						0	
	1						1	
	2						2	
	3						3	
	4						4	
	5						5	
	6						6	
	7						7	
	8						8	
	9						9	
	0						0	

Fig. 2.5. An exposure sheet

2.5 Bar, Route, Model and Exposure Sheets

A great volume of paper flows through an animation studio. In addition to storyboards, already discussed, four main kinds of information sheets are used:

1. **Bar sheets** carry a visual synopsis of the animation sequence; they serve as a guide in every phase of production because they indicate the number of frames allotted per action and the timing of the dialog, mouth actions and music.
2. **Route sheets** list the length, the location, the person responsible and various other statistics of every scene.
3. **Model sheets** show the original characters drawn in a number of representative poses.
4. **Exposure sheets** are the most detailed documents concerning a film. Each frame has a line on the exposure sheet. Camera movements, zooms, and the number of exposures are written here for each frame. An essential tool for the animator and for the cameraman, an exposure sheet is shown in Fig. 2.5.

2.6 Postproduction

Under this term we include all the actions required to transform the shot film into a final product. This includes **processing** and **editing**.

Film processing involves a series of laboratory operations in which the images exposed on film are developed with chemical solutions. Films are made in cellulose acetate and as shown in Fig. 2.6, the standard format is 35 mm, although other formats are available. Table 2.1 lists those currently on the market.

Because production failures can complicate the editing phase, postproduction can imply reshooting. But editing usually consists mainly of assembling, sorting and splicing the film. Sound synchronization also comes into play in postproduction. Fig. 2.7 shows a simple flowchart of the processing of a 16-mm sound film.

Generally, odd-numbered scenes are cut together to form what is called the A roll and even-numbered scenes are similarly spliced into another the B roll. This strategy makes it easier to add superimposition and fade effects during the postproduction phase. Fig. 2.8 shows the A and B rolls.

Table 2.1. Main film formats

Formats	Image size (height $\times$ width)	
70 mm	$1 \times 2, 1 \times 2.33$	
35 mm	$1 \times 2, 1 \times 1.85$	
17.5 mm	9.5×14.5	
16 mm	7.4×10.4	(without sound)
	7.16×9.6	(with sound)
9.5 mm	6.5×8.5	
super-8	5.36×4.01	
8 mm	3.7×5.2	

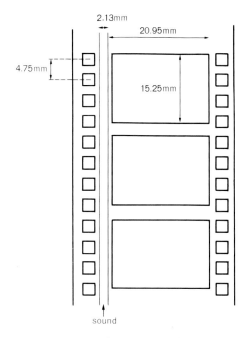

Fig. 2.6. 35 mm format

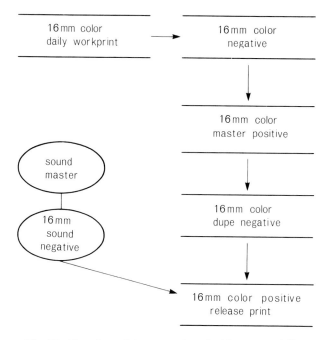

Fig. 2.7. Flowchart of the processing of a 16 mm sound film

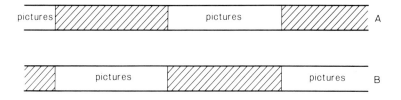

Fig. 2.8. A and B rolls

2.7 Historical Background

Picture animation was invented in 1831 by a Frenchman named Joseph Antoine Plateau. He created the illusion of movement with a machine called a phenakistoscope, a device that consisted of a spinning disc that held a series of drawings and windows that framed the viewer's perception of the drawings.

Then, in 1834, the Englishman Horner extended the phenakistoscope idea and invented the zoetrope. A revolving drum with regularly spaced slits in its sides, the zoetrope held the drawings on its inner walls. When the drum revolved, the viewer could see the drawings through the slits. The zoetrope was refined by the Frenchman Emile Reynaud who developed the praxinoscope. The slits were replaced by mirrors that spun in the center of the drum.

In 1892, Reynaud created the first movie theater in Paris, the Theater Optique. The first animated film, however, was produced in 1906 by the American J. Steward Blackton. It was called *Humorous Phases of a Funny Face*. In 1908, the Frenchman Emile Cohl made black drawings on white paper and took pictures of them. He used the negative on the screen, thus producing the animation of white figures on a black background. One of his most important animated films was *Drame chez les Fantoches*. In 1909, the American Winsor McCay produced *Gertie the Trained Dinosaur*, which can be considered the first cartoon. Although the movie was short, McCay used about 10,000 drawings. During the years 1913–1917, various American cartoon series were produced, the most well-known of them *Felix the Cat*, by Pat Sullivan.

In 1915, the American Earl Hurd introduced the technique of **cel animation**, which took its name from the transparent sheets of celluloid that it used. But, of course, the father of commercial animation is certainly Walt Disney. In the ten years 1928–1938 he produced Mickey Mouse, Donald Duck and the Silly Symphony Series. His first Mickey Mouse short, in 1928, was the first film with fully synchronized sound. Then came the full-length commercial animated cartoon, *Snow White and the Seven Dwarfs*. Meanwhile, other pioneers were developing animated films in different countries; for example, Atamanov, Pashchenko and Ivanov in Russia, Trnka in Czechoslovakia and Bartosch in France. Two very well-known pioneers should be especially mentioned: John Halas in Britain and Norman McLaren in Canada.

2.8 Applications of Animation

There are several areas where animation can be extensively used. These areas can be arbitrarily divided into five categories:

1. **Television**

   A powerful motivator for the rapid development of animation, TV has used it for titles, logos and inserts. But its main uses are in cartoons for children and commercials for a general audience (Fig. 2.9).

2. **Cinema**

   Animation, as a cinematic technique, has always held an important role in this industry. Complete animation films are still produced by the cinema industry. But it is also a good way of making special effects, and is frequently used for titles and generics.

3. **Government**

   Animation is an excellent method of mass communication and governments are, of course, great consumer of such techniques for publicity.

4. **Education and research**

   Animation can be used extensively for educational purposes. Fundamental concepts are easily explained to students using visual effects involving motion. Finally, animation can be a great help to research teams, because it can simulate situations (e.g., in medicine).

5. **Industry**

   The role of animation in industry is very similar to its role in government. Animation is useful for marketing, personnel education and public relations.

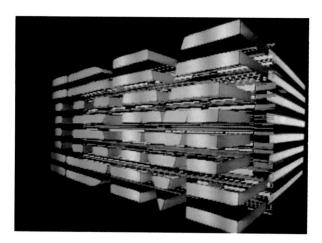

Fig. 2.9. "Journey" by Publicity, IBM Canada. This 10 seconds sequence produced by Computer Image Productions, Inc., Denver, CO USA for IBM Canada involves an intimate journey through the intricate facets of a chip (Producers: Paul Sutherland, Robert Hopp. Agency: Robert Hopp and Associates, Toronto, Canada. Production House: Computer Image Productions, Inc. Director: James Sibley. Animators: Vivian Zezula-Aragon, Brad Jorgensen, Rob Bekuhrs. Tech. Staff: David Cline, Steve Cosgrove, Mike Snyder. Art Director: John Wood, Cliff Erickson. Computers: CAESAR, SCANIMATE, SYSTEM IV)

3. Computer Animation

3.1 The Role of the Computer in Animation

Although computer plays an ever-increasing role in animation, the term "computer animation" is imprecise and can sometimes be misleading. This is because the computer can play a variety of differents roles:

1. **in the creation of drawings**
   i)   key drawings can be digitized
   ii) key drawings can be created with an interactive graphics editor
   iii) complex objects can be produced by programming.
2. **in the creation of motion**
   Inbetweens can be completely calculated or complex motions can be directly generated by the computer.
3. **in coloring**
   Drawings can be painted using an interactive computer system or complex and realistic images can be generated.
4. **in shooting**
   A physical camera can be controlled by computer, or virtual cameras can be completely programmed.
5. **at the postproduction stage**
   Editing and synchronization can be controlled by computer.

3.2 How to Classify Computer Animation Systems?

There are a number of different ways of classifying computer animation systems. First, we can define various levels of systems:

Level 1: used only to interactively create, paint, store, retrieve and modigy drawings. These do not take time into account. They are basically just graphics editors used only by designers.

Level 2: can compute in-betweens and move an object along a trajectory. These systems generally take time into account and are mainly intended to be used by or even replace in-betweeners.

Table 3.1. Functions of computer animation systems

	Computer-assisted animation	Modelled animation
Object creation	– character digitizing – use of a graphics editor	– 3D reconstruction programs – 3D graphics editor – 3D object modelling programs
Motion	– in-between calculation – movement along a path	– 3D motion programming – actor systems
Coloring	– painting systems	– 3D shading systems
Camera	– physical camera control	– virtual cameras
Postproduction	– editing systems – computer-assisted synchronization	– in theory, modelled systems could eliminate the postproduction phase by updating films automatically

Level 3: provide the animator with operations which can be applied to objects: for example, translation or rotation. These systems may also include virtual camera operations like zoom, pan or tilt.

Level 4: provide a means of defining actors; i.e., objects which possess their own animation. The motion of these objects may also be constrained.

Level 5: are extensible and can learn as they work. With each use, such a system becomes more powerful and "intelligent."

Another popular and simpler way of classifying computer animation systems is to distinguish between **computer-assisted** and **modeled** animation.

Computer-assisted animation, sometimes called key-frame animation, consists mainly of assisting conventional animation by computer. Key-frame animation systems are typically of level 2.

Modelled animation means the drawing and manipulation of more general representations which move about in three-dimensional space. This process is very complex without a computer. Modelled animation systems are generally of level 3 or 4. Systems of level 5 are not yet available.

The computer's role in animation is summarized in Table 3.1, which compares the functions of computer-assisted animation systems with those of modelled animation systems.

3.3 Real-time vs. Frame-by-frame

In the preceding sections, we have classified animation systems on the basis of their role in the animation process. Another consideration is the mode of production. Is computer animation just a special case of animation defined as a succession of images, each differing from the one preceding it? In other words, is the computer used to produce each frame individually to be photographed? Or is the "film" produced directly on a terminal? This is a question of time.

To see this, the computer-generated sequences of the film *TRON* can be compared with a video game like PACMAN. Both can be considered computer animation. But in *TRON*, the images are very complex and realistic. This means that several minutes are required to produce one frame. These frames must be recorded (photographed), and then projected at a rate of 24 frames/second. In a video game, on the other hand, animation is immediate; the objects move rapidly and there is complete interaction between the user and his images. This is "real-time" animation, because the moment at which the user makes a decision becomes the moment of materialization. Real-time animation does not require films to be recorded, because the results can be seen directly at a terminal.

Real-time computer animation is limited by the capabilities of the computer. A real-time image must be displayed in less than $\frac{1}{15}$ second, because the illusion of continuous movement breaks down at slower speeds. This is a severe limitation, because only relatively simple calculations can be made in this time. The constraints are imposed by the computer's cycle speed, storage capabilities, word length and instruction set.

One sign of expanding possibilities for real-time computer animation is the development of special hardware like array processors and graphics processors. In the meantime, the following statements can be made:

1. Real-time animation is generally not possible on a multi-user system. PACMAN, for example, can run on an APPLE but not on a main-frame system with one hundred users.
2. Real-time animation has been possible in the past only with vector refresh displays. With raster systems, the rescan of millions of pixels takes too much time.
3. Real-time, three-dimensional shaded animation with transparency and shadows is for tomorrow, not for today.
4. Real-time animation is possible on a microcomputer because it is a single-user machine, but its resolution is poor and its color range is limited.

3.4 Frame Buffer Animation and Real-time Playback

The illusion of real-time animation can be created with a frame buffer, which can be viewed conceptually as a two-dimensional array of pixels. As shown by Booth and MacKay [1982], there are different techniques for limited frame buffer animation. As the time required to rescan all the pixels is too long for animation, only static images are considered. This means that the actual contents of the memory pixels never changes, but the way of interpreting the bits does, causing the illustion of animation.

Color Table Animation
The value of a pixel is generally an index in a look-up table of colors. Animation can be obtained by modifying the look-up table. The modification can be cyclic, alternated or selective. Details of these techniques can be found in a paper by R. Shoup [1979].

Zoom-pan-scroll Animation
Pixel memory can be divided into different regions and the display can cycle through the different images. For example, a 512- × -512 frame buffer can be divided into four 256- × -256 images. By using zoom, pan and scroll operations, the four images can be successively and rapidly displayed.

Several graphics terminals like the AED 767, for example, allow the user to define an image with a virtual resolution of 1024 × 1024. By dividing the memory into four virtual images, it is possible to display successively four real images of 512 × 512 pixels.

Crossbar Animation
The principle of crossbar animation consists of routing any of the bits from pixel memory to any of the input lines in look-up tables.

Real-time Playback
As shown, it is generally impossible to compile frames at the rates required for real-time presentation, especially when images must have a certain degree of realism. However, as it is very difficult to imagine the effects of animation in a frame-by-frame system, the alternative is to compile all the frames in advance at non-real-time rates and save the frames (or the display code) in mass storage. A real-time program then displays the frames. This technique is called **real-time playback**.

3.5 Systems vs. Languages

Computer animation was first developed in the mid-sixties. The early films were produced using programming languages or interactive systems accessible only to computer scientists. Then user-friendly interactive systems were developed, allowing artists to make films without too much intervention by computer scientists. These interactive systems have the great advantage of being dedicated to artists, but they impose limits on the creativity of those who would like to exploit all the computer possibilities. Four arguments can be put forward for the development and use of a programming language for computer animation:

1. Such a language could exploit all the power of the computer.
2. It would permit the easy development of interactive computer animation systems that are compatible with the language, especially in terms of graphical data structures and temporal concepts.
3. Recent developments in the design of programming languages have led to new concepts that are fundamental to the control of motion and temporal events. In particular, research in structured programming and data structures has allowed the design of high-level languages such as PASCAL and SIMULA-67. Work on data abstraction [Liskov and Zilles, 1974; Guttag, 1977] is the basis of abstract data types existing in a number of languages such as ALPHARD, CLU and ADA. Concepts of synchronization and message passing exist in SMALLTALK [Goldberg and Robson, 1983], CONCURRENT PASCAL

[Brinch Hansen, 1975], MODULA-2 [Wirth, 1983] and ADA. Research has also been done on actor systems like PLASMA [Hewitt and Smith, 1975], which has important implications for computer animation.

4. Computer programming knowledge is no longer restricted to computer scientists.

In summary, animator-oriented systems are necessary, because they can attract artists who may be wary of all technology, and computer programming in particular. But computer animation languages must also be developed because they permit more impressive special effects. In addition, research must be done to provide animators with more powerful user-oriented animation systems by using artificial intelligence theory, for example.

4. The Development of Computer Animation in Various Organizations

4.1 The Early Systems: BEFLIX and EXPLOR

During the period 1963–1967, a dozen computer films were made at Bell Telephone Laboratories. Apart from Ken Knowlton [1964, 1965], the most important computer animators at Bell Labs were:

- E. Zajac [1966], who made the first computer-animated film *Two-gyro gravity-gradient attitude control system* in 1963.
- F. Sinden [1967], who made *Force, Mass and Motion*, a film that demonstrates Newton's laws of motion; the programming language was FORTRAN.
- Huggins and Weiner, who made *Harmonic Phasors*, a film concerning the composition of complicated periodic waveforms; the film was produced by programming in PMACRO [Alexander and Huggins, 1967].

Four other animators should also be mentioned:

- McCumber, who made a film illustrating the Gunn oscillation effect in semiconductors.
- Julesz [1966] and Bosche [1967], for their experiments in human vision and perception.
- Noll [1965, 1967], for his films on stereo viewing.

(More details on films and animators can be found in the appendix.)

BEFLIX is a language that was created by Ken Knowlton [1964] on an IBM 7094. The language directly manipulates a matrix of 252×184 "pixels" of three bits, representing eight grey-levels. The primitives are:

- read/write pixel
- manipulation of filling areas bounded by previously drawn lines (copy, move, permutation, zoom, fill, scale, smooth)
- perspective projection
- motion primitives
- grey-scale commands.

For example, PAINT, A, B allows the user to fill up the rectangle defined by two vertices A and B. There are almost no mathematics in BEFLIX. Animation is completed by sending electronic signals (waves) to make image distorsions: sinusoidal, horizontal/vertical deformations, etc.

Several films were produced with BEFLIX:

- a film on BEFLIX by Knowlton (17 min.)
- a film on the list-processing language L6 (2 parts: 16 min. and 32 min.)
- *"Man and his World"*, for EXPO 67 in Montreal (1 min.).

With BEFLIX, the production of one minute of film costs about $500.

As BEFLIX contains little mathematics, Ken Knowlton has combined this language with FORTRAN IV. This produced the FORTRAN IV BEFLIX animated-movie language which was quite powerful for its time.

EXPLOR [Knowlton, 1970] is an acronym for EXplicitly Provided 2D patterns, Local neighbourhood Operations and Randomness. This language, intended for scientific and artistic applications stores pictures in raster-scan format. The artist manipulates a grid of 240×320 cells. A number between 0 and 255 that represents color and intensity is associated with each cell and can be applied to the cells of a rectangle that the user has to specify. For example, in the FORTRAN-coded EXPLOR, CALL PUT(X, Y, W, H, %, N) means "PUT the Nth color in the rectangle of center $\langle X, Y \rangle$, height H and width W. Only a percentage of cells (%) of the rectangle will be randomly colored. Although this system was designed for mosaics and abstract motifs, artist Lilian Schwarz made a well-known 3-minute film *Olympiad* with the system. Over 20 films have been made with EXPLOR, including *Picture From a Gallery*, which involves the manipulation of a family photograph. In short, the originality of EXPLOR lies in the fact that decisions do not define exact patterns but merely the rules for building an image. The rest is filled in randomly.

4.2 Picture-driven Animation: GENESYS

GENESYS is a picture-driven animation system which was developed by Ronald Baecker [1969b] at MIT for his PhD thesis. The system requires that the information defining the image transformation be itself in graphical form. This is the source of the name "Picture-driven animation". Moreover, for Baecker, immediate visual feedback is fundamental.

The hardware consists of a computer, auxiliary mass storage, a locator device and a graphics display. The software has four parts:

- a language for the construction of static pictures
- a language for the specification of picture changes
- a set of programs to produce the sequence of frames
- a set of input/output programs and real-time playback.

The system is based on the following strategy:

1. The animator creates a new film by using the command FORMMOVIE ⟨name⟩

2. The animator sketches the background using the command FORM-BACKGROUND and his locator device.

3. The animator sketches cells and then constructs a coherent object composed of different cells. For example, a woman can be built by the following sequence of commands:

FORMCEL   1   IN CLASS HEAD
FORMCEL   1   IN CLASS BODY
        ⋮

BIND BODY, HEAD...

4. The animator designs motion by sketching a path called a P-curve. Because of the command BIND, the command SKETCHPCURVE BODY creates a path of motion not only for the body but also for the parts to which it is bound.

5. The animator can use PLAYBACK to evaluate the animation sequence.

6. The animator can type a sequence of choices of different positions for any object by using the TYPESELECTION command.

7. The animator can add rhythm to the motion.

What is interesting and new in the GENESYS system is its representation of dynamic behavior. Three concepts are introduced to achieve this:

1. **the P-curves** that define the motion path (this concept will be further discussed in Chapter 5)

2. **the selection descriptions** that define choices of cells from a cell class

3. **the rhythm descriptions** that consist of sequences of instants of display time or intervals between frames. They define temporal patterns marking events.

GENESYS is still considered a useful basic animation system. The concept of picture-driven animation has shown that dynamic information can be abstracted, modeled and generated in the same way as in animated pictures.

4.3 Analog Systems: SCANIMATE and CAESAR

SCANIMATE [Honey, 1971] is an "analog animation system." that allows the animator to modify the signals produced by a video synthesizer. The system, shown in Fig. 4.1, was created by Computer Image Corporation.

The figure shows that the artist can control animation at two points. At point A, the artist can zoom, shrink, rotate and crop the image. At point B, colors and intensity can be easily modified.

SCANIMATE was used for many commercials and films including *2001: A Space Odyssey* and *Yellow Submarine.*

CAESAR [Honey, 1971] stands for Computer-Animated Episodes-using Single-Axis Rotation. Also an analog system, it is more sophisticated and powerful than SCANIMATE because it permits figurative, or cartoon animation. In particular, CAESAR allows the component parts of a cartoon figure to be derived into several sections, each to be shown on a separate portion of the TV display and

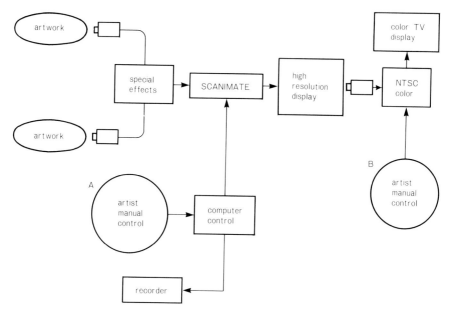

Fig. 4.1. The SCANIMATE system

separately controlled. The animator can store any frame when he is satisfied. CAESAR can also compute the inbetweens of two cartoon figures. CAESAR has been extensively used to produce logos for the TV networks ABC, NBC and CBS. Several cartoons have been produced; the most well-known is probably *Coyote and the Skunk*.

Figs. 4.2 to 4.4 show images produced with SCANIMATE and CAESAR.

4.4 ANIMATOR, ARTA and MOP

ANIMATOR [Talbot et al., 1971] is a two-dimensional interactive film animation system that was developed at the University of Pennsylvania in 1971. As shown in Fig. 4.5, ANIMATOR comes with six modes of operation.

In the **picture definition mode**, the user creates a picture by associating a name to a sequence of picture primitives and previously defined pictures. The primitives are limited to points, lines and circles.

The **motion definition mode** is the most interesting one, because it allows the animator to define parallel and/or sequential motions. These definitions are carried out by constructing operators based on motion, primitives such as translation, rotation and zoom. Primitives can have an absolute or a relative effect. The **scene definition mode** is used to specify the pictures involved in a scene with their absolute starting positions and associated motion. The **movie segment definition**

Fig. 4.2. Three dimensional logo treatment produced off the CAESAR computer for Editel of Los Angeles (Designer/Directors: Susan Crouse-Kemp, Jim Johnson. Animator: Susan Crouse-Kemp. Tech. Staff: Jim Johnson, David Cline. Computers: CAESAR, SCANIMATE. Production house: Computer Image Productions, Inc.)

Fig. 4.3. Music Room. A unique blend of animation and model manipulation produced "Music Room", a generic: 25-second treatment (Producer: Brad Jorgensen. Production house: Computer Image Productions, Inc. Designer/ Directors: Brad Jorgensen, Larry Cole, Jim Johnson. Animators: Susan Crouse-Kemp, Brad Jorgensen. Computers: CAESAR, SCANIMATE)

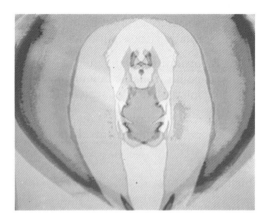

Fig. 4.4. Video vitae. Produced on SCANIMATE at Computer Image Corp. © Pat Lehman 1974

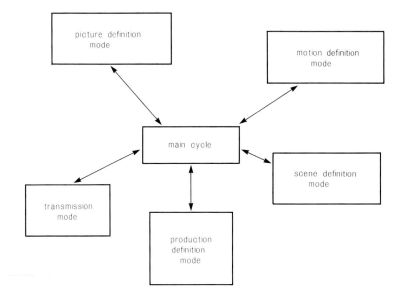

Fig. 4.5. The ANIMATOR modes

mode allows the animator to describe a movie with the relation between scenes. The **transmission mode** is used to enter actions and obtain specific results and the role of the **production mode** is self-evident. The ANIMATOR system is interesting because it is probably the first "modelled" system, although it was only in two-dimensions.

ARTA, also an interactive two-dimensional computer animation system, was created by L. Mezei and A. Zivian [1971] at the University of Toronto. Pictures are entered into the system on punched cards or using a light pen. Accurate work is done by using a grid, vector mode or by sketching freehand. In the vector mode, an interpolation routine could improve the curves by using the Akima algorithm [1970]. ARTA offers 80 menu-prompted commands. These are classified into:

Class A: operations that result in an output figure with the same number of points as an input figure:
rotation, translation, scaling.

Class B: operations that result in an output figure with a different number of points from the input figure:
interpolation, concatenation, texture, addition.

Class C: transformations of the input figure:
random movement, alteration of distances.

Input/output

Figure generators: circle, ellipse, polygon.

Miscellaneous

Animation features were mainly based on two operations:

– the motion of a figure along a path defined by the points of another figure
– in-betweening.

Both operations, still basic operations of computer-assisted animation systems, will be further discussed in Chapter 5.

ARTA has been used in the production of a 10-minute film, *Art from Computers*. But the most well-known film produced with ARTA was *Sosoon*, by Georges Singer. Not a superproduction, the film can be considered as a real "painting in motion." The film consists of the manipulation of simple geometric forms. Transformations are continuous, calm and smooth.

MOP is a three-dimensional computer animation system that was developed by Edwin Catmull [1972] at the University of Utah and considered very advanced for its time. It removed hidden surfaces using the Watkins algorithm [1970] and performed smooth shading with the Gouraud method [1971]. (These concepts will be discussed in detail in Chapter 7.)

In MOP, objects are defined as a group of polygons; a hierarchical collection of objects is called a **body**. MOP is an acronym for MOtion Picture language, implying that some concept of motion forms the basis of the system. In fact, MOP can be considered an attempt at creating an actor system. The language MOP is designed to allow concurrency from the point of view of the user. The rate at which an object moves or changes can be given by a mathematical formulation or in a table of data. For example, a MOP statement can have the following form:

45,144 B ROTATE "WHEEL", 1, 45

This statement means: "rotate the wheel around the axis 1 from an angle of 45° in 100 frames (45 to 144), using the table B." New accelerations can now be defined by modifying table B. Catmull made a movie of a hand to illustrate the MOP system. For a further discussion of that model, see Chapter 9.

4.5 Computer Animation at the National Research Council of Canada

Burtnyk and Wein of the National Research Council of Canada can be considered the pioneers of key-frame animation systems. In a famous paper [Burtnyk and Wein, 1971], they introduced the principles of in-between calculation by computer. Already, in 1967, the Tokyo Computer Technique Group had explored the possibilities of transforming one image into another. The most famous example of their work is *Running Cola is Africa*, which shows the transformation from a runner to a Coca-Cola bottle then to a map of Africa. Burtnyk and Wein integrated this concept into a working animation system called MSGEN [Burtnyk and Wein, 1971b].

In the key-frame animation technique, the animator creates isolated frames at key intervals during a sequence. The in-between frames are computed by interpolation. (The complete technique will be presented in Chapter 5.) The first system produced by Burtnyk and Wein had a menu of commands. Some typical commands are listed:

Start sequence: stores the current picture as a reference start frame.
Interpolation: assigns an interpolation law to each individual cell in the current picture.
Set frame: allows the number of frames to be set from the previous key frame.
Store key: stores the current picture as a key frame on disk.
Read key: brings in the next key frame from disk.

Smooth and fluid movements are very difficult to achieve by linear interpolation. Moreover, the number of frames required is enormous. One way around this is to introduce a non-linear path to control interpolation between the keyframes. However, the use of only one path is too restrictive. Burtnyk and Wein [1976] introduced a new technique for solving this problem: the use of skeleton-derived images. This technique (also discussed further in Chapter 5) is very simple: skeletons, or stick-figures, are used for computing new key images. The animator develops a complex motion sequence with only the skeleton of the image. Because of the simplicity of the skeleton, the degree of interaction can be very high.

The systems developed by Burtnyk and Wein were extensively used by the well-known artist Peter Foldes. A typical example is shown in Fig. 4.6. Foldes' films *Metadata*, *Hunger* and *Visages* have achieved great recognition. In particular, *Hunger* received the Prix du Jury at Cannes in 1974, the Golden Hugo in Chicago and a special prize at the Barcelona Film Festival. The film was also nominated for an Academy award. As shown in Fig. 4.7, the interpolated images have the same artistic style as the first and last key frames.

4.6 Computer Animation at Ohio State University

The Computer Graphics Research Group at Ohio State University is one of the most dynamic groups in computer animation research. Under the direction of Charles Csuri, another pioneer in the area, several computer animation systems have been developed:

1972– GRASS, a user-oriented real-time animation system [De Fanti, 1976]
1975– ANIMA, a 3D real-time animation system [Csuri, 1975]
1977– ANIMA II, a 3D color animation system [Hackathorn, 1977]
1979– ANTTS, a very complex 3D animation system [Csuri et al., 1979]
1982– SAS, the Skeleton Animation System [Zeltzer, 1982, 1982b] oriented towards human motion (Fig. 4.8 and 4.9).

By 1970, Csuri had already developed a real-time animation system on an IBM 1130 [Csuri, 1970 and 1974]. Then a new system, called GRASS, was designed in 1972 [De Fanti, 1976]. This system was particularly "habitable," i.e., the system

Fig. 4.6. "Daphnis and Chloe" re-named "Portrait of a Man" by Peter Foldes

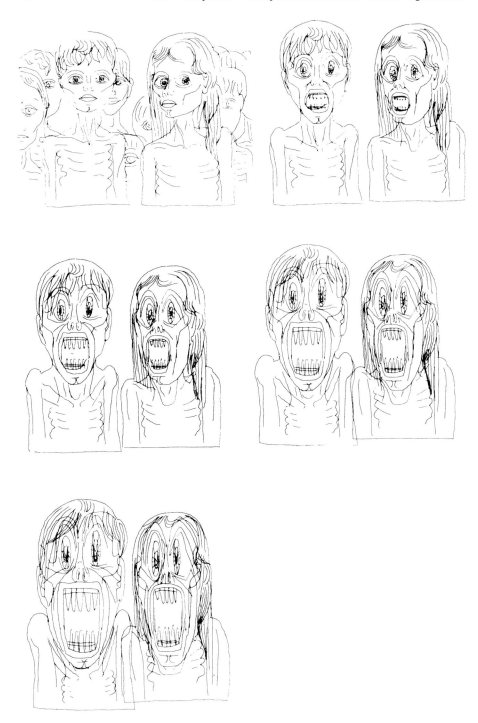

Fig. 4.7. "Hunger" by Peter Foldes (Production: National Film Board of Canada)

4.8

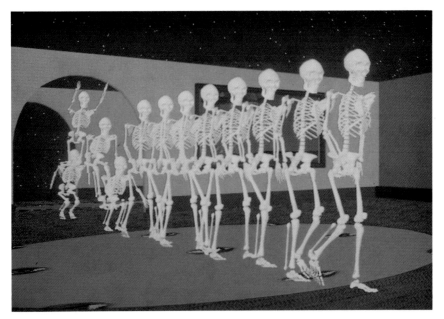

4.9

Figs. 4.8–9. Frames produced with the Skeleton Animation System (Motion control software: David Zeltzer. Skeleton data generation: Donald Stredney)

could be used by a computer novice. Then, based on Csuri's language ANIMA, a new three dimensional real-time animation system was designed. The visual surface system was developed principally by Allan Myers. It provides clipping, perspective, and smooth shading of surfaces. The system also provides surface transparency, although not in real-time.

Hackathorn's ANIMA II, a 3D computer animation system which is not real-time, ran on a PDP-11/45 with a 64K memory and a 44-megaword moving head disk. The graphics terminal used was a 4096- × -4096 Vector General refresh CRT with a joystick, buttons and dials. All software was written in assembler.

ANIMA II provides the animator with 4 major functions:

1. **A real-time interactive geometric modeling program for creating complex objects.** Although the objects are modelled as surfaces composed of polygons, the user is only aware of positioning the objects and deciding their colors.

2. **A set of instructions for writing animation scripts.** Complex motions are broken down into simple changes through space and time. Parallelism is supported by language instructions that are scheduled to be active over a range of time during the animation process. A simple motion is completely controlled by **set** and **change** instructions. For example:

   > set position ⟨name⟩ X, Y, Z at frame ⟨frame number⟩
   > change position ⟨name⟩ to X, Y, Z from frame
   > ⟨frame number⟩ to frame ⟨frame number⟩

   Instead of **position**, key words like **rotation**, **size**, **shape** and **path** can be used to describe the different motions.
   There is no need for loops or conditional statements. Parallel commands provide the ability to schedule language instructions. When the script is ready, it serves to control the whole scene.

3. **An animation language.** The script is analyzed by a preprocessor that builds a data structure for the complete animation sequence. In fact, the preprocessor handles in detail all the preparation of the scene and produces command blocks. The execution of the scene is driven by a scheduler that determines which command blocks must be processed for each frame. An interpreter then modifies the data structure according to the command blocks selected by the scheduler. A compilation routine calculates the color of each face, lighting and perspective and builds an animation file. This file can be displayed in real time on the Vector General terminal, but without color and lighting.

4. **A method of recording frames.** The Csuri group has developed a method of recording the animation files in NTSC format in real time.
   The visible surface algorithm used in ANIMA II is a version of the Myers algorithm, already mentioned in the description of ANIMA. ANIMA II has several drawbacks: limited shading capabilities, no transparency and aliasing problems.

For these reasons, a new system was designed: ANTTS (ANimated Things Through Space). The objectives were:

– to avoid the problems of ANIMA II
– to obtain good response time, but with no real-time requirement
– to allow editing of sequences
– to handle any type of drawing, including lines and 3D surfaces
– to generate textures and clouds.

The most interesting aspect of the ANTTS system is the display algorithm, which processes data in a stream. It uses two large buffers: a run-length and a frame buffer. The algorithm processes data as follows:

1. get a single triangle
2. apply image transformation to the triangle
3. determine the face color
4. compute perspective projection
5. orient the triangle projection with respect to its highest Y value
6. raster-scan the triangle into run lengths
7. pass the run lengths to the buffer by adding them to a list of run lengths at the same Y scan-line
8. when the whole frame is processed, decompose the run-lengths into 3D pixels and compare them with the corresponding pixels in the frame buffer.

This display algorithm is quite efficient. Textured objects can also be produced by defining a three-dimensional perturbation of the object's surface.

ANTTS was implemented on a VAX 11/780 computer with different frame buffers [Csuri et al., 1979]. A subset was also implemented on a PDP-11/23 [Hackathorn et al., 1981].

The Computer Graphics Research Group at Ohio State University is still a leading group in computer animation (Fig. 4.10). Their demonstrations, as well as those of Cranston-Csuri Productions (Fig. 4.11 and 4.12) are always well received at computer animation festivals.

Fig. 4.10. Image produced by Frank Crow, Ohio State University

Fig. 4.11. "Wine Glasses on Mirror" (Animator: Michael Collery, Cranston-Csuri Productions, Columbus, Ohio)

Fig. 4.12. "Pencil City and Balls" (Animators: Shaun Ho and Michael Collery, Cranston-Csuri Productions, Columbus, Ohio)

4.7 From GRASS to ZGRASS

After his PhD from Ohio State University, Tom De Fanti expanded his system, called "the Graphics Symbiosis System," or GRASS [1976]. This three-dimensional real-time system was implemented by a team of 10 people. Written in assembler for a PDP-11/45 with a Vector General display, the GRASS language essentially has two types of primitives:

1. **pictures**
   These are user-defined lists of 3D vectors. The pictures have names; up to 60 can be displayed concurrently.

2. **commands**
   There are two kinds of commands:

   i) commands that do not change the vector list; their functions are performed by the hardware. These include translation, rotations, scaling, etc. (There is also a command for changing intensity and one that moves a picture along a path similar to Baecker's P-curves).

   ii) commands that change vector end-points like smoothing, perspective, chipping, windowing and shading.

   Users can also group pictures together and create a tree. Macros and conditional execution are also available in GRASS.

Several years after GRASS, Tom De Fanti developed the high-level graphics language ZGRASS [Dietrich, 1983]. This was implemented on a low-cost micrographics system, the Datamax UV-1. With 16 2-bit frame-buffers, that system can generate standard NTSC signals. The artist-oriented language offers three different methods of animating an image in real time:

1. **colormap animation**, as described in Section 3.4

2. **bitmap animation**, with:

   i) **additive animation** that consists of adding graphics elements to previous ones

   ii) **snap animation** that basically creates a memorized image (a snapshot) and continuously displays it along a path. 2D 1/2 effects can be easily created with this type of animation.

3. **framemap animation**
   full-screen animation can be produced by taking advantage of the hardware. By cycling through a series of previously designed images, the 16 frame buffers can be used. This arrangement is fully programmable.

Different authors have produced numerous works using ZGRASS. The most well-known are Copper Giloth (Fig. 4.13) and Jane Veeder (Fig. 4.14).

Fig. 4.13. "LIS31" by Copper Giloth

Fig. 4.14. From "MONTANA" by Jane Veeder

4.8 New York Institute of Technology and Lucasfilm

NYIT (New York Institute of Technology) and Lucasfilm are two well-known institutions that produce spectacular computer-animated images. Two of the most well-known specialists in computer animation, Edwin Catmull and Alvy Ray Smith have moved from NYIT to Lucasfilm.

NYIT has produced several computer animation systems in two and three dimensions.

Catmull designed the Computer-Assisted Animation System (CAAS) used at NYIT's Computer Graphics Laboratory. The hardware consists of animation stations, and frame-buffers controlled by several computers including a VAX 11/780 and PDP-11s. Three software packages were developed for assisting conventional animation.

1. TWEEN [Catmull, 1979] is a program that provides a means of generating and manipulating digital forms of character images. The main objective of the system is the production of in-betweens. At any time, the artist can review the in-betweens and modify them with an electronic pen; the computer recalculates the other inbetweens.
2. PAINT [Smith, 1978] one of the most well-known "paint systems," allows an artist to paint by using the pen and tablet and watching the color monitor. (PAINT will be further discussed in Section 5.5.)
3. SOFTCEL [Stern, 1979] is a system that uses frame buffers to replace the conventional operations of hand copying pencil drawings onto cels and painting them. SOFTCEL handles filling operations and painted antialiasing characters that can be merged with a background image. Each frame can be stored on three frame buffers, one for each of the primary colors.

Fig. 4.15 shows an example of the use of the computer in cartoons.

An ambitious project has been under development at NYIT for several years now: a wholly computer-generated feature film, *The Works*. This film is being produced using BBOP [Stern, 1983], a program that interactively animates hierarchically articulated three-dimensional figures.

BBOP is, in fact, a system for three-dimensional key-frame figure animation. There are three major data structures in BBOP: articulated tree-structured models based on polygons or quadric surfaces, a ring of virtual cameras and a list of all the trees and rings for each frame. BBOP is implemented on an Evans and

Fig. 4.15. Cartoon by Edwin Catmull

Sutherland Picture System with a VAX 750 as a host processor. Image rendering is performed by a shell program provided by the UNIX operating system. Hidden surface removal is performed by z-buffering (see Chapter 7); anti-aliasing techniques, lighting models and texture mapping are also included.

Another area of expertise at the NYIT Computer Graphics Lab is human face modelling. This research has been carried out under the leadership of F.I. Parke and is described in Section 9.6.

Lucasfilm is a commercial film production house. However, the special effects in films like *Star Trek II* and *Return of the Jedi* [Duff, 1983] are demonstrations of the state of the art in computer animation. As well as Catmull and Smith, Bill Reeves and T. Duff have also contributed greatly to the development of computer animation. Reeves [1983] has produced a method for modelling fuzzy objects such as fire, clouds and water. The technique, called **Particle Systems** was used in the Genesis Demo sequence from the movie *Star Trek II* and for the explosion caused by the destruction of the Death Star's power generator in *Return of the Jedi*. (Particle systems will be further discussed in Section 8.5.) Software developed at Lucasfilm used the C language; Figs. 4.16 and 4.17 show images produced there.

4.9 MAGI/Synthavision, Robert Abel, Triple I and Digital Effects

These four companies produced computer-generated imagery for the film *TRON*, done at Disney Studios. Information International Inc. (Triple I) has now left this business, but the three other companies are still very active and they regularly present demo reels of their work in commercial productions.

MAGI (Mathematical Applications Group Inc.) has been deeply involved in the animation and entertainment fields since 1966. Their application package, called SynthaVision, converts models of quadric surfaces, polygons and other geometric forms into three-dimensional images. These can be shaded and textured. A "Director's Language" allows the animator to assign motions to objects, cameras and light. These techniques are, of course, highlighted in the work done on *TRON*.

Robert Abel and Associates is a commercial production house from Los Angeles. Some of their best computer-generated work includes numerous logos for TV programs such as the CBS Evening News. Since 1978, they have used an Evans and Sutherland Picture System II. Their animation software was developed by a team under the direction of Bill Kovacs. The film *TRON* incorporated their vector computer effects.

Information International Inc., (Triple I) also played a large past in the production of computer-animated images for *TRON*. The company has produced some of the best computer-generated images. In 1976, for example, they created a 40-second sequence film for "Futureworld" in which a clone of Peter Fonda was created. However, management decided to stop work on computer animation at the end of 1982.

The software Tripe I used was very powerful, especially ASAS, the Actor/Scriptor Animation System developed by Craig Reynolds [1982]. This

Fig. 4.16. "SIGGRAPH Watch" by Rob Cook, Lucasfilm and Stuart Sechrest, Cornell University

Fig. 4.17. "Road to Point Reyes" directed by Rob Cook, Lucasfilm Ltd. This landscape was defined using patches, fractals, particle systems, and a variety of procedural models. The various elements were rendered separately and later composited. Rob Cook designed the picture and did the texturing and shading, including the road, hills, fence, rainbow, shadows and reflections. Loren Carpenter used fractals for the mountains, rock and lake, and a special atmosphere program for the sky and haze. Tom Porter provided the procedurally drawn texture for the hills and wrote the compositing software. Bill reeves used his particle systems for the grass and wrote the modelling software. David Salesin put the ripples in the puddles. Alvy Ray Smith randered the forsythia plants using a procedural model. The visible surface software was written by Loren Carpenter and the anti-aliasing software by Rob Cook. The picture was rendered using an Ikonas graphics processor and frame buffers, and was scanned on a COLOR FIRE 240, courtesy of MacDonald Dettwiler and Associates Ltd. The resolution is 4K × 4K, 24 bits/pixel

Fig. 4.18. "The Juggler" by Omnibus/Triple I 3D simulation

programming language, described further in Section 10.5, is a programming language extension of LISP. It allows the technical director to animate objects, colors, shading parameters, light sources and the camera. Fig. 4.18 shows an image produced by Information International Inc.

Digital Effects is another production house that worked on *TRON*. They used a laser-scanning system to digitize, store and reproduce images. Judson Rosebush, president of Digital Effects, is the primary designer of APL VISION and FORTRAN VISION, two computer animation packages that are currently used. Numerous commercials have been produced by Digital Effects. The images from Times Square, produced in 1979, are especially spectacular.

4.10 And the Others?

This chapter has discussed the most important computer animation systems and languages since the development of this art. However, numerous computer animators and organizations have been omitted and we would like to briefly mention some of these. Information about movies, systems and languages can be also found in the appendices and of course readers are invited to explore the numerous references at the end of the book.

Among the earliest computer animation systems, three important systems have not been described:

– CAMP [Citron and Whitney, 1968] is a language for computer-assisted production of animated film sequences based on mathematical curves
– CAFE [Nolan and Yarbrough, 1969] is a conversational system for describing geometrical forms and the sequence of such forms
– ANTICS [Kitching, 1973] is a key-frame animation system.

For more recent productions, the traditional SIGGRAPH film festival is certainly the place where the most comprehensive list of computer animation teams can be found. We would like to single out the work of a few individuals and organizations:

– James Blinn of the Jet Propulsion Laboratory—specialist in space travel simulation.
– Nelson Max of the Lawrence Livermore Laboratory, who produced several films on molecules. Fig. 4.19 shows a frame of his film *Carla's Island*.
– NHK, the Japanese television network, which produced an excellent film, *Four Seasons*, under the direction of Mayumi Yoshinari. Fig. 4.20 to 4.22 show frames from this film.
– Pacific Data Images [Chuang and Entis, 1983] a new Californian company.
– Digital Productions, a firm created by John Whitney Jr.; they use a Cray-1 computer to produce their images.
– Sogitec, a French company. Fig. 4.23 shows an image in industrial design.

Finally, we must mention our own work at the University of Montreal which will be discussed in later chapters of this book.

Fig. 4.19. "Carla's Island" by Nelson Max, Lawrence Livermore National Laboratory and Department of Energy

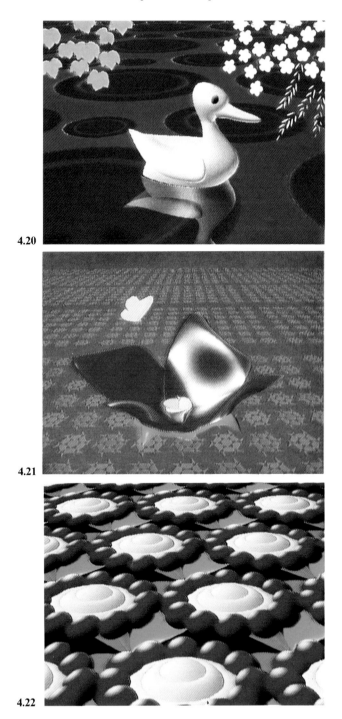

4.20

4.21

4.22

Figs. 4.20–22. Frames from "Four Seasons of Japan" (Director: Mayumi Yoshinari. Art Director: Tatsuo Shimamura. Technical Director: Junnosuke Kutsuzawa. © NHK)

Fig. 4.23. Synthesized watch by Sogitec Audiovisuel, Paris

5. Key Frame and Painting Systems

5.1 Computer-assisted Animation

We showed in Chapter 3 that numerous steps in conventional animation can be assisted or improved by computer. In particular, the computer can be used:

1. to input drawings
2. to produce in-betweens
3. to specify the motion of an object along a path
4. to color the drawings and create a background
5. to synchronize motion with sound
6. to initiate the recording of a sequence on film.

These different aspects will be studied in detail.

5.2 The Input of Drawings

In conventional animation, it has long been a general practice to draw the different objects or parts of objects involved in a scene on separate celluloid transparencies (**cels**). Frames are produced by photographing a stack of cels.

With computers, the process of creating drawings can be improved by using a graphics editor. Although the graphics editor is less used in computer-assisted animation than in modelled animation, it allows the designer to create drawings, save, retrieve, modify and delete them.

Typically, animators use free-hand drawings in cartoons; however, these can be combined with more regular drawings which can easily be created with a graphics editor. Moreover, graphics editors sometimes offer operations to improve drawings. This is the case of the graphics editor GRAFEDIT [N. Magnenat-Thalmann et al., 1981], which provides the user with an IMPROVE command based on local interpolation fit [Akima, 1970] and Bezier polygons [Bezier, 1972]. Fig. 5.1 shows an example of the use of the IMPROVE command of GRAFEDIT with the final

Fig. 5.1. The IMPROVE command in GRAFEDIT (Akima interpolation)

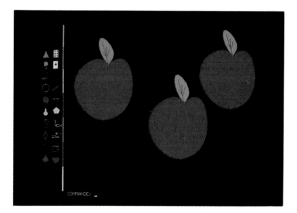

Fig. 5.2. Final results of an Akima interpolation

results given in Fig. 5.2. A list of commands available in a graphics editor such as GRAFEDIT is given in Table 5.1.

Although the process of making input drawings can be helped by computer, the major advantage is in the production of inbetweens, after two key frames have been created.

5.3 In-between Calculations

Basically, the "in-between" technique works as follows: the animator specifies two key drawings and the computer calculates additional drawings between them by computing linear distances between two corresponding points, as shown in Fig. 5.3. However, the process cannot work properly if the correspondence between both key drawings is not well defined. As key drawings do not generally have the same number of lines, this means that each drawing must be broken down into small line segments.

The process is explained more formally below based on the original ideas of Burtnyk and Wein [1971].

Table 5.1. The GRAFEDIT commands

STORE	– stores a diagram or a catalog in a file
RETRIEVE	– retrieves a diagram or a catalog from a file
CATALOG	– enters a diagram into the catalog
REMOVE	– removes a diagram from a catalog
PLACE	– puts a copy of a diagram from the catalog to the diagram area
DIAGRAM	– allows the user to draw an original diagram
POLYGON	– draws a regular polygon
TEXT	– enters graphical text
ERASE	– erases diagrams
TRANSLATE	– performs a translation
SCALE	– performs a scaling
ROTATE	– performs a rotation
INTERPOLATE	– performs a Akima interpolation
SYMMETRY	– performs a symmetry
CLIPPING	– performs a clipping
JOIN	– joins independent diagrams
LINES	– draws lines, arrows
ARC	– draws an arc of circle
FOUNT	– modifies the dimension of the current character fount
STYLE	– selects a linestyle
PEN	– selects a current color
REFERENCE	– modifies the reference point for ROTATE and SYMMETRY
IDENTIFY	– identifies diagrams
GRID	– draws/erases a grid for measures
END	– terminates the session
UNION	– performs a union between two diagrams
INTERSECTION	– performs an intersection between two diagrams
DIFFERENCE	– performs the difference between two diagrams
COLOR	– changes the color of a diagram
SURFACE	– puts a diagram in POLYGON mode
RUBBER	– performs a rubber transformation (Skeleton technique)

Key drawings are decomposed into cels and in-betweens are calculated by interpolation between cels. Each cel is itself composed of strokes that are defined as sequences of visible line segments. To perform an interpolation from a cel C1 with N1 strokes to a cel C2 with N2 strokes, the following algorithm must be applied:

If the number of strokes of both cels are the same $(N1 = N2)$ and the number of points of the corresponding strokes also match, in-betweens can be calculated. Otherwise a preprocessing step is required. This preprocessing step can be separated into two parts:

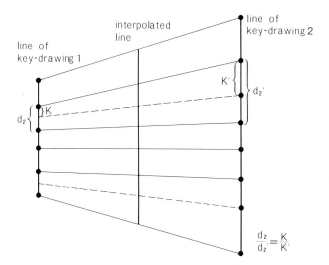

Fig. 5.3. The "in-between" technique

1. **Preprocessing for cels with a different number of strokes**

    if N1 > N2 (for N2 > N1, the algorithm is the same with
                N1 and N2 interchanged)

    then, N1 − N2 strokes must be added to C2. These sections are added as
    follows:

    i) N1 *modulo* N2 strokes of C2 are broken into N1 *div* N2 + 1 strokes
    ii) the other strokes of C2 are broken into N1 *div* N2 strokes. Fig. 5.4 shows
        an example with N1 = 4 and N2 = 2.

2. **Preprocessing for two corresponding strokes with a different number of points**

    If both the cels to be preprocessed have the same number of strokes, all
    corresponding strokes must have the same number of points (NP1 = NP2).
    If this is not the case, for example:

    if NP1 > NP2

    then the following numbers are computed:

    $$RT := (NP1 - 1)\, div\, (NP2 - 1)$$
    $$RS := (NP1 - 1)\, mod\, (NP2 - 1)$$

    RT points are added to the first RS line segments of the stroke of the
    second cel and RT − 1 to the others.

Fig. 5.5 shows an example where NP1 = 12 and NP2 = 5. Two points are added
to the three first segments and 1 to the last.
When preprocessing is finished, the interpolation process begins.

Interpolation

To compute an in-between, an intermediary point is calculated by interpolating between two corresponding drawings. Fig. 5.6 shows an example that explains the technique. Interpolation is linear: this means that the distance between two corresponding points is always regularly divided. Other divisions are possible by using other interpolation laws.

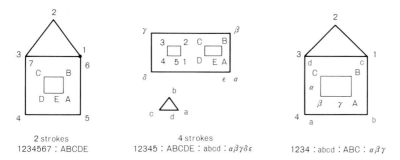

Fig. 5.4. Preprocessing of cels for in-betweening

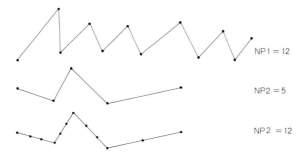

Fig. 5.5. Preprocessing of strokes for in-betweening

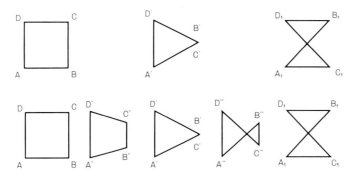

Fig. 5.6. Linear interpolation

```
program INTERPOLATION;
const
   NBINBETWEEN = 17; (* number of inbetweens +1 *)
   LAWX        =  4; (* linear interpolation in x *)
   LAWY        =  4; (* linear interpolation in y *)
var
   FILEC:FIGFILE;    (* file containing both cels *)
   FIRSTCEL,         (* cel 1 *)
   LASTCEL,          (* cel 2 *)
   RESULT:FIG;       (* result of the interpolation *)
   CURRENT:INTEGER;  (* current inbetween number *)
   FRACTION:REAL;    (* phase fraction of the interpolation *)
begin
   WINDOW(ORIGIN, << 719,359 >>);
   VIEWPORT(ORIGIN, << 1,0.5 >>);
   RESET(FILEC);
   READBINFIG(FILEC,FIRSTCEL);
   READBINFIG(FILEC,LASTCEL);

   PREPROCESSING(FIRSTCEL,LASTCEL);

   for CURRENT:=0 to NBINBETWEEN do
   begin
      FRACTION := CURRENT / NBINBETWEEN;
      RESULT:= INBETWEEN(FIRSTCEL,LASTCEL,FRACTION,LAWX,LAWY);
      draw RESULT;
      TAKEPICTURE;
      erase RESULT
   end
end.
```

Fig. 5.7. Program that draws in-betweens

Fig. 5.7 shows a program that computes and draws in-betweens. This program first reads two cels (FIRSTCEL and LASTCEL) and then performs the preprocessing phase. It then computes and draws the inbetweens by using the function INBETWEEN. The parameter law can be 0, 1, 2 or 3, corresponding to the different possible interpolation functions described in the next section.

5.4 The Laws of Animation

Four fundamental laws have been used in interpolation; they allow motion between two key frames to occur at a constant speed, to accelerate, decelerate or to accelerate then decelerate. Fig. 5.8 shows a PASCAL function called LAW (OP, MAXVAL, FRACT) that gives a real value corresponding to a fraction (FRACT) of the total time expressed in number of images. OP is the operation (1 = CONSTANT, 2 = ACCELERATION, 3 = DECELERATION, 4 = ACCELERATION then DECELERATION). The value must vary in the range 0 to MAXVAL. Fig. 5.9 shows how such a function is used in an animation program.

```
function LAW(OP:INTEGER; MAXVAL,FRACT:REAL):REAL;

begin
    case OP of
        1: (* constant velocity *)
            LAW := MAXVAL*FRACT;

        2: (* acceleration *)
            LAW := MAXVAL*(1-COS(PI*FRACT/2));
        3: (* deceleration *)
            LAW := MAXVAL*SIN(PI*FRACT/2);
        4: (* acceleration then deceleration *)
            LAW := MAXVAL*(1-COS(PI*FRACT))/2
    end
end.
```

Fig. 5.8. The animation laws

```
create OBJECT(...);
for IMAGE := 1 to NBFRAMES do
begin
    FRACTION := IMAGE/NBFRAMES;
    VAL := LAW(OPERATION,MAXVAL,FRACTION);

    .. transformation using VAL to modify OBJECT into OBJ2 ..

    draw OBJ2;
    TAKEPICTURE;
    PAGEGRAPH
end;
```

Fig. 5.9. An animation program (excerpts)

5.5 Skeleton Techniques

There are problems with the technique of in-betweening presented above. The first is that the motion of each point in the image is along a straight line and the same law is applied to each point. The second is that motion design requires several key frames and there is discontinuity at these frames. Various techniques can be used to overcome these problems.

The idea behind the skeleton technique [Burtnyk and Wein, 1976] is that "skeletons" of the figures, rather than the figures themselves can be used as a basis for in-betweening. A skeleton, or stick figure, is a simple image composed of only a few points, describing only the form of movement required. This allows the animator to create many key-frames consisting only of skeletons. The computer can create much better in-betweens because the key frames are much more similar; details can be added to the skeletons by computer according to a single model. In fact, this approach corresponds to how manual in-betweeners mentally use key frames as guides without using all the detailed information contained in them.

The best way of defining a skeleton is to use a network of 4-sided polygons. Relative coordinates can be associated with each vertex. Suppose that any progression in a direction from one vertex to the next corresponds to a change of one unit, as shown in Fig. 5.10.

Relative coordinates of a point P (L and W) are defined as the fractional distance along each axis which is occupied by a line passing through P intersecting the two opposing edges of the polygon at this fractional distance. Consider Fig. 5.11, with

$$P_1 = \langle\!\langle X_1, Y_1 \rangle\!\rangle \qquad P_2 = \langle\!\langle X_2, Y_2 \rangle\!\rangle$$
$$P_3 = \langle\!\langle X_3, Y_3 \rangle\!\rangle$$

and $\qquad P_4 = \langle\!\langle X_4, Y_4 \rangle\!\rangle \quad$ and $\quad P = \langle\!\langle X, Y \rangle\!\rangle$

We have

$$P^1 = P_1 + L(P_2 - P_1) \qquad (5.1) \text{ with } P^1 = \langle\!\langle X^1, Y^1 \rangle\!\rangle$$

and

$$P^{11} = P_3 + L(P_4 - P_3) \qquad (5.2) \text{ with } P^{11} = \langle\!\langle X^{11}, Y^{11} \rangle\!\rangle$$

As the line $P^1 P^{11}$ passes through P, the following equation holds:

$$\frac{X - X^{11}}{Y - Y^{11}} = \frac{X - X^1}{Y - Y^1} \tag{5.3}$$

By eliminating X^1, X^{11}, Y^1, Y^{11} from equations 5.1 to 5.3, we obtain the relative coordinate W.

$$W = \frac{X - X_1 - L(X_2 - X_1)}{(X_3 - X_1) - L(X_2 - X_1 - X_4 + X_3)} \tag{5.4}$$

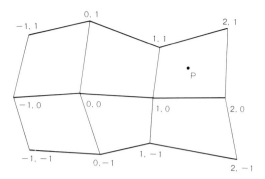

Fig. 5.10. Skeleton

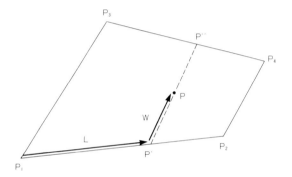

Fig. 5.11. Relative coordinates

Generally, the axes are chosen in such a way that there are only two units in the W direction. This restricts the transverse distance and allows better control. Fig. 5.12 shows examples of skeleton-derived images.

5.6 The Path of Motion and P-curves

Linear interpolation techniques are very convenient to transform the shape of an object; they can produce good in-betweens when the initial and final key frames are given. This method is the basis of the excellent film *Hunger* by Peter Foldes. However, because of the problems of continuity discussed in section 5.4, linear interpolation is not suitable for producing classical movements involving a modification of location. This problem can be solved by programming all physical laws that drive this movement. However, this approach requires thorough knowledge of both physics and computer science. Moreover, physical equations for many motions are quite difficult to express.

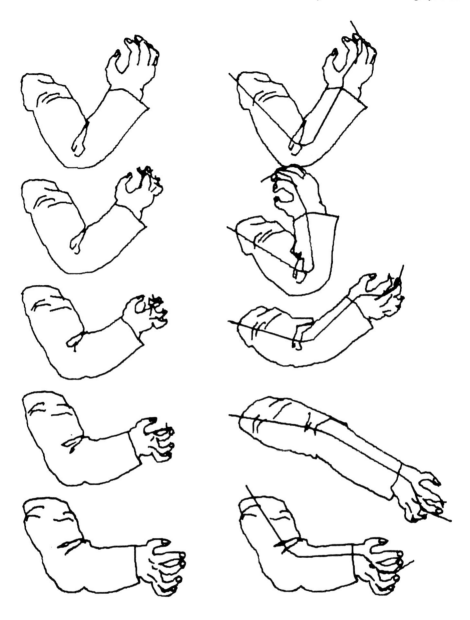

Fig. 5.12. Skeleton Technique Animation System by M. Wein and N. Burtnyk, National Research Council of Canada

An interesting technique that can be combined with interpolation, as shown in Section 5.7, involves the use of path descriptions and P-curves, as first introduced by R. Baecker [1969] in his GENESYS system.

A dynamic picture is obtained by continuously altering of a static picture. These alterations are obtained by specifying the temporal behavior of a parameter. For example, the temporal behavior of the position of a point can easily be represented by a P-curve.

A P-curve defines both the trajectory of the point and its location in time. In an example suggested by Baecker [1969], a person goes from one corner A of a square room to the diagonally opposite corner C by walking along two adjacent walls. Fig. 5.13 shows the situation and the trajectory, $Y = f(X)$, is shown in Fig. 5.14. However, no indication of time is given here.

It is also possible to represent the two curves corresponding to the variation of X and Y with time $X(t)$ and $Y(t)$, as shown in Fig. 5.15.

We observe that there is almost no motion between t_1 and t_2; that is not shown on Fig. 5.14. A P-curve allows the animator to express the information contained in Fig. 5.14 and Fig. 5.15 on a unique graph. In our example, the P-curve has the shape of the trajectory, but a trail of symbols is used instead of a continuous line to depict the path. The symbols are spaced equally in time. This means that the dynamics are represented by the local density of the symbols, as shown in Fig. 5.16.

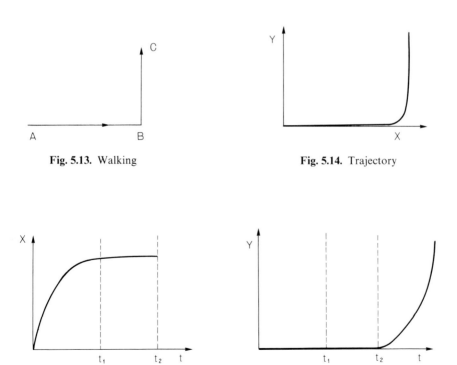

Fig. 5.13. Walking   Fig. 5.14. Trajectory

Fig. 5.15. $X(t)$ and $Y(t)$

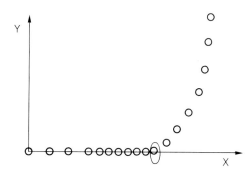

Fig. 5.16. P-curve

5.7 In-betweening Using Moving Point Constraints

As discussed, in-betweening often provides bad results, because of the use of linear interpolation. Even if a non-linear law is used, this is a non-linear variation in time only and not in space. In fact it is not sufficient to specify the speed of interpolation, it is also desirable to specify a non-linear path. Reeves [1981] has proposed a method of in-betweening using moving point constraints. This method is meant to allow the specification of multiple paths and speeds of interpolation and to reduce motion discontinuities at key frames.

The principle of the technique is to associate a curve varying in space and time with some points of the animated object. This curve is called a moving point and it controls the trajectory and the dynamics of the point similarly to P-curves.

Fig. 5.17 shows an example with three key frames (K1, K2 and K3) and three moving points (M1, M2 and M3). The shape of the curves specifies the path of interpolation; for example, A1 is transformed into A2 using the moving point M1. B1 is transformed into B2 and then into B3 using the moving point M2. C1 is transformed into C2 and then into C3 using the moving point M3. Symbols along the curves indicate timing. Each symbol represents an equal length of time.

With such a strategy, only the moving points need to be defined; the curves in the key frames do not have to be numbered and counted.

Several different in-betweening algorithms can be applied in the Reeves technique: the Miura algorithm [Miura et al., 1967], the Coons algorithm [1974] and the cubic metric space in-between algorithm [Reeves, 1980].

The three algorithms must operate on complete path networks. Fig. 5.18 shows such a network corresponding to Fig. 5.17. Reeves [1980] has tested several simple algorithms for completing the networks.

In Fig. 5.19 we consider one patch, defined by four curves, involving parts of two key frames (e.g., K1 and K2) and two moving points (e.g., M1 and M2).

The in-betweening problem is to find the curve K(t) that represents the in-between part corresponding to K1 and K2 at time t.

The Miura algorithm consists of the following steps:

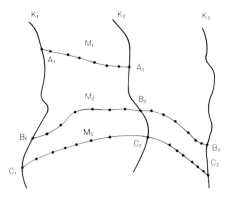

Fig. 5.17. In-betweening using moving point contraints

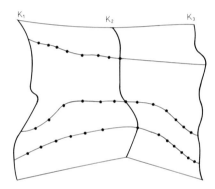

Fig. 5.18. Patch network

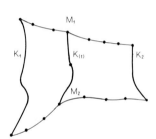

Fig. 5.19. One patch

1. Approximate the curves K1 and K2 by two segment lines L1 and L2 with the same extremities as K1 and K2.
2. Find the transformation T_1 that transforms L1 into L(t) where L(t) is the approximation of K(t) with the same extremities.
3. Find the transformation T_2 that transforms L2 into L(t).

The transformations T_1 and T_2 are composed of translation, rotation and a scaling. In parametric notation, the curve K(t) can now be expressed as:

$$(1 - t)T_1 + tT_2 \qquad (5.5)$$

The Coons algorithm is based on the Coons representation for three-dimensional objects used in computer-aided design. It defines each patch defined by its four boundaries and normal derivative functions at these boundaries. Interpolation is performed by calculating a surface which will satisfy the boundary conditions. This means that adjoining patches will be curvature continuous across their common boundary.

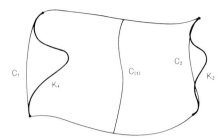

Fig. 5.20. Parametric curves

The cubic metric space in-betweening algorithm is similar to the Miura algorithm but it produces much better continuity along boundaries between patches. Instead of using segment lines L_1, L_2, $L(t)$, Reeves uses cubic curves C_1, C_2, $C(t)$. As shown in Fig. 5.20, the parametric curves C_1 and C_2 match the positions of the key frames K_1 and K_2 at their two end points, but they also match the first derivatives. $C(t)$ is also a parametric cubic curve defined in such a way that the endpoints are the positions of the moving points at time t and its endpoint slopes are the time-weighted average of the slopes at the corresponding endpoints of K_1 and K_2.

The in-between shape $K(t)$ is obtained by applying to K_1 and K_2 the transformation that transforms C_1 into $C(t)$ and C_2 into $C(t)$ with the conditions that $K(t)$ must match $C(t)$'s position and slope at its end points.

5.8 Coloring Techniques

The use of color in cartoons is very important. When the number of cels that have to be colored is considered, it can be seen that the computer can play an important role relieving the tedium and expense of hand coloring. The principle is very simple: the artist points to an area on the color display by using a locator device, and the area is colored. The color has, of course, to be chosen beforehand by the artist. Generally, that is also accomplished by pointing to a selection in a menu of colors, called the **palette**. This operation of area filling or coloring is one operation of more general interactive systems called **paint systems**. These systems will be discussed in detail in the next section. The coloring operation is also often implemented in graphics editors. Fig. 5.21 shows an example made with the graphics editor GRAFEDIT [N. Magnenat-Thalmann et al., 1981]. There are two kinds of coloring algorithms:

1. **Region-filling algorithms,** which are used to fill regions defined by pixel values in a frame buffer.
2. **Polygon-filling algorithms,** which are used to fill polygons defined by their vertices.

Region-filling algorithms are much faster because they work directly with pixels. However, they cannot be easily used in systems that manipulate objects by complex transformations. This means that region filling algorithms are very suitable for coloring backgrounds, but they are not very adequate for coloring any cel.

A region-filling algorithm has to solve the following problem: given a connected set of pixels of color C1 bounded by pixels of different colors (all different from C1), change these and only these pixels from color C1 to a different color, C2. We consider that pixels are 4-connected, meaning that any pixel can be reached from another one by a sequence of any of the four one-pixel moves: up, down, left, right. A simple algorithm consists of first determining whether the pixel at $\langle X, Y \rangle$ is still of color C1. If so, the value is changed to C2 and the four neighboring pixels are then examined. The process is typically recursive.

Alvy Ray Smith [1979] has developed a more efficient algorithm (tint-filling) that is based on the same basic principle. However, instead of recursion, the algorithm works with runs. A run is defined as a horizontal group of adjacent pixels within the region. In this method, the contiguous horizontal run containing the starting pixel is colored with C2. Then by examining the row above the just-filled run from left to right, the right-most pixel of each run is found and stacked. The same process is applied to the row below the just-filled run. After processing a run, the next run is given by the pixel address at the top of the stack. The algorithm is finished when the stack is empty.

A typical polygon-filling algorithm is based on a scan-line method. The polygon is scanned by horizontal (scan) lines. For each scan-line, there are three steps:

1. Find the intersection of the scan-line with the edges of the polygon.
2. Sort the intersections by increasing x-coordinates.
3. Color all pixels that remain within pairs of intersections.

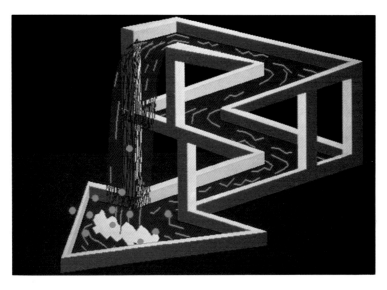

Fig. 5.21. An example produced with GRAFEDIT. © N. Magnenat-Thalmann and D. Thalmann

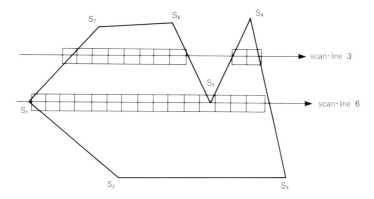

Fig. 5.22. Scan-line algorithm

Fig. 5.22 shows an example: at scan-line 6, there is a problem with the pixel at the vertex S_5; it must be counted twice.

As the calculations of intersections can be very expensive, edge coherence can be used. This is based on the principle that if a scan line intersects an edge, there is a great probability that it also intersects the next scan-line. An active edge table is then maintained which contains all edges intersected by the current scan-line.

5.9 Paint Systems

A paint system is much more than an interactive system with area filling or coloring facilities. It simulates the normal tools of a painter. Typically, a paint system is a menu-driven program for handpainting two-dimensional images. The painter uses a stylus, or pen. First, he chooses a color from a palette, i.e., a color menu. Then, the artist selects a "brush" that can have any 2-dimensional shape. Painting is accomplished by moving the stylus. A stroke is drawn as a succession of copies of the brush.

One of the most well-known paint systems is PAINT [Smith, 1978] which was developed at the New York Institute of Technology. The system offers several menus and many commands. In particular, the following is included in PAINT:

- different modes of painting: simple, rubber stamping, smearing, filtered, anti-aliased
- automatic filling (with the tint-fill algorithm)
- brush creation and storage
- palette creation and storage
- picture storage
- a way of recording actions
- an input scanner
- drafting aids like smoothing.

Several other existing paint systems are described in the journal *Computer Graphics World* [CGW, 1982].

5.10 Color Simulation and Dithering

Coloring and painting systems can theoretically be implemented for any color raster terminal. However, very realistic images can only be produced using expensive devices. It is difficult to produce good images with a low-resolution screen, such as those currently available on popular home computer systems. But with a fairly reasonable resolution, say 512×512 pixels, it is possible to produce good images in two dimensions if colors, intensity and so on are not too restricted.

For example, let us consider a terminal which has a resolution of 420×640 pixels. It has a choice of 64 different colors but only 8 can be displayed at the same time. This drastically limits the production of realistic effects. However, the terminal has 120 patterns that can be programmed. These patterns have 8×14 pixels and allow the user to control colors at the pixel level. In this project, tools have been developed for using these pattern facilities:

- to obtain more than eight colors at the same time on the screen
- to obtain all color possibilities by simulation with patterns
- to obtain color gradations (discussed in Section 5.11).

Color simulation is the heart of the project developed by Magnenat-Thalmann et al., [1984]. We can obtain a very large number of "simulated colors" by using the eight colors (chosen from among 64) and the 120 patterns. The procedure that simulates the colors is called MIXCOLORS.

We input to this procedure N colors along with their weights and intensity in the mixture. MIXCOLORS then produces a matrix of colors and transmits it to the procedure DEFPAT that builds the convenient command for the terminal. To fill a polygon P with the mixture, we use the procedure FILLCOLOR (P, NUMPAT) where NUMPAT is the pattern number defined in MIXCOLORS.

The procedure MIXCOLORS can be defined in the PASCAL language as:

procedure MIXCOLORS (INFOCOL:*dynamic* TABCOLOR;
INT:INTENSITY; NUMPAT:LIMITPAT);
- NUMPAT is the pattern number defined in the range LIMITPAT $= 0..119$.
- INT is the intensity of the mixture defined by the type
INTENSITY $= record$
               FORCE:REAL;
               BLACK, WHITE:COLNUMBER
       end;

where FORCE is the density of the mixture (between 0 and 1)

BLACK and WHITE are the color numbers used to add black or white pixels to the mixture.
- INFOCOL is a dynamic (conformant) array; this array can be defined as:

type DESCRCOLOR = *record*

H, L, S: REAL;

WEIGHT: REAL;

NUM: COLNUMBER

end;

TABCOLOR = *array* [INTEGER] *of* DESCRCOLOR;

The array defines the colors in the mixture by giving the color value in the HLS system, the relative weight in the mixture and the color number that is used.

To record the colors in the N × M matrix, we consider this matrix as a width tape of N × M "cells". Each "cell" has a color number. The tape is followed by putting in a color number every X "cells" according to the distribution of the color in the mixture. This distribution is a function of the relative weights and density of the mixture and is calculated as follows:

- add all the color weights
- compute the relative weights of each color, depending on the density, by using:

INFOCOL [K] . WEIGHT := (INFOCOL [K] . WEIGHT/ WEIGHT_SUM) * DENSITY

where DENSITY is

$$(1 - INT . FORCE) * 2 \text{ if INT . FORCE} > 0.5 \text{ and INT . FORCE} * 2$$
$$\text{if INT . FORCE} < 0.5$$

- compute the distribution step, a correction and a correction frequency. The last two values are only used when there are collisions in the color distribution process described below.

For each color K do

TEMP := 1/INFOCOL [K] . WEIGHT;

STEP := TRUNC(TEMP);

with COLOR [K] *do*

begin

if ROUND(TEMP) = STEP

then begin

STEPROUND := STEP;

CORRECTION := STEP + 1

end

else begin

STEPROUND := STEP + 1;

CORRECTION := STEP

end;

if ABS(TEMP-STEPROUND) < EPSILON

then FREQCORRECTION := number of pixels in a pattern + 1

(*this means there is no correction*)

else FREQCORRECTION := ROUND (1/ABS (TEMP-STEPROUND))

end;

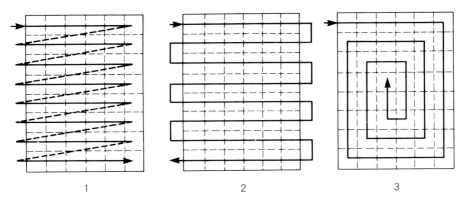

Fig. 5.23. Three methods of color distribution

Once distribution steps for each color have been computed, they must be used in the distribution process. But how is the pattern followed? How does the imaginary tape advance through the pattern? Three methods were studied, as shown in Fig. 5.23. The third method (spiral) was choosen because it produces the most homogeneity.

During the distribution process, collisions are possible; this means that a color number is assigned to a "cell" that is already occupied. We proceed as follows:

if the "cell" is occupied (collision)
then if we may go back *then begin* go back;
        if the cell is free
        then put in the color number
        else go forward to the next free cell
        end
    else go forward to the next free cell

We consider that we can go back if the actual step is the maximum of the distribution step (STEPROUND) and the correction. The actual step is computed as the corrected step if COUNT modulo the correction frequency is equal to zero, otherwise it is computed as the distribution step. COUNT is a counter that is incremented during the progress of the imaginary tape.

Another way of simulating colors by pattern can be based on techniques used for halftone images like the **ordered dither technique**, which is used to display an m-x-m image on an m-x-m bi-level display (Judice et al., 1974). In this method, a pixel (x, y) is the desired intensity at the point (x, y) and D_{ij} is an element of the n-x-n dither matrix D_j. The indices i and j are calculated by the equations:

$$i = x \ modulo \ n \quad \text{and} \quad j = y \ modulo \ n$$

The dither matrices, calculated by Judice et al.(1974), are matrices where each of the integers 0 to n^2-1 appear once in matrix.

5.11 Gradation Techniques

To produce realistic images in two-dimensions, one of the best methods is the use of gradation. Many pictures can be represented by using gradations to simulate special effects such as shading, light effects, reflections and so on. Typical examples of drawings with gradation include sunsets, sea, landscapes, trees and mountains.

Gradation techniques start from an initial figure and "converge" to another, for example a line segment or a point. The gradation is obtained by coloring intermediate figures. At each step, the color is lighter or darker, depending on the parameters.

Three procedures have been implemented:

POINTGRAD: gradation from a figure F to a point P
LINEGRAD: gradation from a figure F to a line segment with vertices S1 and S2
FIGGRAD: gradation from a figure F to another figure F2.

Apart from the specific parameters F, P, S1, S2 and F2, the following parameters have to be given for the three procedures: the initial intensity INTINIT, the final intensity INTFINAL and the array of colors INFOCOL (as defined in Section 5.10).

We also have to establish a rule for changing the intensity at each step. Four types of rules were tested, based on the animation laws (Section 5.4):

– acceleration then deceleration
– acceleration
– deceleration
– linear progression.

The number of steps in the gradation is defined as $PATI - PAT2 + 1$ where PAT1 and PAT2 are two pattern numbers.

Algorithms

1. **Gradation to a point P**
   The gradation is obtained by the following steps:
   i)   The initial figure is filled with the mixture defined by the array of colors INFOCOL and the initial intensity.
   ii) A ratio R of homothesis is computed based on the number of steps.
   iii) Intermediate figures are computed by homothesis with ratio R and center P and are then filled with the mixture defined by the array of colors INFOCOL. The intensity is calculated by using the chosen rule.
   Fig. 5.24 shows an example.

2. **Gradation to a line segment $S_1 S_2$**
   This method uses the two-figure interpolation technique introduced by Burtnyk and Wein [1971] and presented in Section 5.3. It requires that the initial and the final figures have control points that allow a correspondence between them. In the gradation example presented (Fig. 5.25), we have to add two control points to the initial figure F. These points correspond to the two

Fig. 5.24. An example of gradation to a point: "a candle" (Designer: N. Chourot. © N. Magnenat-Thalmann and D. Thalmann)

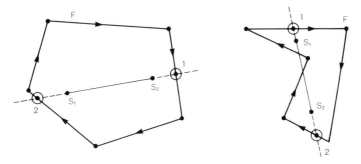

Fig. 5.25. Gradation to a line segment

intersections between F and the line passing through the segment $S_1 S_2$, as shown. We also build a circular segment C that includes S_1 and S_2 as control points. Then the interpolation process starts between the figures F and C. All intermediate figures calculated by the interpolation process are displayed and filled with the mixture obtained by using the array of colors INFOCOL and the intensity calculated with the chosen rule. Fig. 5.26 shows an example.

3. **Gradation to another figure F2**

   This method uses the same interpolation technique between the two figures. To suit both figures to the interpolation process, the following algorithm is applied:

   i) *if* F1 is counterclockwise *then* reverse (F1)

       if F2 is counterclockwise *then* reverse (F2)

Fig. 5.26. An example of gradation to a segment: "spheres in the sky" (Designer: N. Chourot. © N. Magnenat-Thalmann and D. Thalmann)

   ii)   *look for* the left-most point P_{L2} of F2
         if P_{L2} is on the left of the highest point of F1
         and on the left of the lowest point of F1
         then look for the point P_{L1} of F1 that is the nearest to
         P_{L2} *else* look for the left-most point P_{L1} of F1
   iii) add P_{L1} as control point of F1
         add P_{L2} as control point of F2

When this algorithm has been applied, the interpolation and color process is the same as in the previous gradation method.

5.12 A Case Study: The Multiple Track Animator System

MUTAN [Fortin et al., 1983] is an interactive system for independently animating three-dimensional graphical objects (or parts of graphical objects), as in a scene. Its main purpose is to define, by key positions, the best motions for a graphical object. For example, MUTAN can synchronize motion with sound, light or smell. Suppose, for example, that an animator would like to produce a film sequence in which two little girls are skating to music. There are two problems: the motion must be synchronized with the music and the two girls must be synchronized with each other.

To synchronized the motion with the music, marks are associated with appropriate frame numbers. These marks indicate that at this moment in time, the character is performing exactly a specific motion. As the intermediate frames are produced, it is not necessary to start again if the synchronization is found inadequate. The marks merely have to be moved.

An animator might also wish to adjust the motion of one individual without modifying the motion of the others. To solve this problem, we introduced the concept of a TRACK (as in sound reproduction). All animation constraints of a graphical object are recorded on each track.

The name MUTAN stands for "MUltiple Track ANimator," which means that the system can handle several tracks. It also provides a visual image that allows the animator to see exactly what is being done.

During an interactive session with MUTAN, the screen is divided into three areas:

1. **The chronogram/visual area**
   This displays either a schema of the tracks with the marks (chronogram mode) or a specific frame (visual mode), depending on the command.
2. **The animator-computer dialog area**
   Here the user may enter commands and receive error messages.
3. **The information area**
   This contains information about the tracks or about the current frame when it is displayed.

Table 5.2. The MUTAN commands

ADD	– adds a certain number of frames
BACKWARD	– moves backward along the film
CREATE	– creates a track
CHRONOGRAM	– displays a part of film in the chronogram area
CUT	– cuts frames on one or several tracks
DELETE	– deletes a track
END	– ends the session
ERASE	– erases a mark
FILM	– produces the frames on a file
FORWARD	– moves forward along the film
GET	– memorises a mark
IDENTIFY	– selects invisible marks
LOOK	– looks at any frame in the visual area
MARK	– creates or modifies a mark on a track
MENU	– displays a file indicated by an index
PUT	– replaces a mark on a track
READ	– reads mark information
TRACKS	– displays tracks in the chronogram area
WRITE	– writes mark information

There are presently 19 commands in the MUTAN system, as shown in Table 5.2. Almost all commands have similar parameters:

- a track or a set of tracks
- a mark or a set of marks
- a frame number.

CREATE ⟨track⟩, as the name implies, allows the animator to create a new track. This track of course has no marks. The command DELETE ⟨track⟩ is similarly self-explanatory.

If a film consists of a little girl MELANIE playing with a dog, the animator will use the commands CREATE MELANIE and CREATE DOG. These commands will initialize the tracks. To display them, the command TRACKS MELANIE DOG must be entered. Following this command, two red lines are displayed in the chronogram area. Each line identifies a track.

Now the marks must be placed on the tracks to define animation constraints. The command MARK ⟨frame number⟩ ⟨track⟩ allows the animator to create or modify a mark on a track and to define the frame number where the mark is placed. For example, suppose the dog hears a whistle, stops running and then starts again. Two marks would be used.

MARK 15 DOG
MARK 18 DOG

For each MARK command, the animator receives the following message in the dialog area: "ENTER THE NAME OF THE FRAME"; he/she then types respectively "DOG STOPS", "DOG STARTS".

The MARK command can also be used without parameters. In this case the animator enters the mark on the red line representing the track. The principle is valid for other commands.

When the MARK command is used, the animator has to enter in the dialog area the name of a key position which identifies an image. The key positions can be created with a graphics editor by using the graphical programming language MIRA-3D [N. Magnenat-Thalmann and D. Thalmann, 1983] or by digitizing. The different key positions can be grouped into indices. The command MENU ⟨index⟩ shows the animator which key positions are available on the file indicated by the index.

A mark can be erased with an appropriate command, while the command GET memorizes a mark before erasing it and PUT replaces it on the track.

The animator can move a window along the film by using the command CHRONOGRAM. This command has different forms. For example, CHRONOGRAM 50 75 MELANIE DOG, displays the frames 50 to 75 for the tracks MELANIE and DOG. At the same time, information about the different marks on this part of the film are displayed in the information area. If there are too many marks to display, only some of them are visible; others can be seen by using the command IDENTIFY.

As the work of an animator is essentially sequential, two commands have been added to move forwards and backwards along the film. FORWARD or

BACKWARD performs a shift to the right or left, moving the same number of frames as that presently displayed in the chronogram area.

The animator can cut one or several frames on one or several tracks by using the command CUT ⟨set of frames⟩ ⟨set of tracks⟩. All marks will be shifted to the left.

Conversely, the command ADD ⟨frame number⟩ ⟨set of tracks⟩ adds a certain number of new frames to the right of the frame specified and on the chosen tracks. The number of frames added has to be entered by the animator in the dialog area.

The LOOK command allows the animator to look at any frame of the film in the visual area. For the frames where no marks exist, an interpolation is performed. It is also possible to select only one or several tracks: In this case, only a part of the frame is displayed.

The command FILM produces the frames on a file to be recorded on a videorecorder or to be displayed for a camera.

There are also commands to read and write MARK information on a file.

6 Modeled Animation

6.1 What Is Modeled Animation?

While computer-assisted animation is a highly valuable and interesting process, computer modeled animation is even more fascinating. Here the computer becomes more than a support, playing a basic role in the creation of a three-dimensional world. Man, in fact, has always found it difficult to represent three-dimensional space in drawings; few people can draw in true perspective. Furthermore, it is simply impossible to produce all the tens of thousands of drawings needed for an animated film by hand. In this sense, the computer is not replacing man, since it does jobs which simply cannot be performed manually. Modeled animation has been used in television advertisements (Crow, 1978) and for special effects in films like *2001: A Space Odyssey, Return of Jedi* and especially *TRON*. Three-dimensional computer animation involves three main activities:

1. **Object modeling:** this consists of describing or constructing three-dimensional objects. Two kinds of computer models can be implemented:

   - wire-frame models based on three-dimensional line drawings
   - solid models based on two and three-dimensional surfaces.

   For each of these two types of models, there are three ways of creating the objects:

   - digitization
   - graphics editing
   - programming.

2. **Motion specification and synchronization:** to animate an object is to make it move, or to change its shape or position over a period of time. Consider a very simple example which illustrates how the computer can be used for this purpose. Suppose we want to move an object 300 meters in 5 seconds. Knowing that 24 images per second will be required (i.e., 120 images altogether), the object will have to be moved a distance of 2.5 metres per image (i.e. 300 meters divided by 120). The computer must therefore be instructed to repeat the following sequence 120 times:

- move the object 2.5 metres
- draw the object
- take a picture
- erase the object.

The same principle applies to more complex movements, as long as provision is made for changes in pace, pauses, etc.
Not only must the movements be created for all the actors involved in each scene, but all these movements must be synchronized.
When making an ordinary video film, movements can be filmed of course, but the camera itself can also be moved. The same principle applies to three-dimensional computer animation, although instead of wielding a real camera, a dummy, or "virtual," camera is simulated. The location of the camera, its positioning and even focus are programmed. Furthermore, all these parameters can be varied or combined so that any camera motion can be simulated (pan, tilt, zooms). An example is presented in Section 11.3.

3. **Image rendering:** this is the process of producing a realistic image by removing hidden surfaces and adding effects like shading, shadows, transparency and texture. These techniques will be discussed in detail in Chapters 7 and 8.

6.2 Object Modeling

The oldest and simplest type of three-dimensional model is the **wire-frame model**. This is composed of a list of points given by their coordinates or by a sequence of instructions of the type:

moveabs $\langle\langle X, Y, Z \rangle\rangle$ – move to a new location.
lineabs $\langle\langle X, Y, Z \rangle\rangle$ – draw a line from the current location
                            to the new location.

Consider the tetrahedron shown in Fig. 6.1. This can be represented by:

moveabs $\langle\langle 3, 0, 1 \rangle\rangle$;
lineabs $\langle\langle 5, 0, 1 \rangle\rangle$;
lineabs $\langle\langle 6, 0, 5 \rangle\rangle$;
lineabs $\langle\langle 3, 0, 1 \rangle\rangle$;
lineabs $\langle\langle 4, 3, 6 \rangle\rangle$;
lineabs $\langle\langle 6, 0, 5 \rangle\rangle$;
moveabs $\langle\langle 5, 0, 1 \rangle\rangle$;
lineabs $\langle\langle 4, 3, 6 \rangle\rangle$;

A wire-frame model is frequently too simple and cannot be used to achieve a great degree of realism. For this purpose, a **solid mode** is used that is based on surface descriptions. Three categories of descriptions are used, depending on the objectes shape:

- description by a set of polygons
- description by the equation of an algebraic surface
- description by patches

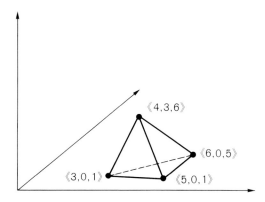

Fig. 6.1. A tetrahedron

The most well-known technique involves describing a solid by a **collection of polygons**. Lists of point and polygons are specified, where each polygon is defined by its vertices, identified by their rank in the list of points. For example, the tetrahedron of Fig. 6.1 can be defined as:

POINT $\langle\langle 3, 0, 1\rangle\rangle$
POINT $\langle\langle 5, 0, 1\rangle\rangle$
POINT $\langle\langle 6, 0, 5\rangle\rangle$
POINT $\langle\langle 4, 3, 6\rangle\rangle$
POLYGON   1, 2, 4
POLYGON   2, 3, 4
POLYGON   1, 3, 4
POLYGON   1, 2, 3

Polygons can model any object. However, if the object is curved, a large number of polygons may be required. For this reason, algebraic surfaces and patches are often used.

Algebraic surfaces are curved surfaces described mathematically by an equation. The most popular include the quadric surfaces like spheres (Fig. 6.2), cones, cylinders and ellipsoids (Fig. 6.3). A new and powerful family of parametric shapes had recently extended these basic quadric surfaces: the superquadrics [Barr, 1981]. These generalize the basic quadric surfaces by producing a continuum of useful forms with rounded edges and filleted faces. Angle-preserving transformations operate on a predefined surface or space curve, bending and twisting the object into a new form.

For representing car bodies or airplane surfaces, a good procedure is to use bivariate surface **patches**. Surfaces are constructed piecewise, sewing the patches together with specified continuity conditions.

The two most well-known surface patches are the work of Coons and Bezier.

In the technique introduced by Coons (1964), a surface patch is determined by four boundary curves, $P(U, 0)$, $P(U, 1)$, $P(0, V)$, $P(1, V)$ where U and V are in the range 0,1 and by a linear interpolation between these four curves:

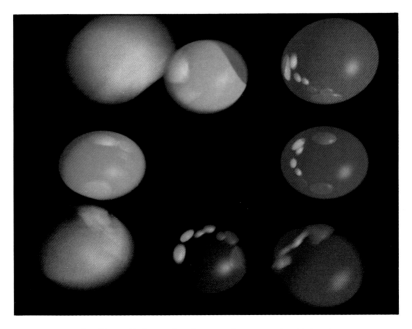

Fig. 6.2. Balls in motion by Tom Porter and Rob Cook

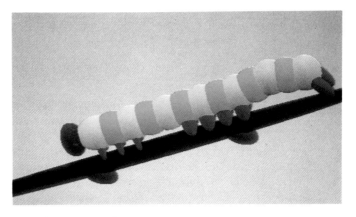

Fig. 6.3. Caterpillar by Don Herbison-Evans, Univ. Sydney

$$Q(U, V) = P(U, 0)F_{00}(V) + P(U, 1)F_{01}(V) + P(0, V)F_{00}(U)$$
$$+ P(1, V)F_{01}(U) - P(0, 0)F_{00}(U)F_{00}(V)$$
$$- P(0, 1)F_{00}(U)F_{01}(V)$$
$$- P(1, 0)F_{01}(U)F_{00}(V) - P(1, 1)F_{01}(U)F_{01}(V) \qquad (6.1)$$

where the functions $F_{ij}(U)$ serve to blend the boundary conditions to form a surface.

In the method introduced by Bezier (1972), a surface is calculated from N curves given by M points. These points P_{ij} are called control points and the surface is calculated as:

$$Q(U, V) = \sum_{i=0}^{N} \sum_{j=0}^{M} P_{ij} B_{iN}(U) B_{jM}(V) \qquad (6.2)$$

where U and V are in the range [0; 1].

$$B_{iN}(U) = \frac{N!}{i!(N-i)!} U^i (1-U)^{N-i} \qquad (6.3)$$

$$B_{jM}(V) = \frac{M!}{j!(M-j)!} V^j (1-V)^{M-j} \qquad (6.4)$$

Fig. 6.4 shows an example of a Bezier surface in a line drawing.

It is important to note that an object is often built up as a combination of simpler objects that can be modeled in different ways. Fig. 6.5 shows a wire-frame giraffe that is modeled as follows:

head................. box
neck................. series of circular cones
thigh .... truncated elliptic cone
knee-cap............. sphere
foreleg.............. cylinder
hoof................. two bodies of revolution
tail .... cylinder and truncated cone

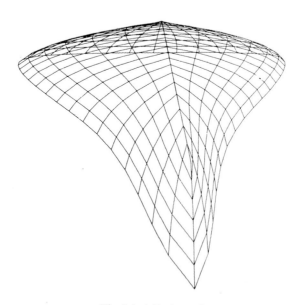

Fig. 6.4. A Bezier surface

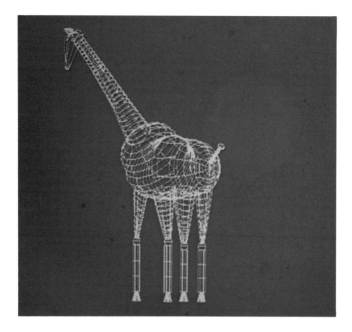

Fig. 6.5. A giraffe

The construction of three-dimensional objects based on these different models is generally a complex task. A powerful new type of surface called β-spline surfaces has been introduced by Brian A. Barsky [1985]. An example of this and other surfaces is shown in Fig. 7.9 and Fig. 7.10.

6.3 Object Creation

There are three ways of constructing three-dimensional objects, according to the kind of object and it degree of complexity:

– digitization
– graphic editing
– programming.

Digitization
Digitization consists of taking a photograph or making a drawing of an object (for example a car), tracing a grid on this object, and then photographing it from various viewpoints—front, side, top and bottom. The points of intersection of the grid are then numbered in such a way that the same point on several photographs bears the same number. The various photographs are then digitized, using a program which reconstructs the image in three dimensions. This technique is used particularly for objects with highly irregular shapes. (Complete examples are

given in Sections 11.4 and 12.3.) Another method based on pictures taken from two different distances is described by Blum [1979].

Graphics Editing

With a graphic editor, objects can be constructed in three dimensions by assembling and combining simpler objects. This is necessarily an interactive operation, since the user must be able to see immediately the effect of the commands given. As an example, we present the BODY-BUILDING [Magnenat-Thalmann et al., 1985] general-purpose three-dimensional graphic editor. It can be used to create three-dimensional objects, to modify them by geometrical transformations and to assemble them to obtain a complete drawing. The drawing can be stored on a file; later, it can be retrieved for further modifications, or a hard copy can be obtained. BODY-BUILDING is strongly user-oriented and does not require a background in computer science. The user communicates with the editor by a set of simple commands, guided by various messages and other feedback. Thus, a BODY-BUILDING, session involves a friendly dialogue between user and editor.

At the beginning of a session, the editor divides the screen into two areas:

1. **The drawing area**, where the user creates his or her drawing
2. **The command/message area**, which is an alphanumeric area; the user may enter commands and receive messages.

The commands can be classified into six categories:

1. **Environment relation commands**, which allow objects to be saved and retrieved.
2. **Visual parameter definition commands**, which allow the user to select interactively the visual parameters which define the projection used for the drawing. BODY-BUILDING also offers a standard projection for the user who is not familiar with three dimensional graphics.
3. **Creation/deletion commands**, which allow the user to create or delete objects. There are three ways of creating an object:
   i) **by direct graphical input with a locator device**
      In this case, the user draws an original diagram. 3D input is similar to the polyhedron input of PICAX [Liardet, 1978].
   ii) **by combining existing diagrams**
      (concatenation, join ...).
   iii) **by generating ruled surfaces and patches**
      Most commands and lines of commands may be preceded by a repetitive factor, allowing the user to write little "programs" that create drawings based on very regular patterns.
4. **Transformation commands**, which allow the user to modify the objects by various geometrical transformations: rotation, translation, symmetry, scaling, union, and so on.
5. **Special commands**, which allow the user to select various global options— transparency, color, lights—or to examine the values of variables.

Table 6.1 shows the commands in BODY-BUILDING.

Table 6.1. The BODY-BUILDING commands

ALIGN	ERASE	PUT	SHADE
BETA	EXECUTE	READFILE	SHOW
COLOR	HELP	READGRAPH	SOURCE
CONE	LIST	REDRAW	TEXT
COONS	MOVE	REFLECTANCE	TRANSLATION
COPY	PARACONIC	REVOLUTION	TRANSPARENCY
CREATE	PARCAMERA	ROTATION	UNION
DELETE	PERCAMERA	SAVE	
END	POSITION	SCALE	

Programming

For objects based on complex and repeated patterns or mathematical functions, we use **programming**. Such an object could be a bridge. The superstructure is generally based on repeated patterns (lattice, cantilever, suspension). The piers are composed using mathematical figures like cylinders or cones [Thalmann et al., 1982b]. We have, in fact, developed a graphical type called BRIDGE that allows the programmer to reproduce almost any kind of bridge (explained in detail in Section 11.1). Abstract graphical types [Thalmann and Magnenat-Thalmann, 1979] certainly provide the best way of structuring the definition of graphical objects. For example, a graphical type can be defined by using the syntax of the MIRA language [Magnenat-Thalmann and Thalmann, 1982, 1983]

$\langle$figure type$\rangle ::= $ *figure* $\langle$formal parameter list$\rangle$; $\langle$block$\rangle$

The formal parameter list and the block are similar to the corresponding elements in a procedure. However, statements in the block must build the graphical object either by line drawing specifications or surface specifications (for the removal of hidden surfaces and shading).

To define a figure type, the following steps must be carried out:

1. The characteristics of the figure are determined, which then become the parameters.
2. An algorithm is developed to build the figure with the help of the parameters. For example:

type TETRAHEDRON = *figure* (A, B, C, D: VECTOR);
                  begin
                        moveabs A; *lineabs* B, C, A, D, C;
                        moveabs B; *lineabs* D
                end;

These graphical types provide the following advantages to the programmer:

1. Operations may be restricted to specific types (e.g., the angle between two planes may be defined, but not the angle between two spheres.)

2. Figures can be used just like other types (e.g., we may define an array of cubes or a record with figure fields.)

Various attributes may be given to a figure; the most important are linestyle, intensity, linewidth and color. Graphical variables are defined as variables of graphical type. Four fundamental statements allow the user to manipulate these variables:

– *create* ⟨figure⟩ (⟨actual parameter list⟩)
– *delete* ⟨figure⟩
– *draw* ⟨figure⟩
– *erase* ⟨figure⟩

The first operation creates the figure by giving values to the corresponding type parameters; the figure may then be drawn, erased or deleted.

6.4 Motion Specification

Motion in cartoon animation is often restricted to stretching, twisting, bending and changing of shape. These can generally be performed by using interpolation techniques. Other movements can be decribed by paths like p-curves. In modeled animation, the transformations used in cartoon animation are sometimes employed, but modeled objects also need to be rotated and moved through a dynamic perspective view.

One of the most difficult problems in three-dimensional computer animation is specifying motion with synchronization and parallelism. For us, the term "motion" may mean several different kinds of animation events:

1. physical motions like rotations or translations of an object
2. physical transformations like alterations of the shape, size or color of an object
3. virtual camera motion.

First, these motions must be expressed precisely. For example, to move a car a distance of 300 meters in 5 seconds along the X axis, 120 frames are required (we assume 24 frames/second). If car speed is constant, the car has to be translated 2.5 meters per frame. This can be done with a loop statement in a programming language like MIRA-3D [Magnenat-Thalmann and Thalmann, 1983].

```
create CAR(...);
for FRAME := 1 to 120 do
    begin
        draw CAR;
        TRANSLATION (CAR, ⟨⟨2.5, 0, 0⟩⟩, CAR);
        TAKEPICTURE;
        CLEARGRAPH
    end;
```

The car motion given above is very easy to produce with a user-oriented system. However, when a car moves its wheels also have to rotate at a given angular speed.

This can easily be programmed. In the above program, for example, we would add wheel rotation in the loop statement. However, the most appropriate concept for animating an object like a car with rotating wheels is that of "actor." An actor possesses its own animation. This concept was first introduced in ASAS [Reynold, 1982] and then generalized by the definition of **actor types** in the CINEMIRA language [Magnenat-Thalmann and Thalmann, 1984]. For example, a CAR type can be defined as:

```
type CARTYPE = actor (SPEED:VECTOR; T1, T2:REAL);
              time T1..T2;
              type TPOS = animated VECTOR;
                   ...
                   TANGLE = animated REAL;
                   ...
              var POS: TPOS;
                  ALPHA: TANGLE;
                  I: INTEGER;
              begin
                init POS, ALPHA;
                create CAR(...);
                for I:= to 4 do create WHEEL[I] (...);
                TRANSLATION (CAR, POS, CAR);
                include CAR;
                for I:= 1 to 4 do
                  begin
                    TRANSLATION (WHEEL[I], POS, WHEEL[I]);
                    ROTATION (WHEEL[I], CENTER, WHEEL[I]),
                    ALPHA, WHEEL[I]);
                    include WHEEL[I]
                  end
              end;
```

In this excerpt, we see that the position POS of the CAR and the angle ALPHA of rotation of the wheels are defined as **animated** types. This means that POS and ALPHA are values that vary with time. Of course, the laws of variation governing the two are not independent. When an actor type is defined, variables of this type can be initialized by an **init** statement. For example:

```
var CAR1, CAR2: CARTYPE;
  ⋮
init CAR1 (《0, 30, 0》, 3, 5);
init CAR2 (《10, 40, 0》, 4, 6);
shoot until 6;
```

This means that two cars have been initialized with different speeds and different time limits. The statement **shoot** performs the shooting phase, whereupon actors are automatically placed. In this example, the upper time limit of the scene is 6 seconds, while the lower time limit is the upper limit of the previous scene.

These concepts will be further discussed in chapter 10.

7. Hidden Surfaces, Reflectance and Shading

7.1 Hidden Surfaces

A three-dimensional line drawing is generally rather unrealistic, except in a few cases (see the Eiffel Tower in Fig. 7.1). To achieve realism in a computer-generated image, lines which could not really be seen by an observer first must be removed. This process has been a common research theme since the first three-dimensional systems; numerous algorithms have been proposed to solve the problem [Sutherland et al., 1974]. They can be classified into three major categories:

1. **Object space**
   Such algorithms are based on calculations and comparisons between the geometric elements as defined by the user in the three-dimensional space or object space. Although very accurate, their cost grows very fast with the

Fig. 7.1. The Eiffel tower (from *Dream Flight*. Directors: P. Bergeron, N. Magnenat-Thalmann, D. Thalmann)

complexity of a scene. Although several of these algorithms are well-known (Appel, 1967; Galimberti and Montanari, 1969), they are not yet well used. The Appel algorithm, however, is conceptually interesting because it has applications in shadow generation (see Section 8.6) and is also considered to be the first to perform "ray tracing" (see Section 8.1). The Appel algorithm is based on the concept of quantitative invisibility, i.e., a count of the number of surfaces hiding a vertex of the polygonal objects represented. A line segment is visible only if all points on it have a quantitative invisibility of zero. This technique detects changes in quantitative invisibility along a segment and draws the visible portions.

2. **Image space**

   These algorithms make extensive use of hardware. They are based on the principle that objects are composed of polygonal faces and one must decide which face is visible at each pixel of the screen. Much more efficient than the previous algorithms, they are also limited in cost because the number of pixels remains constant and does not depend on the complexity of the scene. Moreover, these algorithms tie in well with raster technology, which is becoming ever more popular. The most well-known image space algorithms are the work of Watkins [1970] and Warnock [1969].

3. **List priority**

   These algorithms represent a compromise between object space and image space algorithms. They involve two steps:

   – in object space, processing mainly consists of building a priority list between objects according to their depths.
   – in image space, processing mainly consists of determining object visibility.

The most well-known list-priority algorithms have been developed concurrently by Schumacker et al. [1969] and Encarnacao [1970].

We briefly summarize some major algorithms that are currently used in computer animation:

– Warnock subdivision
– Scan-line
– Depth buffer
– Run-length buffer [Csuri et al., 1979].

Warnock Subdivision

In this algorithm, the screen is divided into **windows**; three cases are considered for each:

1. There is nothing to be seen in the window—there is no problem.
2. What is visible in the window is easy to draw—there is no problem.
3. What is visible is too difficult to draw—the window must be subdivided into four smaller windows.

The algorithm is typically recursive, ending it processing under one of three conditions:

1. There is nothing to see—the window is colored with the background color.
2. The window is reduced to a pixel—since no further subdivision is possible it must be colored with the appropriate color.
3. The window is easy to color; this is possible
    i) when a polygon surrounds the window. In this case the window is colored with the appropriate color.
    ii) only one polygon intersects the window. In this case the window is colored partly with the background color and partly with the appropriate color for the polygon.

Scan-line

This algorithm is based on the same principle as the color-filling algorithm described in Section 5.8; the major difference being that several polygons need to be processed instead of only one.

More generally, scan-line algorithms [Wylie et al., 1967; Bouknight and Kelley, 1970; and Watkins, 1970] are based on the following schema coded in a PASCAL-like language.

We consider two arrays:

INTENSITY: *array* [1 .. LENGTH] *of* PIXEL;
DEPTH: *array* [1 .. LENGTH] *of* REAL;

1. For each pixel IX on the scan-line

    DEPTH [IX] := background value;
    INTENSITY [IX] := maximal value;

2. For each polygon in the scene, find the pixels of the scan-line that are within the polygon.
    For each of these pixels IX:
    i) calculate the depth Z of the polygon at $\langle\langle X, Y \rangle\rangle$
    ii) *if* Z < DEPTH [IX]
        then begin
            DEPTH [IX] := Z;
            INTENSITY [IX] := corresponding polygon shading value
        end;

3. At the end of the processing of one scan-line, the array INTENSITY contains the good values and is displayed.

This basic scan-line algorithm can be much improved by taking advantage of scan-line and edge coherence. For example, the Watkins algorithm consists of two parts:

1. determination of sample spans.
    A sample span is a section of scan-line on which no change in visibility can occur.
2. determination of visibility.
    The algorithm sorts a list of span segments along the X and Z axes for each Y scan-line.

Depth Buffer

Developed by Catmull [1975], this algorithm is the simplest method of hidden-surface removal. However, it requires a depth buffer (or Z-buffer) that consists of an array containing the Z-value for each pixel. The algorithm is similar to the basic scan-line, but the intensity values are stored in a two-dimensional array (frame buffer) instead of a one-dimensional array. We have:

INTENSITY : *array* [1 .. HEIGHT, 1 .. LENGTH] *of* PIXEL;   (*frame buffer*)
DEPTH : *array* [1 .. HEIGHT, 1 .. LENGTH] *of* REAL;   (*Z-buffer*)

1. For each pixel $\langle\!\langle IX, IY \rangle\!\rangle$:

   INTENSITY [IX, IY] := background value;
   DEPTH [IX, IY] := maximal value;

2. For each polygon in the scene, find all pixels $\langle\!\langle IX, IY \rangle\!\rangle$ that are within the projected polygon. For each pixel:

   i) calculate the depth Z in $\langle\!\langle IX, IY \rangle\!\rangle$
   ii) *if* Z < DEPTH [IX, IY]   (*polygon nearer*)
       then
         begin
           DEPTH [IX, IY] := Z;
           INTENSITY [IX, IY] := corresponding polygon shading value
       end;

3. At the end of the processing of the scene, the array INTENSITY contains the required frame.

Run-length Buffer

This algorithm was specially developed for the ANTTS animation system [Csuri et al., 1979]. It is based on the use of a **run-length frame buffer** that stores run-lengths, or sequences of pixels with the same value on a scan-line. The run-length buffer is a list of fixed memory arrays, one for each scan-line of the display. This is a unified approach to the display of data: polygons and solids modeled with polygons can be divided into triangles and then broken down into run-length segments. Lines can also be broken down into run-lengths of length 1 and points, and patch points are run-lengths of length 1.

After the conversion of objects into run-lengths, the algorithm passes each run-length to the run-length buffer. When the frame has been completely processed, the run-lengths are decomposed into three-dimensional pixel values. The Z-values are compared with the same XY values in the pixel buffer, effecting brute force hidden surface removal.

The run-length buffer is, of course, stored in main memory. The pixel buffers, in mass storage, contains the color and depth of each pixel and other information like image type, light information, and object identification. This approach, requires far less main memory than the Z-buffer algorithm.

7.2 Light Reflection Models

If we eliminate the hidden faces of a sphere approximated by polygons and color all the visible polygons with the same red color, we will obtain ... a red circle! This is because our perception of the third dimension is greatly improved by the reflection of light. In the case of the sphere, the different points on its surface do not reflect light in the same way if there are point sources of light. This means that the sphere must not be colored with a uniform color.

Theoretically, there are two extremes of surface types:

– ideal specular reflectors that are like perfect mirrors
– ideal diffuse reflectors that correspond to dual matte surfaces.

In fact, most real surfaces are neither ideal specular reflectors nor ideal diffuse reflectors. For this reason, reflectance models have been developed. These models break reflection into three components: ambient, diffuse and specular. The ambient component corresponds to light that is uniformly incident and that is reflected equally in all directions by the surface. The diffuse component consists of light that emanates from a point light source, but is scattered equally in all directions. The specular component represents the highlight, i.e., light concentrated around the impact point of the incident ray. The highlight has the color of the source light.

The first light model that took into account these components was devised by Bui-Tuong Phong [1975]. Intensity in this model is given by:

$$I = I_a + I_d + I_s \tag{7.1}$$

where I is reflected intensity, I_a is reflection due to the ambient light, I_d is diffuse reflection and I_s is specular reflection. Diffuse reflection is defined as:

$$I_d = K_d \sum_{1}^{ls} \vec{N} \cdot \vec{L}_j \tag{7.2}$$

where
    K_d is the diffuse reflection coefficient
    $\vec{N}$ is the unit surface normal
    $\vec{L}_j$ is the vector in the direction of the jth light source
    ls   is the number of light sources.

Specular reflection is defined as:

$$I_s = K_s \sum_{1}^{ls} (\vec{N} \cdot \vec{L}'_j)^n \tag{7.3}$$

where
    K_s is the specular reflection coefficient
    $\vec{L}'_j$ is the vector in the direction halfway between the viewer and jth light source
    n   is an exponent that depends on the surface (typically n varies from 1 to 200 and would be infinite for a perfect reflector).

Note that the empirically-derived term for I_s contains a dot product to the nth power which in fact reduces to $\cos^n \alpha$ where α is the angle between the direction of reflection and the viewpoint. This means that the highlight is only important when α is near zero and n is small.

There are two dot products in Equation 7.1 and Phong [1975] has developed an efficient method for their incremental evaluation along a scan line.

Although the Phong model is very realistic, the specular reflection component is not exact and this has a noticeable effect for non-metallic and edge-lit objects. This is due to the fact that the intensity of the highlight does not change with the direction of the light source. According to Blinn [1977], this fault is especially apparent in computer animation.

Blinn has shown that the theoretical model designed by Torrance and Sparrow [1967] is more realistic. In this model, the surface to be drawn is assumed to be a collection of small mirrors, like facets, that are randomly placed all over the surface. The specular component is considered as reflections coming from all facets oriented in the direction of $\vec{L_j}$. The amount of specular reflection K_s is calculated as:

$$K_s = \frac{DGF}{\vec{N} \cdot \vec{E}} \tag{7.4}$$

where $\vec{N}$ is the unit surface normal, $\vec{E}$ the eye direction, D the distribution function of the directions of the facets on the surface, G the amount by which the facets shadow and mask each other and F the Fresnel factor. Blinn [1977] discusses these factors in detail.

Whitted [1980] has proposed a simpler model based on global illumination information. The new model takes into account the transmission of light through transparent objects. The model is defined by:

$$I = I_a + I_d + I_s + I_t \tag{7.5}$$

where I_t is the transmitted intensity.

The diffuse term I_d is calculated like Phong by equation (7.2). The specular term is defined as:

$$I_s = K_s S \tag{7.6}$$

where K_s is the specular reflection coefficient and S the intensity of light incident from the specular direction. The transmitted intensity will be further discussed in Section 8.2.

Whitted has applied this model of light in a technique called "ray tracing," which is presented in Section 8.1.

Hall and Greenberg [1983] have improved the Whitted model, as will be shown in Section 8.2.

Cook and Torrance [1982] have proposed a reflectance model that describes the behavior of light in terms of energy equilibrium and electronic wave theory. In this model, the brightness of an object is related to the intensity and size of each light source that illuminates it. The intensity of reflected light is given by:

$$I = I_a + \sum_j I_{ij}(\vec{N} \cdot \vec{L_j}) dw_{ij} (K_s R_s + K_d R_d) \tag{7.7}$$

where I_a, $\vec{N}$, $\vec{L_j}$, K_s and K_d have the same meaning as in the other models and dw_{ij}

Fig. 7.2. A copper vase by Rob Cook, Cornell University

represents the solid angle of a beam of incident light coming from the jth source. R_s is the specular bidirectionnal reflectance and R_d is the diffuse bidirectionnal reflectance. A bidirectionnal reflectance is defined as the ratio of the reflected intensity in a given direction to the incident energy from another direction. Cook and Torrance have also introduced an ambient reflectance, R_a, that is a linear combination of R_s and R_d. R_a, R_s and R_d all depend on the wavelength and as there exist numerous measures of reflectance spectra, a procedure for calculating RGB values from spectral energy distributions has been developed by Cook and Torrance. Fig. 7.2 shows an example.

7.3 Shading

We have already shown that there are three kinds of descriptions for solid models (Section 6.2):
– a set of polygons
– the equation of an algebraic surface
– patches.

For each of those descriptions, shading can be calculated using the reflection models presented in the previous section. However, reflection models do not directly provide ways of calculating the complete shading of an object, but only the intensity of light at specific points. The shading techniques used depend on the type of object.

For polygon meshes, three basic ways of shading objects have been developed: constant shading, Gouraud shading and Phong shading.

Constant Shading
This model involves calculating a single intensity for each polygon. It implies the following assumptions:

1. The light source is at infinity.
2. The observer is at infinity.
3. The polygon is not an approximation of a curved surface.

The two first assumptions are required so that the dot products $\vec{N} \cdot \vec{L}_j$ and $\vec{N} \cdot \vec{L}'_j$ are constant in the calculation of intensity. The third assumption is made because each polygonal facet of an object will have a slightly different intensity from its neighbors. This produces good results for a cube, but very poor ones for a sphere. Moreover, constant shading produces the Mach band effect, described by E. Mach, in 1865 as follows:

> "Wherever the light-intensity curve of an illuminated surface (the light intensity of which varies in only one direction) has a concave or convex flection with respect to the axis of the abscissa, that particular place appears brighter or darker, respectively, than its surroundings."

Fig. 7.3 shows an example of constant shading.

Gouraud Shading
Gouraud [1971] introduced an intensity interpolation shading method that eliminates the discontinuities of constant shading. However, the Mach band effect is still visible where the slope of the shading function changes. The principle of Gouraud shading is as follows:

1. For each vertex common to several polygons, the normal to each polygon is computed as a vector perpendicular to the plane of that polygon.
2. For each vertex, a unique normal is calculated by averaging the surface normals obtained previously (see Fig. 7.4).
3. Vertex intensities are calculated by using the vertex normals and one of the light models presented in Section 7.2.

Fig. 7.3. 3D shaded text (constant shading)

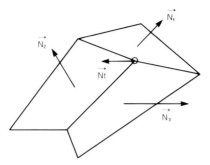

Fig. 7.4. Calculation of the vertex normal $\vec{N}_t = (\vec{N1} + \vec{N2} + \vec{N3})/3$

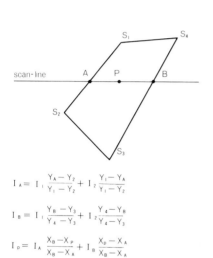

$$I_A = I_1 \frac{Y_A - Y_2}{Y_1 - Y_2} + I_2 \frac{Y_1 - Y_A}{Y_1 - Y_2}$$

$$I_B = I_1 \frac{Y_B - Y_3}{Y_4 - Y_3} + I_2 \frac{Y_4 - Y_B}{Y_4 - Y_3}$$

$$I_p = I_A \frac{X_B - X_P}{X_B - X_A} + I_B \frac{X_P - X_A}{X_B - X_A}$$

Fig. 7.5. Intensity interpolation (Gouraud shading)

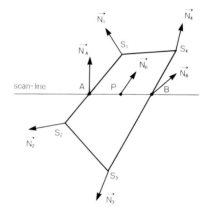

Fig. 7.6. Normal interpolation (Phong shading). $\bar{N}_P$ is calculated by linear interpolation between $\bar{N}_A$ and $\bar{N}_B$; $\bar{N}_A$ is calculated by linear interpolation between $\bar{N}_1$ and $\bar{N}_2$ and $\bar{N}_B$ is calculated by linear interpolation between $\bar{N}_3$ and $\bar{N}_4$

4. As each polygon has different shading at each vertex, the shading at any point inside the polygon is found by linear interpolation of vertex intensities along each edge and then between edges along each scan-line (Gouraud shading is based on a scan-line algorithm like Watkins' algorithm). Fig. 7.5 shows an example of interpolation calculation.

Phong Shading

Bui-Tuong Phong [1975] has proposed a normal-vector interpolation shading method. This means that instead of interpolating intensities like Gouraud, Phong interpolates the surface normal vector (as shown in Fig. 7.6). With this approach, the shading of a point is computed from the orientation of the approximated normal. With Phong shading, a better approximation of the curvature of the surface is obtained and highlights due to the simulation of specular reflection are much better rendered. However, the method requires more computation. For this reason, the animator may prefer to choose a different type of shading, according to the kind of object used. The next section will show how it is possible to make this choice in a structured way.

Apart from computation time, there is another great problem in the computer animation of shaded objects with the Gouraud and Phong algorithms. If an object and its light source are rotated together in the image plane, the shading of the object can change contrary to expectations. This is due to the fact that the interpolation of intensities (or normals) is carried out using values on a scan-line, and when objects and lights are rotated, the scan-lines do not cut the edges at the same points. Duff [1979] has proposed to alleviate this problem by interpolating intensities (or normals) in a rotation-independent manner; this would mean avoiding the use of values on a scan-line and adopting an appropriate interpolator depending only on the vertices of the polygon.

7.4 Structured Shaded Graphical Types

MIRA-SHADING [Magnenat-Thalmann et al., 1984] is an attempt to develop a structured method for defining realistic objects in a programming language.

Figures are high-level graphical types that define the composition of a three-dimensional object. In MIRA-SHADING, an object is modeled as a combination of faces, vertices and edges. For example, a CUBE must be declared with the following specification:

figure of 8 *vertices*, 6 *faces*, 12 *edges*

The syntax of the **figure** type is shown in Fig. 7.7.

The characteristics of the figure are defined in a list of formal parameters that specify the object **for the user**. For example, to create a SPHERE, the user must give the center and the radius:

e.g.   *type* SPHERE = *figure* (CENTER : VECTOR; RADIUS : REAL)

These characteristics are the only ones that the user needs to know.

The user need not know that the SPHERE is actually constructed using 250 faces! However, the construction of the object must be carried out in the type through statements using the parameters and any declaration that may be useful (constants, variables, types, procedures, functions). The specification section defines the name of the figure, the type of shading and the main characteristics: number of vertices, faces and edges. As these numbers may need to be calculated, statements are allowed in the specification section. For example:

type STRANGE = *figure* (N: INTEGER; ...);
                    var N2: INTEGER;

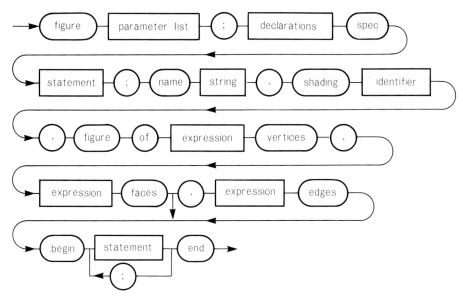

Fig. 7.7. Syntax of the figure type

> *spec*
>   N2 := N * N;
>   *name* 'STRANGE', *shading* **PHONG**
>   *figure of* N2 *vertices*, N *faces*, N + 2 *edges;*
> *begin*
>   . . .
> *end;*

The role of the statement part in a figure type is to define the vertices, the faces and the edges. Vertices are specified in an assignment-like statement:

$$vertices := A, B + C, \langle\!\langle 4, 2, 5 \rangle\!\rangle$$

defines the values of the first three vertices of the figure and the statement

$$vertices \; 4 := D, E \; cross \; F$$

defines the values of the vertices 4 and 5.

The statement **createface** allows the programmer to specify the number of edges for a face and also optionally the color of the face in the RGB system. For example:

> *createface* 3 *with* 5 *edges*
> *createface* 1 *to* 6 *with* 6 *edges col* $\langle\!\langle 0, 0, 1 \rangle\!\rangle$

The last statement creates six faces with six blue edges. The different faces are also built using an assignment-like statement where the vertices are given by their rank in the **vertices** statement:

$$face \; 1 := 3, 4, 5, 7;$$

defines the first face with 4 edges 3-4, 4-5, 5-7 and 7-3.

For example, we present below a BOX type defining a parallellepiped object characterized by four vertices.

The **figure** type is as follows:

type BOX = *figure* (A, B, C, D, COLO: VECTOR);
                var CORI, BORI, DORI: VECTOR;
                spec
                    name 'BOX', *shading* CONSTANT,
                    figure of 8 *vertices,* 6 *faces,* 12 *edges;*
                begin
                    CORI := C − A;
                    BORI := B − A;
                    DORI := D − A;
                    vertices := A, C, B + CORI, B, D, C + DORI, D + BORI
                    + CORI, D + BORI;
                    createface 1 *do* 6 *with* 4 *edges;*
                    face 1 := 1, 2, 3, 4;
                    face 2 := 2, 6, 7, 3;
                    face 3 := 3, 7, 8, 4;
                    face 4 := 5, 1, 4, 8;
                    face 5 := 1, 5, 6, 2;
                    face 6 := 6, 5, 8, 7;
                    COLOR (COLO);
                end;

The whole object is colored with the color COLO.

Creation of Figure Variables

Graphical (or figure) variables are defined as variables of graphical type, as already shown in Section 6.3. For example,

                        var B: BOX;
                            S: SPHERE;

The user characteristics of the variables are given with the statement **create** that requires the values of the actual parameters corresponding to the formal parameters in the graphical type. For example, the user must give the value of the center and the radius of a sphere:

create S($\langle\!\langle\!\langle 4, 5, 3 \rangle\!\rangle\!\rangle$, 12);
− creates a sphere of center $\langle\!\langle\!\langle 4, 5, 3 \rangle\!\rangle\!\rangle$ and radius 12
create B(A, B + D, $\langle\!\langle\!\langle 2, 4, 1 \rangle\!\rangle\!\rangle$, C, $\langle\!\langle\!\langle 1, 0, 0 \rangle\!\rangle\!\rangle$);
− creates a red colored box with vertices A, B + D, $\langle\!\langle\!\langle 2, 4, 1 \rangle\!\rangle\!\rangle$ and C.

MIRA-SHADING provides the three kinds of shading presented in the previous section: constant, Gouraud and Phong.

However, in order to establish a way of specifying the type of shading when creating objects, we have introduced the data type TYPSHADE which is predefined as:

$$type \ \text{TYPSHADE} = (\text{CONSTANT, GOURAUD, PHONG});$$

A figure type can thus be defined as:

$$type \ \text{ELLIPSOID} = figure\,(\text{A, B}:\text{VECTOR}; \text{X, Y}:\text{REAL}; \text{SHA}:\text{TYPSHADE});$$

$$\vdots$$

$$spec$$

$$\vdots$$

$$name \ \text{`ELLIPSOID'}, \ shading \ \text{SHA},$$
$$figure \ of \ \text{X} \ vertices, \ \text{Y} \ faces, \ \text{Z} \ edges;$$

$$\vdots$$

Colors can be defined in different ways:

1. The object can have a single color, which is defined using the COLOR standard procedure.
2. Each face of the object can have a different color, which is specified in the **createface** statement; this is well adapted to constant and Phong shadings, but is not convenient for Gouraud shading.
3. A color is defined for each vertex of the figure; this color must be specified in the **vertices** statement and this procedure is only appropriate for Gouraud shading. For example:

$$\text{vertices} := \text{A} \ col \ \langle\!\langle 1, 0, 0 \rangle\!\rangle, \ \text{B} \ col \ \langle\!\langle 0.8, 0, 0.2 \rangle\!\rangle$$
$$\text{C} \ col \ \langle\!\langle 0.6, 0, 0.3 \rangle\!\rangle, \ \text{D} \ col \ \langle\!\langle 0.5, 0.1, 0.4 \rangle\!\rangle;$$

A certain number of shaded figure types have been implemented;
i)   CUBE, BOX, regular polyedra with constant shading.
ii) SPHERE is defined with Phong shading.
iii) cylinders are predefined by

$$\text{CYLINDER} = figure \ (\text{F}:\text{FIG}; \text{D}:\text{LINE}; \text{H}:\text{REAL})$$

where the cylindrical body is defined by the displacement of a line segment of direction D and length H along a curve F.

4. Cones are predefined by

$$\text{CONE} = figure \ (\text{F}:\text{FIG}, \text{D}:\text{VECTOR}; \text{FRACT}:\text{REAL})$$

where the conical body is defined by the displacement of a segment line along the curve F passing through D; FRACT is a parameter that allows the representation of truncated cones.

5. Revolving bodies are defined by the rotation of a figure F around a line D and can be created using the following predefined type:

$$\text{REVOLUTION} = figure \ (\text{F}:\text{FIG}; \text{D}:\text{LINE}; \text{ALPHA}:\text{REAL})$$

The angle α can be used to limit the revolution to less than $360°$. Fig. 7.8 shows an example with Phong shading.
6. Patch surfaces are also predefined using five figure types: parametric surfaces, Coons surfaces, Bezier surfaces B-spline surfaces and β-spline surfaces. Fig. 7.9 and 7.10 show examples.

Fig. 7.8. Revolution bodies implemented as graphical types MIRA-SHADING (Designers: N. Magnenat-Thalmann, D. Thalmann)

Fig. 7.9. Logo produced using B-splines (Designers: André and Xavier Pintado. © N. Magnenat-Thalmann and D. Thalmann)

Fig. 7.10. Examples of MIRA-SHADING graphical types (Designers: André and Xavier Pintado. © N. Magnenat-Thalmann and D. Thalmann)

7.5 Rendering of Parametric and Patch Surfaces

Curved surface segments (also called patches) can be used instead of polygons to model free-form curved surfaces. Catmull [1975] has proposed a method for producing computer-shaded pictures of such curved surfaces. This method involves three steps:

1. Establishing a correspondance between points on the surface and the pixels
2. Removing hidden parts of patches
3. Calculating light intensities.

The hidden-surface algorithm used was Catmull's Z-buffer algorithm. Calculation of light intensity can be performed with the Phong method by using an intensity function or by mapping intensities from a picture or a photograph.

The first step is solved by a recursive subdivision algorithm similar to the Warnock algorithm discussed in Section 7.1.

According to Catmull [1975], the algorithm can be described as follows:

"If the patch (or subpatch) is small enough so that its projection covers only one sample point, then compute the intensity of the patch and write it into the corresponding element of the frame-buffer; otherwise, subdivide the patch into smaller subpatches and repeat the process for each subpatch."

This method is time-consuming; in practice, it can be used only with bicubic patches. However, it is of interest because it produces images of superior quality. Carlson [1982] has proposed a modified recursive subdivision to find the space curve which is the intersection of two bicubic patches.

More general algorithms for producing shaded images of parametric surfaces are based on scan-line methods. Three different algorithms have been proposed and compared [Lane et al., 1980]: the Blinn, the Whitted and the Lane-Carpenter algorithms. In each patches are surfaces defined by three bivariate functions:

$$X = X(u, v)$$
$$Y = Y(u, v)$$
$$Z = Z(u, v)$$

Patches are then transformed to a display space with X going to the right, Y going up and Z going into the screen. Silhouette edges are defined as curves in the surface for which the Z-component of the normal is Zero.

Blinn Algorithm

This is an algebraic approach that generalizes the concept of scanning a polygon to scanning a patch. In a first phase, boundary curve and silhouette edge intersections with the current scan-line are determined. All intersection calculations are performed using bivariate Newton-Raphson solutions of the equations. The process results in a list of boundaries for the current scan-line. In a second phase, the boundaries are sorted in order of x value on the scan-line. For each picture element, the Z information for the surface is generated and the required shading can be represented. This algorithm tends to be generally robust and relevant, except when the Newton iteration fails.

Whitted Algorithm

In this algorithm, bicubic surface patches are defined in terms of "edges" that are cubic curves. Patches have four cubic edge curves. Extremely curved patches may also have additional interior curved edges which subdivide the patch into sub-patches. The silhouette curve is approximated by a cubic hermite interpolation function. After the silhouettes have been determined, intersections of the edges with the scan-line are calculated using Newton's method. Depth and surface normals are then linearly interpolated between the endpoint values of scan line segments. Visibility is calculated for each segment by comparing the average depth of segment endpoints to establish the priority of segments. Shading is computed using the Phong model. The major disadvantage of the Whitted algorithm is that it fails if it tries to find silhouettes that do not intersect the boundary of the patch.

Schweizer and Cobb [1982] have proposed an algorithm that is partially based on the Whitted algorithm. Their approach consists of essentially two parts:

1. Preprocessing steps for converting bivariate cubic surface descriptions into a standard internal form and deriving curved-edge polygons; a general surface intersection method is used to detect silhouette edges.
2. Rendering of the curved-edge polygons by calculating a cubic approximation to the normal surface and performing an interpolation of the bounding edge normals across the scan-line.

Lane-Carpenter Algorithm

In this algorithm, a polygonal approximation to the smooth surface is derived and the polygons are rendered. A subdivision technique similar to the Catmull algorithm, combined with a polygon scan-line algorithm, this method can be summarized as follows:

1. Patches are sorted by maximum possible y values.
2. As each scan-line is processed, patches with this maximum possible y value are subdivided until:
   i) any one piece no longer overlaps the scan line and therefore is placed in the inactive patch list; or
   ii) the patch is within a set of tolerances of being a four-sided planar polygon, at which time it may be processed with a polygon scan-line algorithm.

A variant of the Lane-Carpenter algorithm has been described by Riesenfeld et al. [1981].

The algorithms described above deal with bivariate parametric surfaces generated by three functions of two variables. Another class of surfaces includes shapes like spheres, cones, or hyperboloids of revolution. These fall into the class of quadric surfaces that is a subset of implicit surface solutions to some equation:

$$F(X, Y, Z) = 0$$

Blinn [1982] has proposed a general solution to the imaging problem for such surfaces. The implicit form is ideally suited to raster conversion algorithms. The pixel coordinates are substituted for X and Y and the equation is solved for Z. Blinn has also shown how to solve the problem for the summation of several Gaussian density distributions.

The method has been applied to the representation of electron density maps of molecular structures. The results more closely resemble what a real electron density cloud might look like for a covalent bond than do classical molecular models based on intersections of spheres and cylinders [Knowlton and Cherry, 1977; Porte, 1978; Max, 1979]. Although classical models are suitable for animation, as shown by the films produced with Atom LLL [Max, 1979], bond-stretching and breaking is more easily controlled with the density distribution approach. Fig. 7.11 shows a beautiful picture produced by N. Max.

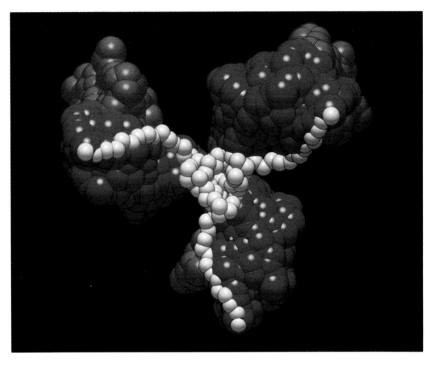

Fig. 7.11. Molecule by Nelson Max, Lawrence Livermore National Laboratory and Department of Energy

8. Transparency, Texture, Shadows and Anti-aliasing

8.1 Ray-tracing Algorithms

Ray tracing is an old technique, based on the numerical simulation of geometric optics. Intuitively, it can be seen that light rays could be traced from a light source along their paths until they reach the observer. However, this is a rather wasteful approach, because only a few rays coming from a given source actually arrive at the observer. This is why the first algorithms involving ray tracing carried out the process in the opposite direction. Rays are traced from the observer to the objects in the scene, as shown in Fig. 8.1. The first practical use of the ray-tracing technique in computer animation was the MAGI system [Goldstein and Nagel, 1971], which used the algorithm developed by Appel [1968].

A ray-tracing algorithm consists of shooting pixel rays, computing the intersections of these rays with the objects in the scene and obtaining the photometric information required to color the current pixel.

At each surface struck by a ray, a reflected and/or refracted ray may be generated. For each of these new rays, the process must be recursively applied to determine which other surfaces they intersect. For each pixel, an intersection tree

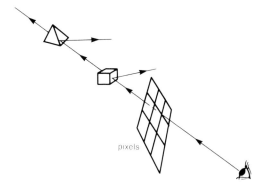

pixels

Fig. 8.1. Principle of ray tracing

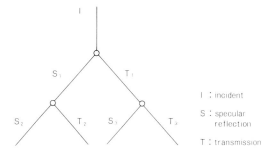

Fig. 8.2. Intersection tree

must be constructed (See Fig. 8.2). When the tree has been created, it is traversed applying an equation at each node to calculate intensity. With the recursive process, the intensity for the current node is obtained when all its sub-nodes have been evaluated.

The equation applied at each node to calculate intensity is one of those already presented in Section 7.2: Phong [1975], Whitted [1980] or Hall and Greenberg [1983].

But the heart of a ray-tracing algorithm lies in its intersection algorithms. Whitted [1980] stated that up to 95% of CPU time in computing a ray-traced image is spent on the intersection calculations. Kajiya [1982, 1983] has described methods for calculating the intersection of different objects with rays.

Sphere
Because of the sphere's symmetry, it is a fairly simple process to compute its intersections with a ray. An intersection may be tested by finding the minimal distance between the ray and the center of the sphere. If this distance is less than the radius, there is an intersection. As such calculations only require a few floating operations, the sphere is often used as a primitive to model more complex objects like ellipsoids.

Polygonal Surfaces
For this type of surface, the intersecting point between the ray and the plane of each polygon is first calculated. Then, the algorithm checks if the point is in the interior of the polygon.

Algebraic Surfaces
An algebraic surface is a surface defined by the equation:

$$P(X, Y, Z) = \sum_{ijk} a_{ijk} X^i Y^j Z^k = 0 \tag{8.1}$$

If we substitute the ray equation $R(t) = R_0 + V \cdot t$ where R_0 is the origin and V a unit vector pointing in the direction of the ray, we obtain a polynomial equation in t which can be solved by various methods of numerical analysis. Pat Henrahan [1983] has developed a method to automatically derive the equation of intersection between the ray and the surface. Fig. 8.3 shows an example.

Parametric Patches

There are two main methods for calculating the intersection between parametric patches and rays.

1. The recursive method of Whitted [1980] generates bounding spheres for each patch. If the bounding sphere is pierced by a ray, then the patch is subdivided into subpatches and bounding spheres are produced for each subpatch. The process continues until the intersected bounding sphere is smaller than a predefined minimum or no more bounding spheres are intersected. This algorithm is similar to Catmull's [1974]. The method of using a hierarchy of bounding spheres has been generalized by Rubin and Whitted [1980] in a method whereby the object space is represented entirely by a hierarchical data structure consisting of bounding volumes.
2. The algebraic method of Kajiya [1982] transforms the problem of computing a ray-patch intersection into the problem of intersecting two sixth-degree algebraic curves. The solution of this problem is given by Bezout's theorem [Walker, 1950].

Surfaces of Revolution and Cylinders

For this kind of object, the problem can be reduced to two-dimensions. For surfaces of revolution, a cut plane is defined as passing through the ray and parallel to the axis of revolution. Intersections between the ray and the curves formed by intersecting the cut plane with the surfaces are then computed. For cylinders, the ray is projected onto the base plane. Then intersections between the projected ray and the boundary curve of the base are calculated. In both types of

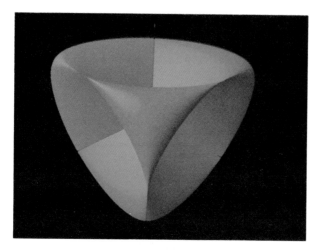

Fig. 8.3. The Steiner surface: an algebraic surface ray traced by programs developed by Pat Hanrahan

objects, the solution of the two-dimensional ray-tracing problem is obtained using strip trees [Ballard, 1981], a hierarchical structure which represents the curve at varying resolutions.

Of all synthetic images, those rendered by ray tracing are the most realistic. However, the method is still very expensive in terms of floating point computation. With the development of new hardware and refinement in the algorithms, we can expect considerable improvement in the performance of these techniques.

8.2 Transparency

A surface may allow some light to be transmitted through it from behind. Depending on the type of material used, the transmittance can be specular (transparent material) or diffuse (translucent material). Little work has been done with diffuse transmission.

Specular transmission methods have been developed. However, they often do not take the whole phenomenon into account.

Physically, the three Descartes laws fix the rules concerning reflection and refraction of light. According to Fig. 8.4:

1. The reflected and refracted rays are in the plane passing through the normal and the incident ray.
2. The incident angle i_1 is equal to the reflected angle r.
3. For monochromatic light, Snell's law is applied:

$$n_1 \sin i_1 = n_2 \sin i_2 \qquad\qquad (8.2)$$

where n_1 and n_2 are refraction indices.

The simplest transparency algorithms have two major drawbacks:

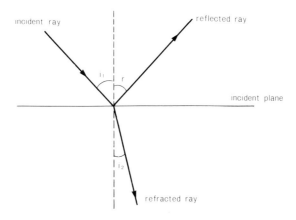

Fig. 8.4. Reflexion and refraction of light

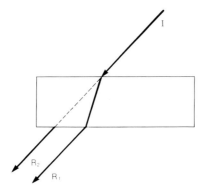

Fig. 8.5. Refraction through an object with depth

1. The intensity of light transmitted through the object does not take into account the depth of the object.
2. Refraction is ignored; this means that, in Fig. 8.5, ray R_2 (which is incorrect) would be used rather than ray R_1.

These simple algorithms simulate transparency by modifying a background image. The color C of the modified pixels is calculated (Newell et al., 1972) by the following expression:

$$C = tC_1 + (1 - t)C_2 \tag{8.3}$$

where C_1 is the color of the pixel on the background image, C_2 is the color that would be applied to the transparent object if it were opaque and t is the transparency of the object (0 for completely opaque, 1 for completely transparent).

This technique can be easily applied in shading algorithms like Gouraud and Phong. For example, during the operation of a scan-line algorithm, when a given polygon in the foreground is transparent, the nearest of the other polygons behind it is visible. The intensity I is calculated as a weighted sum of the individual intensities I_1 and I_2 calculated for the two polygons:

$$I = tI_1 + (1 - t)I_2 \tag{8.4}$$

If the transparent object is curved, this algorithm is very inaccurate. One way to improve realism is to decrease the transparency near the edges, using a function like:

$$t = (tmax - tmin)(1 - (1 - n_z)^p) + tmin \tag{8.5}$$

where tmax and tmin are the extreme values of the transparency t for the object, n_z is the z component of the unit normal vector to the surface and p is the cosine power factor.

Kay and Greenberg [1979] have proposed an algorithm, based on ray tracing, which takes refraction into account. This means that each ray is modified whenever it strikes a new transparent surface. In a slight modification of the simple algorithm seen in equation 8.3, the value C_2 is not necessarily at the same X, Y location as the new value C and the transparency t is a function of the thickness of the material through which the light ray must travel.

To trace the path of a ray through thick material, Kay and Greenberg use the following process:

1. Find a unit vector $\bar{U}$ that defines the direction of the refracted ray by using an approximation of Snell's law (equation 8.2).
2. Find the distance D that the ray must travel within the transparent material.
3. Multiply $\bar{U}$ by D to obtain the ΔX and ΔY shift values.
4. Add ΔX and ΔY to the X, Y location. This gives the location of the sight ray as it emerges from the transparent material.

The following equation calculates the intensity of a transmitted ray:

$$t = T^d \tag{8.6}$$

where t is the transparency for the path of the current ray, T is the transparency for one unit distance and d is the number of distance units making up the path through the transparent material.

This refraction solution was implemented with a Z-buffer algorithm. However, several iterations were required, because the surfaces must be processed in inverse order. Fig. 8.6 shows an image created by Kay and Greenberg.

As already indicated in Section 7.7, Whitted [1980] also used ray tracing to determine the global illumination in an image plane. In equation 7.5 there is a transparency term I_t, which is calculated as:

$$I_t = K_t T \tag{8.7}$$

where K_t is the transmission coefficient and T is the intensity of the transmitted ray. The direction of this ray is calculated using Snell's law.

Fig. 8.6. Simulated transparent vase by D.S. Kay and D. Greenberg, Cornell University

Fig. 8.7. Images of gallery with mirrored walls and local light sources by R. Hall and D. Greenberg, Cornell University

Hall and Greenberg [1983] have further improved the model by including Fresnel's relationships for wave-length and angle-of-incidence as suggested by Cook and Torrance [1982], as well as the scattering of transmitted light from sources and the attenuation of previous nodes. The model is as follows:

$$K = K_d \underbrace{\sum_j (\vec{N} \cdot \vec{L}) R_d I_j}_{\substack{\text{diffuse from} \\ \text{light sources}}} + K_s \underbrace{\sum_j (\vec{N} \cdot \vec{H})^n R_f I_j}_{\substack{\text{specular from} \\ \text{light sources}}}$$

$$+ K_s \underbrace{\sum (\vec{N} \cdot \vec{H}')^n T_f I_j}_{\substack{\text{transmitted from} \\ \text{light sources}}} + \underbrace{A R_d}_{\substack{\text{global} \\ \text{diffuse}}} + \underbrace{K_s R_f R F_r d_r}_{\substack{\text{global} \\ \text{specular}}} + \underbrace{K_t T_f T F_t d_t}_{\substack{\text{global} \\ \text{transmitted}}} \qquad (8.8)$$

$\vec{H}$ is the unit mirror-direction vector based on the reflected ray and $\vec{H}'$ is the unit mirror-direction vector based on the transmitted ray; R_f is the Fresnel reflectance, T_f the Fresnel transmissivity, A the intensity of global ambient illumination, R the intensity of the reflected ray, T the intensity of the transmitted ray, F_r the transmittance per unit length of material of the reflected ray, F_t the transmittance per unit length of material of the transmitted ray, d_r the distance travelled by the reflected ray and d_t the distance travelled by the transmitted ray. All other terms are defined as in Section 7.2. Fig. 8.7 shows an example.

8.3 Texture

Computer-generated images can achieve a high degree of realism with hidden surface removal and shading. However, in many cases they tend to look artificial because surfaces appear very smooth. Images of metallic or plastic cups, for example, look very realistic, but images of oranges or human skin do not. Almost all physical surfaces, in fact, have a microstructure visible to the human eye. This microstructure, called **texture**, provides a great deal of information about the nature of the surface.

Catmull [1975] has shown with his algorithm (see Section 7.5) that photographs, drawings or any picture can be mapped onto bivariate patches. However, this approach fails when the number of points to be displayed on a patch is less than the number of elements in the picture to be mapped. Catmull suggests alleviating this problem by mapping areas onto areas rather than points onto points, subdividing the patch and the picture at the same time.

Blinn and Newell [1976] have extended the Catmull technique by introducing a more sophisticated filtering method; in effect, applying a controlled blur to the pattern to be mapped. This is implemented by computing a weighted average of regions in the pattern definition function. The shape of this weighting function is determined using digital signal processing theory. The quadrilateral formed in texture definition space by the (U, V) corners of the pixel forms the base of a square pyramid which is used to weight the texture values. This function was originally used by Crow [1977] to solve the aliasing problem in computer-synthesized shaded images, as it will be shown in Section 8.7.

For a sample object, Blinn and Newell use a plain teapot constructed of 26 bicubic patches. They discuss different techniques for creating and mapping texture patterns such as (U, V) functions, hand drawings and scanned photographs. Techniques for simulating texture and reflection are combined to produce images of objects having patterned shiny surfaces. The amount of light coming from a given direction is modeled to the texture mapping and then added to the intensity obtained from the texture mapping.

Schweizer [1983] also describes a texturing technique that approximates the changes caused by distance and orientation without attempting to exactly render a realistic surface texture. Since it does not reproduce the actual texture pattern, it is called an **artificial texture**. It is an inexpensive aid for visualizing the shape of a shaded surface.

These approaches are quite interesting but they do not simulate rough surfaces. One application of textured-surface representation is in the area of flight simulators [Schachter, 1981]. Schachter distinguishes two basic categories of textures: natural and man-made. For the first category, he proposes [Schachter, 1980] Gaussian random patterns to model natural phenomena. For man-made textures which are more regular, Schachter [1980b] uses patterns modeled with an equation involving a priority function.

Blinn [1978] has developed a method which uses a texturing function to slightly alter the direction of the surface normal before using it in the intensity calculations. This technique was previously used by Batson et al. [1975] to generate shaded relief images. Blinn uses a function $F(u, v)$ that measures the displacement of the irregular surface from an ideal smooth one. A new point P' on the wrinkled surface is given by the following equation:

$$P' = P + FU \tag{8.9}$$

where P is the original point and U the unitary normal vector. Fig. 8.8 shows a cross section of a smooth surface (v is constant), the function $F(u)$ and the corresponding cross section of the wrinkled surface.

The choice of the function F is very important. Blinn has proposed different techniques:

- F is defined analytically as a bivariate polynomial or bivariate Fourier series; this is generally an expensive approach because of the large number of coefficients required.
- F is defined by a lookup table using a doubly indexed array of values between 0 and 1; the results are not very smooth unless an enormous array is used.
- F is defined by a lookup table as in the previous case and an interpolation is performed for values between table entries; B-splines can be used, but Blinn has shown that a cheaper, continuous interpolation scheme for derivatives consists of taking the difference of the interpolated function along the parametric directions.

Table entries can be generated algorithmically. However, when irregular textures are required, the best approach is to construct a table manually. This can be achieved with a video frame buffer and a painting program that utilizes a digitizing tablet to control the alteration of the table values. The user "paints" in the function values; black areas correspond to small values of the table and white areas to large ones.

Another important way of producing texture is based on fractal surfaces, to be discussed in the next section.

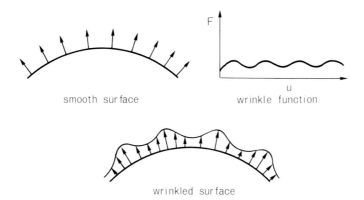

smooth surface   wrinkle function

wrinkled surface

Fig. 8.8. Cross section of a smooth surface

8.4 Fractals

Modeling techniques generally assume that an object is a collection of lines or polygons, or that it can be described by high-order polynomials like Bezier, Coons or B-spline patches. While these techniques efficiently model solid objects like cars, roads and houses, they are not well adapted to the representation of natural features like terrains, snow, sand or smoke. The representation of snow by a collection of polygons is not only too expensive but also too regular to be realistic. Based on the theoretical work of Mandelbrot [1975, 1977, 1982], Fournier et al. [1982] have modeled both primitives and their motion as a combination of deterministic and stochastic elements. With this approach, the surface of an object can be a polynomial function or a stochastic function of predetermined location. Motion can also be a smooth function or it may vary irregularly.

A stochastic model of an object represents that object by a sample path of some stochastic process of one of more variables. Stochastic objects can be constructed from several stochastic modeling primitives. In summary, stochastic modeling requires:

- an object or a phenomenon to be modeled
- a stochastic process
- an algorithm to compute the sample paths of this process.

A very common natural entity to be represented is terrain, which is characterized by randomly distributed features. To model it, a stochastic process is required. Mandelbrot has introduced a fractal model of terrain as an application in computer graphics of a family of one-dimensional Gaussian stochastic processes called a **fractional Brownian motion**. A family of random functions $B_H(u, w)$, forming what Mandelbrot and Van Ness [1968] call reduced fractional Brownian motion, have been introduced. In these functions, u is a real parameter, w the set of all values of a random function taken from a sample space W, and H is a real parameter where $0 < H < 1$. When $H = 0.5$, ordinary Brownian motion is obtained.

Fractional Brownian motion can be chosen for modeling terrain, but an algorithm for computing sample paths must be found. This algorithm must be efficient, because up to 10^6 sample points frequently have to be generated. Mandelbrot has proposed several methods for calculating discrete approximations to Fractional Brownian motion. These methods are based on three approaches: a fractional Poisson field, a modified Markov Process and an inverse Fourier transformation.

Because all these methods are very costly in terms of computation, Fournier et al. have proposed a recursive subdivision algorithm to generate approximations to the sample paths of one-dimensional fractional Brownian motion.

One-dimensional Fractals

The algorithm corresponds to the construction of a "fractal polyline" primitive from an initial deterministic line segment. It recursively subdivides the interval, as shown in Fig. 8.9, and generates a scalar value at the midpoint. This value is taken as a displacement of the midpoint at each step in the recursion and is used as an

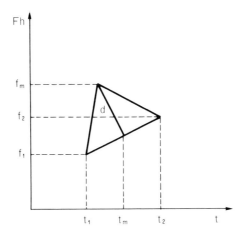

Fig. 8.9. One-dimensional fractal

offset from that midpoint along a vector normal to the original line segment. This offset d is calculated by the following equation:

$$d = s \cdot gauss(sd, tm) \qquad (8.10)$$

where s is the current standard deviation, gauss is a function that returns a Gaussian random variable with zero mean and unit variance, sd is the seed and tm is the middle of the interval $((t1 + t2)/2)$.

One-dimensional fractal primitives can be combined in arbitrary ways to represent natural phenomena like rivers or coastlines. By choosing an appropriate value for H, it is possible to generate realistic shapes.

Two-dimensional Fractals

Fractal polygons can be created similarly to fractal polylines. For example, surfaces consisting of triangles can be easily used to represent stochastic surfaces. Each triangle is subdivided into four by connecting the midpoints of the sides, as shown in Fig. 8.10. The positions of the midpoints are obtained by the same process as for polylines. A similar method can be used to subdivide quadrilaterals and the process can be generalized to a mesh of triangles or quadrilaterals.

Fournier et al. also show how to generate stochastic parametric surfaces by defining a surface description which is stochastic in nature rather than deterministic. Fig. 8.11 shows an example.

Three-dimensional Fractals

Norton [1982] has described a system for generating and displaying geometric fractals in three dimensions. The algorithm used to generate the surfaces, well adapted for an array processor, requires space and time. As three-dimensional surfaces are assumed to have an interior and an exterior, the technique is based on "point determinations;" this means that calculations determine whether a point is inside or outside a specified invariant set. The technique involves iterating a

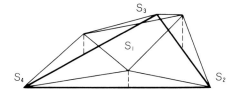

Fig. 8.10. 2D fractal subdivision. The midpoint of each edge of the triangle is displaced in x by a random variable

Fig. 8.11. Planets produced using a stochastic model by Alain Fournier, University of Toronto

function repeatedly and keeping track of the points which satisfy certain criteria. A three-dimensional grid is used; the output of the algorithm consists of a list of boundary points on the grid. The surface is displayed using a two-stage method:

1. Assign illumination intensities to each vertex by imagining a light source.
2. Produce an image depending on viewer direction.

The display process is based on Z-buffers. Fig. 8.12 and 8.13 show examples of three-dimensional fractals.

Four-dimensional Fractals
The introduction of fractals to model motion can be very effective in handling complex irregular moving objects, such as a leaf in the wind. Used by Loren Carpenter in the film *Vol Libre* (see appendix C) to model the path of a lightning

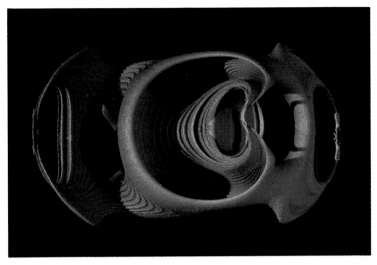

8.12

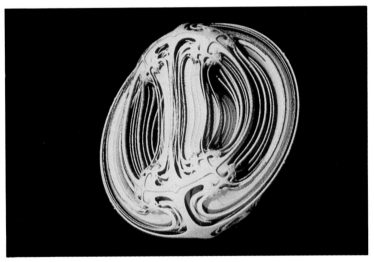

8.13

Figs. 8.12–13. By Alan Norton, IBM Research. These mathematical shapes result from the dynamics of simple formulas in 3 dimensional space. Repeatedly applying such a formula is like a process of erosion: We see here what remains after the process is repeated many times. The resulting object is a fractal [Mandelbrot, 1982], possessing roughness and fragmentation at all scales of magnification. The generation technique, described in [Norton, 1982], effectively simulates the erosion process inside the memory of a computer, then displays the resulting shape by simulating the reflections of light from such a surface. Calculations were performed on an IBM 3033 computer using an FPS 190L array processor. Pictures were displayed at resolution 1024 × 1280 on a RAMTEK 9400 system

bolt, the sequence of positions was created by extending fractional Brownian motion from one dimension into three and by changing the random numbers generated. The complete path was obtained by interpolation as in key-frame systems. Fig. 8.14 shows an image created by Loren Carpenter.

Fractal Surfaces with Ray Tracing

Kajiya [1982] has introduced a method of intersecting rays with fractal surfaces. The algorithm, which involves calculating all the intersections between rays and polygons, is of course impractical, because a typical scene requires the tracing of a million rays on a surface of a million polygons. To dramatically cut the number of intersections to be computed, Kajiya proposed generating the fractal surface and tracing it at the same time, thereby discarding very early the parts of the surface which do not contribute to the current pixel.

The Kajiya rendering algorithm maintains a list of active nodes which are to be traced by the current ray. A facet is a polygon representing the surface at this level of recursion, and the extent encloses the surface given by the subtree at N. A node is active if its extent intersects the ray and no primitive polygonal facet shadows it. Assume that the fractal surface can be represented as a tree of branching ratio four, with a facet and an extent associated with each node.

The algorithm works as follows:

Remove the closest node N from the active node list. For each of the four extents E_i, if there is an intersection with the ray, add the corresponding nodes N_i to the active node list. If the new nodes contain primitive facets that intersect the ray, then remove all nodes shadowed by the closest facet from the active node list.

Fig. 8.14. Synthetic fractal mountain. © Loren Carpenter 1980

8.5 Fuzzy Objects Modeling and Particle Systems

Fuzzy objects, as defined by Reeves [1983], are objects that do not have smooth, well-defined and shiny surfaces. Their shapes are irregular and ill-defined and may change with time. In computer animation these objects, most importantly clouds, smoke, fire and water, are frequently required but difficult to represent. Fuzzy objects can of course be represented by geometric primitives. For example, Schachter [1983] describes the simulation of cumulus cloud layers by a concatenation of cloud groups, each consisting of about 75 sunshaded ellipsoids confined to a circular envelope. Schachter also shows how smoke trails can be simulated by strings of long, thin, translucent ellipsoids. The results, however, are quite unrealistic, although they are useful especially in the case of flight simulators.

Csuri et al. [1979] have proposed a model for representing a cloud of smoke. The cloud is first generated by a three-dimensional mathematical approximation. Then a two-dimensional array of the intensities is created by ray tracing. A procedure model, the technique has been well described by Marshall et al. [1980] and is one of the first attempts to model objects as collections of particles. Blinn [1982b] has produced images of the rings of Saturn using light reflection functions for simulating clouds and dusty surfaces. The technique consists of simulating light passing through and being reflected by layers of particles.

A systematic method for modeling fuzzy objects has been developed by Reeves [1983], called the **particle systems** method.

A particle system is a collection of particles that together represent a fuzzy object. Over a period of time, particles in the system are born, move, change and die. Reeves describes how to compute each frame in a motion sequence with the following steps:

1. Generate new particles and assign them individual attributes.
2. Extinguish particles whose lifetime is over.
3. Move and transform the remaining particles according to their dynamic attributes.
4. Render the image of the living particles in a frame buffer.

Particles are generated by means of controlled stochastic processes. The number of particles generated at a given frame can be determined by an equation involving either the mean number generated at a frame and it variance or the mean number generated per unit of screen area and its variance. For each new particle generated, values are determined for the following attributes: initial position, velocity, size, color, transparency, and shape and lifetime. Global dynamic attributes like "rates of change" are also defined in the particle system to control motion and transformations. A particle is killed when its lifetime reaches zero, accomplished by decrementing the current lifetime at each frame.

Particle rendering can be complex because particles can hide each other and transparency and shadows are also often required. However, for explosions and fires, Reeves describes a very simple algorithm based on the assumption that each particle is displayed as a point light source.

A pixel gains light when it is covered by a particle; the amount depends on attributes like the particle's transparency and color. A particle's size and shape determine the covered pixels. A hierarchy of particle systems can also be defined to control complicated fuzzy objects.

Particle systems were used to produce the Genesis Demo sequence (see appendix C) from the Lucasfilm Ltd. movie, *Star Trek II: The Wrath of Khan*. Fireworks have also been modeled using particle systems. A case study on fireworks is further described in Chapter 11.

The modeling of clouds as particle systems is much more complex because particles cannot be rendered as point light sources but must be considered individual light-reflecting objects. Cloud models are also very complex because of their shape, atmospheric factors and shadows. This problem remains unsolved up to now.

8.6 Shadows

As noted by Crow [1978], algorithms for shadows require considerable computation time and are rarely used in computer-animated films.

However, unless the light source is located at an eyepoint, or illumination is very diffuse, as with an overcast sky, an image is not complete without shadows.

Before studying several algorithms for implementing shadows, we must define the term "shadow." This is the darkness cast by an object that intercepts light. This shadow falls from the side opposite the source of light and, as already mentioned, it is only visible when the eyepoint moves away from the light source.

The first algorithm for generating shadows was suggested by Appel [1968] as an extension of his hidden-line algorithm [1967]. The segment parts that lie in shadow are determined by computing for all vertices the quantitative invisibility with repect to the light source.

Bouknight and Kelley [1970] have designed a method that scans an object row by row to determine visibility. When a polygon boundary is crossed, the polygonal surface nearest the observer is found by a depth sort. A secondary scan is used to detect shadow boundaries calculated by projecting edges upon the surfaces being scanned.

Another way of generating shadows is to use a hidden-surface algorithm to detect which surfaces are hidden from the light source. As this information (on shadow boundaries) must be used in a second pass to generate an image, an object-space hidden-surface algorithm such as that described by Sutherland et al. [1974] must be used. Calculations can be optimized by using hierarchical data description as proposed by Clark [1976], because the shadow algorithm may be driven by the hierarchical organization of the data. A priority order is used to treat groups of objects.

Nishita and Kakamae [1974] have proposed a method for generating shadows by using a convex polyhedron-clipping algorithm in a first step, and then a method similar to that used by Bouknight and Kelley to remove hidden surfaces.

An algorithm based on a "shadow volume" approach was designed by Crow [1977b]. The boundary surface of the shadow volume is obtained, as shown in

Fig. 8.15, by all planes defined by the light source and the contour edges of the original object. Then the volume is clipped by the viewbox (bounds of the field of view). When the shadow volume has been determined, any hidden surface algorithm can be used to create the display. The shadow data is considered as the original data but it is invisible.

The best approach is probably the polygon shadow generation algorithm proposed by Atherton et al. [1978]. The method is based on an object space polygon-clipping algorithm designed by Weiler and Atherton [1977] for hidden surface removal. This algorithm removes all surfaces that lie behind each unique polygonal area and within its borders. Shadows are created in three steps:

1. Shadow descriptions are found by viewing the environment from the light source.
2. By using the hidden surface removal algorithm, illuminated polygons are detected. These polygons are those that are not in shadow and they are determined by considering hidden surfaces removed when viewed from the light source.
3. Illuminated polygons are added to the original polygons.

The transformations are performed using view and shadow matrices. The first shadow matrix transforms the polygonal data environment to the environment from a viewpoint at the light source position. Illuminated surfaces are then obtained by using hidden surface removal. The second shadow matrix is used to obtain illuminated surfaces and a copy of the environment at any orientation. This results in a complete shadowed data file. By applying view matrices and the hidden surface removal algorithm, hidden-line removed vector displays or hidden-surface removed halftone displays can be obtained.

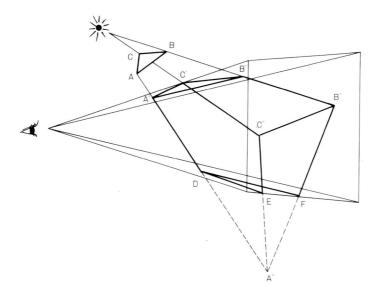

Fig. 8.15. Shadow volume

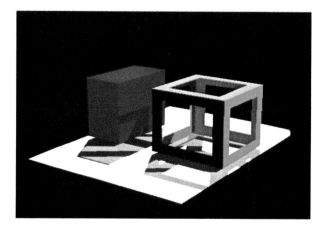

Fig. 8.16. Shadowed image display with two light sources at different locations by P. Atherton, K. Weiler and D. Greeberg, Cornell University

By using the hidden surface removal algorithm for each light source, shadowed images with several light sources can be produced, as shown in Fig. 8.16.

8.7 Spatial Anti-aliasing

A phenomenon called **aliasing** is a major enemy of the computer animator. The term refers to the fact that this phenomenon occurs when a low-frequency signal appears as an "alias" of a high-frequency signal after sampling. Practically, this means that resolution in the object space is infinite when compared with resolution in the display space.

Typically, the effects of the aliasing problem are as follows:

1. A **stairstepping** effect exists along the edges of a line drawing or border of two contrasting surfaces.
2. Small objects can disappear between the dots because is possible that no part of them will coincide with a sample point.
3. There is a line breakup effect, wherein the width of a stripe is on the order of a pixel and misses the center of this pixel.

These problems become very obvious in computer animation, where the main anomalies are:

– objects appearing and disappearing
– shapes of objects changing
– a scintillation effect.

Aliasing effects were mentioned early on by Shoup [1973] and Catmull [1974]. However, the problem was first systematically studied by Crow [1977], who proposed three general classes of anti-aliasing algorithms:

1. As the aliasing problem is due to low resolution, one possibility is to increase that resolution, causing sample points to occur more frequently. However, this approach has severe limits, because it also increases the cost of image production.
2. The image may be generated at high resolution, and then digitally filtered. This method, called **supersampling**, eliminates the high frequencies that are the source of aliases. The technique has been used with excellent results [Crow, 1981]. However, it requires a high-resolution copy of the image.
3. The image can be calculated by integrating intensities over neighborhoods to yield pixel values. This kind of algorithm is called a **prefiltering algorithm**. It has been successfully employed by Crow [1977] and Catmull [1978]. In both approaches, the reduction of aliasing effects is obtained by using a display algorithm with a filtering process in the rendering algorithm. Crow [1977] discusses the application of filtering to hidden-surface algorithms. He properly computes the intensity at a sample point. He proposes the implementation of a filtering tiler for convex polygons. Catmull [1978] has proposed a hidden-surface algorithm at the pixel level. The area of a pixel is viewed as a window, against which all nearby polygons are clipped. This determines the area of the pixel covered by each polygon.

The elimination of all aliasing is theoretically possible by limiting the frequency of the input image in the spatial domain to one-half of the sampling frequency [Oppenheim and Shafer, 1975]. However, this requires convolving the image with $\sin(x)/x$ functions, which is not feasible with traditional hardware. The function $\sin(x)/x$ must be approximated; the least costly method involves intensity-averaging by area. The intensity of the pixel is computed as a weighted average of the intensities of each region that covers the pixel, as shown in Fig. 8.17.

Such a technique is also applicable to line drawings where each pixel overlapped by the line must have an intensity proportional to the area of the pixel covered by the line. To compute the fraction of each pixel overlapped by the line, algorithms have been proposed by Crow [1978] and Fuchs and Barros [1979].

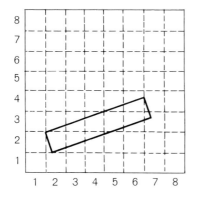

pixel	intensity
2,2	0.7
3,2	0.6
4,2	0.3
5,2	0.05
2,3	0.15
3,3	0.6
4,3	0.85
5,3	0.9
6,3	0.7
7,3	0.1
5,4	0.25
6,4	0.55
7,4	0.05

Fig. 8.17. Spatial antialiasing

Research in anti-aliasing methods is still making progress and different directions are being explored. Piller [1980] and Gupta and Sproull [1981] have proposed parallel processing approaches using special hardware. Fiume et al. [1982] have proposed a parallel scan conversion algorithm for a general-purpose "ultracomputer". In this approach, a parallel anti-aliasing algorithm approximates the subpixel coverage by edges using a look-up table. Turkowski [1982] has introduced a method of calculating antialiasing through the use of coordinate transformations. He has studied the use of the perpendicular point-line distance in evaluating the two-dimensional anti-aliasing convolution. This means that the anti-aliasing filter kernel is approximated by a one-dimensional function of the perpendicular distance from a pixel to a line. Extension to polygon rendering has also been described.

Bloomenthal [1983] has presented algorithms for the detection and smoothing of edges and the filtering of an image in accordance with the inferred edges, obtained from the set of vertical and horizontal segments which form the staircase of the aliased line.

Other interesting anti-aliasing techniques have been applied to texture by Blinn and Newell [1976], Dungan et al. [1978] and Feibush et al. [1980]. Whitted [1980] and Roth [1982] have also studied the problem of aliasing in highlighting and Whitted [1983] has described a method of displaying anti-aliased lines by painting with an anti-aliased brush.

The antialiasing techniques discussed in this section are spatial in nature. They help to reduce the problem of creating images by sampling processes in the space domain. However, we have not discussed the problem vis à vis time.

8.8 Motion Blur and Temporal Anti-aliasing

As we have seen, spatial aliasing is an effect of spatial undersampling. Temporal undersampling can also be disturbing. Szabo (1978) distinguishes three different temporal effects: the interlace effect, the frame rate update effect and the stroboscopic effect.

The **interlace effect** is present in all interlaced television. When an object moves up or down the screen of a CRT, it appears to break up into a series of parallel bands. In particular, if the object travels at a rate of one scan line per field time, only half the number of scan lines appears. The interlace effect can be overcome by using a wide spatial filter which scans two pixels and two scan lines; of course, this reduces the resolution. The effect can also be reduced by sampling at the frame rate instead of the field rate. However, this introduce another effect, the **frame rate update effect**: when an object (for example, a vertical stripe) moves horizontally to the right, it will appear twice on the eye retina if the position of the stripe is calculated at the frame rate. The **stroboscopic effect** occurs when an object which is supposed to spin so rapidly that it appears as a blur to the eye, seems to be stationary when generated on a display.

Lipscomb [1981] has studied temporal aliasing problems in real time refresh vector systems. In particular, with many refreshes per update, motion can appear reversed, jerky or erratic.

More recently, the problem of temporal anti-aliasing in computer animation, also called motion blur, has been investigated by several authors.

Potmesil and Chakravarty [1983] attempt to model motion blur, which they define as "an effect caused by the movement of objects during the exposure time of the camera, and often used to give the viewer the illusion of the motion of objects." In fact, the principle is simple: a movie camera opens its shutter for a short interval of time and motion is represented as a slight blur of the image of the moving object. In computer-animated films, this motion blur is required if the object moves rapidly. This is also the case when the virtual camera moves rapidly.

Potmesil and Chakravarty [1982] have earlier described a technique for modeling the effects of a lens and aperture in a virtual camera. Their model allows the generation of synthetic images which have a depth of field and can be focused on an arbitrary plane. Also optical characteristics of a lens can be incorporated. This approach is quite interesting in computer animation, because it allows selective highlighting through focusing or other optical effects and permits special techniques like fade-in, fade-out, lens distortions and filtering (see Section 2.4) to be simulated. Image generation consists of two stages:

1. generation of point samples of intensity in the image using a geometric pin-hole camera; points are generated by the ray-tracing hidden-surface algorithm [Whitted, 1980] discussed in Section 8.1.
2. conversion into a raster image by a focus processor.

Image (de)focusing is obtained by introducing circle of confusion as a projection of a point onto the image plane. Diffraction effects are studied by determining the light intensity distribution within the circle of confusion for defocused points.

The raster image is generated using the point samples, the geometric camera model and the lens and aperture parameters. Potmesil and Chakravarty have extended their model to motion blur by redefining the two stages of image generation for computer animation as:

1. The ray-tracing hidden surface program generates intensity sample points of an instantaneous image, identifying points which are in motion and giving the image path of the projected motion.
2. A processor generates motion blur by convolving moving points with optical system-transfer functions; these functions are derived from the path and the velocity of the objects and the exposure time of the virtual camera.

Korein and Badler [1983] have incorporated motion blur into computer-animated sequences by using two forms of algorithms. The first approach is based on intervals during which each object covers each pixel. For each pixel, objects that cover it during the filtered interval are determined. Subintervals, during which each of these objects projects onto that pixel, are also determined and subintervals associated with occluded intervals are removed. The pixel intensity function is obtained using the remaining subintervals and corresponding object attribute functions. The implementation of the algorithm has been limited to objects composed of spheres like Bubbleman [Badler et al., 1979], which will be further discussed in Section 9.3.

8.18

The second approach is based on supersampling. The technique is similar to the corresponding spatial anti-aliasing technique, but multiple intensity buffers for a single frame are generated, each one corresponding to a different point in time. The intensities of each pixel in the different buffers form a function that can be digitized at a greater resolution than the output frame rate. It may then be filtered to obtain the final image. Although Korein and Badler note a few undesirable effect, the technique is simple to implement and can be used with different methods of image rendering. Fig. 8.18 shows the effect of temporal anti-aliasing.

The particles in the particle systems introduced by Reeves [1983] and presented in Section 8.5 are motion-blurred. Particle positions are calculated at the beginning and about halfway through the frame, and an anti-aliased straight line is drawn between the corresponding screen coordinate positions in the frame buffer.

Fig. 8.18. Temporal anti-aliasing by Jan Korein and Norman I. Badler, University of Pennsylvania

9. Human Modeling and Animation

9.1 Stick, Surface and Volume Models

As stated by Norman Badler [1982], one of the best-known specialists in this area, modeling realistic human forms remains one of the most difficult and challenging problems.

There are two reasons for this:

1. Geometric and mathematical models used in computer graphics are not very suitable for the shape of the human body.
2. The movement of joints is difficult to model, in particular because of the role of muscle action.

For these reasons, in computer animation, two-dimensional and two-and-a half dimensional models are often used, although they are quite unrealistic. One way of representing realistic human bodies and motions is by reconstructing three-dimensional images from two-dimensional projections of bodies and motions from the real world. For example, the "juggler" in the Information International Demo 82 is quite realistic. However, he is not modelled by computer, but only reconstructed from projections of an existing real "juggler." The technique is called three-dimensional rotoscopy; its main drawback is that it can only generate motions which have been previously performed by human beings.

In fact, to obtain realistic three-dimensional movements, three-dimensional models must be used. There are three general methods for modeling the human body in three dimensions [Badler and Smoliar, 1979]:

– stick figures
– surface models
– volume models.

Stick Figures
A stick figure like a skeleton, is made up of a collection of body segments and joints. Realism suffers because depths are difficult to evaluate. Several movements are impossible to represent, like twists and contacts. The most well known stick model was designed by Withrow [1970]. The hero of the film *Dream Flight* [Thalmann et al., 1982], Hipi is also a stick model. This is further described in Section 12.4. Fig. 9.1 shows Hipi flying.

Fig. 9.1. Hipi flying (from *Dream Flight*)

Surface Figures

Skeletons can be surrounded by surfaces that are composed of planar or curved patches. Movement that modify these surfaces are now visible and hidden lines can be removed.

Various models have been designed for surface figures. In 1968, Fetter [1982] introduced his first man model with seven segments (parts) for studying the Boeing 747 Instrument panel. A second more fully articulated man was introduced in 1969. Then the third man and woman were designed by Fetter as a hierarchy of figures whose complexity depends on the application and the point of view. The fourth man (Fig. 9.2) and woman (Fig. 9.3) are based on the most recent work of Fetter on the visual effects of hemispheric projections [1981]. These models can be shaded with Phong's algorithm.

Other models are based on data obtained by anthropometrists [Dooley, 1982].

Boeman (Boeing Corporation) is based on a 50th-percentile three-dimensional human model. He can reach for objects like baskets but a mathematical description of the object and the tasks is assumed. Collisions are detected during Boeman's tasks and visual interferences are identified. Boeman is built as a 23-joint figure with variable link lengths.

Buford (Rockwell International) is based on the 50th-percentile three-dimensional model of Dreyfus. He has difficulty moving and has no vision system. Buford is composed of 15 independent links that must be redefined at each modification.

Cyberman (Chrysler Corporation) was designed for the automobile industry. Although he was created to study the position and motion of car drivers, there is

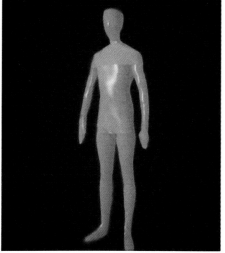 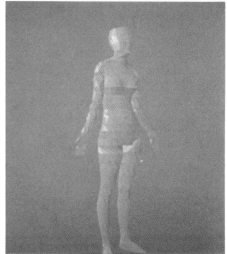

Fig. 9.2. "Fourth Man" by William Fetter, Steven Williams, Craig Wittenberg, James Wallace SIROCO, Bellevue, Washington, USA

Fig. 9.3. "Fourth Woman" by William Fetter, Steven Williams, Craig Wittenberg, James Wallace SIROCO, Bellevue, Washington, USA

no check to determine whether his motions are realistic. It is based on 15 joints; the position of the observer is predefined.

Combiman (Aerospace Medical Research Center) was specifically designed to test how easily a human can reach objects in a cockpit. Motions have to be realistic and the human can be chosen at any percentile from among three-dimensional human models. The vision system is very limited. Combiman is defined using a 35 internal-link skeletal system.

Sammie was designed in 1980 at the University of Nottingham. This is, so far, the best parameterized human model and it presents a choice of physical types: slim, fat, muscled, etc. The vision system is very developed and complex objects can be manipulated by Sammie, based on 21 rigid links with 17 joints.

Volume Figures
In this approach, the body is decomposed into several primitive volumes. Three kinds of elementary volumes have been used to create such models:

- cylinders by Evans [1976] and Poter and Willmert [1975]
- ellipsoids by Herbison-Evans (see Section 9.2)
- spheres by Badler (see Section 9.3).

The use of cylinders is very difficult, because of the joints and hidden-surface removal is very time-consuming. For these reasons, we examine only the two other models in the next two sections.

9.2 The NUDES System

The NUDES system (Numerical Utility Displaying Ellipsoid Solids), designed by Don Herbison-Evans [1978, 1980, 1982], provides real-time animation of human figure drawings with hidden lines omitted. The human figures are stick figures fleshed out by ellipsoids. Fig. 9.4 and 9.5 show examples of such human figures.

The principle behind the use of ellipsoids is very simple. Assume we have two ellipsoids, A and B, where B hides part of A (Fig. 9.6a). The points where the elliptical outlines disappear and reappear must be of one of the following types:

Fig. 9.4. "Rina" by Don Herbison-Evans. Figure from the "Computers and Dance" program at the University of Sydney

Fig. 9.5. "Horse and Jockey" by Don Herbison-Evans, University of Sydney

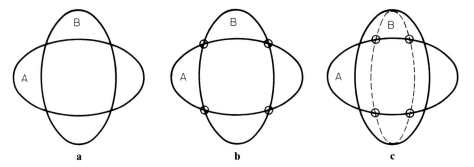

Fig. 9.6. Two intersecting ellipsoids. **a** two ellipsoids. **b** obscuration points. **c** interpenetration points

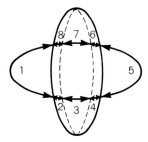

Fig. 9.7. 8 possible arcs

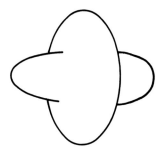

Fig. 9.8. Visibility of intersecting ellipsoids

1. **Obscuration points**—these are intersection points between the elliptical outlines (Fig. 9.6b).
2. **Interpenetration points**—these are the intersections between the outline of ellipsoid A and the section of ellipsoid B which is cut by the plane of the outline of ellipsoid A (Fig. 9.6c).

These points can generate eight possible arcs (Fig. 9.7). We now have to decide which ones should be visible.

A very simple algorithm involves testing to see whether the center of the arc should be visible; if so, the arc must be visible. For example, in Fig. 9.8, arcs 1, 2, 5 and 8 are visible.

9.3 The Badler Bubbleman

Designed by N. Badler et al. of the University of Pennsylvania [1979, 1980], Bubbleman is a three-dimensional human figure consisting of a number of spheres or **bubbles**. The model is based on the overlap of spheres and the appearance (intensity and size) of the spheres varies depending on the distance from the observer. The spheres correspond to a second level in a hierarchy; the first level is the skeleton.

Skeleton

The Bubbleman skeleton is a set of joints and segments organized in a tree structure. The nodes are the segments and the edges are the joints. One segment is defined as the reference segment.

To simplify processing, the logical window concept was introduced. The segments taken into account in the computation of motion are only those which fall within the logical window, or those along a path from the reference segment to some segment within the logical window. For example, if we assume that the logical window includes only the left elbow, the head segments, right arm and legs will not be involved in motion processing. The shape and size of each segment is described independently, and each has its own local coordinate system. The origin of the coordinate system is the center of gravity of the segment. The notation used follows the conventions of Labanotation, discussed in Section 9.4.

Spheres

It would be possible to draw the human figure by representing each segment by a line linking joints. However, this is quite unrealistic. A simple but advantagous way of improving the figure is to use overlapping spheres. Spheres are useful for three reasons:

1. Sphere projections always produce circles on vector displays and can be represented by shaded discs on raster displays.
2. Hidden-face removal can be implemented with a z-buffer method.
3. Unlike cylinders or ellipsoids, spheres have no privileged direction.

Spheres are used to create a kind of skin for each segment. In the current Badler model, 310 spheres are used. They are produced with a decomposition algorithm [O'Rourke and Badler, 1979], and then the choice is interactively improved. Spheres that belong to a segment are linked to it. Positioning the segment positions all the spheres. Any transformation on the segment is applied to the center of the sphere. The radius remains unchanged. Spheres of adjacent segments may overlap.

One important property of spheres is that they have the same shape from any point of view. Their projection is always a circle or a disc; the radius does not change for an orthographic projection nor decrease in perspective when the observer is far away.

Hidden surfaces and shading can be economically processed using a depth buffer algorithm as described in Section 7.1, but adapted to the topology of the sphere. The screen is considered as an array of pairs of values: depth and intensity. At the beginning, the array is initialized with a maximum depth and 0 intensity (black) at each point.

Each sphere is processed as a solid disk, using the value of the nearest point to the observer as the depth value. For each processed sphere, values in the depth buffer are only modified if the depth of this sphere is less than the current value.

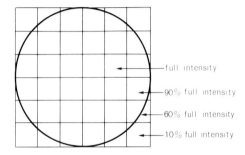

Fig. 9.9. Anti-aliasing in a spherical representation

With this approach, hidden parts are erased in the depth buffer by overlapping parts. Overlapping spheres have of course similar depth and thus similar intensities; the result is a smoothly shaded picture.

Aliasing problems are solved using a technique similar to that presented in Section 8.7. Fig. 9.9 indicates the main principles of the method. The screen is considered to be an array of cells; a cell which is completely covered by a disc receives the full intensity; a cell that is partly covered has an intensity in proportion to the area of the cell covered.

Problems with the model and methods for dealing with the intersection of spheres associated with different segments are described in Badler et al., 1979.

9.4 Labanotation

Computer-modelled human motion can only be improved by studying real human movement. Two forms of notation for recording human movement have been established and may form the basis for computer-represented human movement. These are Labanotation or Kinetography Laban [1966] and Eshkol-Wachmann notation [1958]. In Labanotation, the body is viewed as a set of joints connected by limbs. In Eshkol-Wachmann notation, limbs are connected at joints. Only Labanotation, which provides an abstraction of the human body as shown in Fig. 9.10., will be discussed in this text.

For each joint, a position is specified with respect to a set of axes that can be oriented in many ways. Two specific joints have a role: the **distal joint** is the active joint and the **proximal joint** is the one from which movement is carried out. Movement of the distal joint is expressed through operations that are classified into five categories:

1. **direction signs** that describe the translation of joints
2. **revolution signs** that describe the rotations of joints
3. **facing signs** that describe the orientation of points on surfaces (e.g. the orientation of a palm)

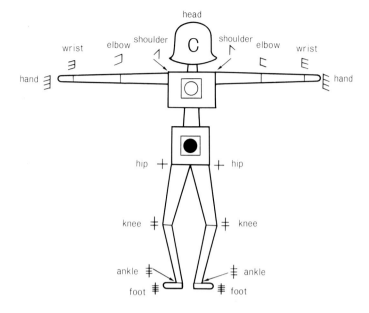

Fig. 9.10. Labanotation

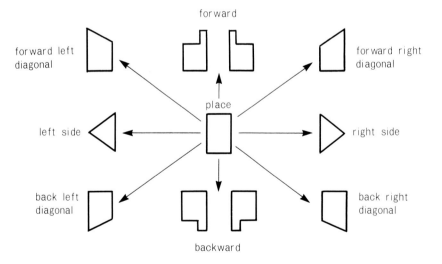

Fig. 9.11. The direction symbols

4. **contact signs** that describe the contact of two body parts or the contact of a body part with an object.
5. **shape signs** that describe the tracing of a path or formation of a shape by some body part.

In Labanotation, symbols have been introduced to describe the operations of these five classes. Each symbol has a shape to describe the movement, an intensity to express its level, and a size to define the duration of the motion. For example, Fig. 9.11 shows the shape of the nine direction symbols in a plane.

To describe the 27 three-dimensional space directions, shading is used, as shown in Fig. 9.12.

The description of the movement of a human body is noted in columns. One column represents one body part, as shown in Fig. 9.13.

Fig. 9.14 shows an example of a walking cycle. Interactive editors and programming languages based on Labanotation have been developed [Weber et al., 1978; Smoliar and Tracton, 1978; Smoliar and Weber, 1977; Calvert and Chapman, 1978; Calvert et al., 1980, 1082, 1982b].

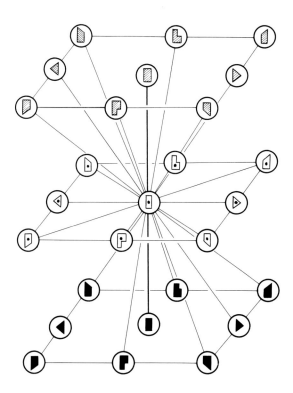

Fig. 9.12. 3D space directions

arm
body
leg gesture
left support
right support
leg gesture
body
arm
head

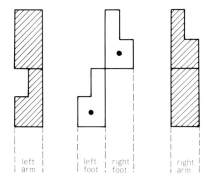

Fig. 9.13. Simplified description of the movement of a human body

Fig. 9.14. A walking cycle

9.5 Hand Representation

As the hand is the most useful tool for the human being, it is not surprising that computer scientists have been interested in its modelling and animation. Two specific attempts are the Catmull and the Badler models. In the MOP system designed by Catmull [1972], hands are decomposed into polygons. Then the Watkins algorithm is applied to remove hidden surfaces. Gouraud shading allows the designer to achieve realism (Fig. 9.15 shows examples).

The Badler model [Badler and Morris, 1982] is based on the same principle. However, a B-spline surface is computed, based on the skeleton of the hand, to improve the simulation of palm movements. Spheres are linked to the B-spline surface, which does not itself appear on the image. It is only used for the placement of the spheres.

9.6 Facial Animation

The animation of the human face is extremely difficult to model by computer. There are two problems:

1. the representation of the face itself. It is difficult to make a realistic image with natural-looking skin.
2. the modelling of motion. This is very complex, because of the interdependence of different parts.

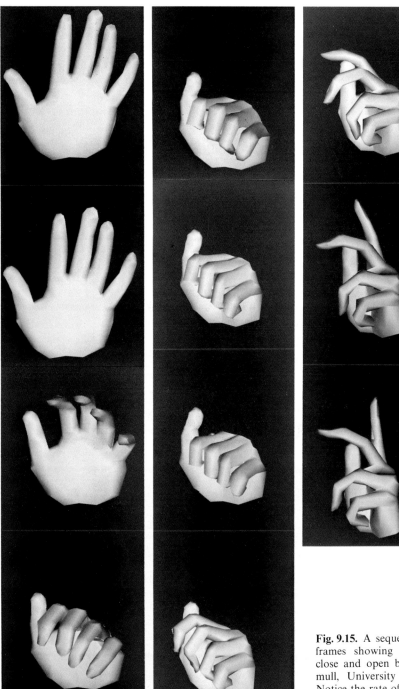

Fig. 9.15. A sequence of 11 frames showing the hand close and open by E. Catmull, University of Utah. Notice the rate of change is not constant

The most well known specialist in facial animation is Frederic I. Parke of the New York Institute of Technology. For him there are two main approaches to applying computer graphics techniques to facial animation [1982]:

1. using a key-frame system: This means that a certain number of face images are specified and the inbetweens are calculated by computer, as shown in Section 5.3.
2. using parameterized facial models: In this case the animator can create any facial image by specifying the appropriate set of parameter values.

The use of key-frame systems in two dimensions gives good results and is used

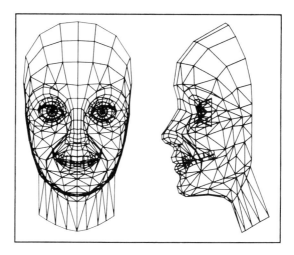

Fig. 9.16. Front and side views of the polygonal network, or topology, used to generate the image shown in Fig. 9.17

Fig. 9.17. Image of facial animation (Phong shading) by Frederik I. Parke, New York Institute of Technology

in cartoons [Stern, 1979; Reeves, 1981]. Parke used this technique in three dimensions [1972], but it is was not very efficient, as too many key frames were required.

Parameterized models, as introduced by Parke [1975, 1982], are based on the concept of basic parameterization and a model of image synthesis. Basic parameterization consists of choosing the appropriate set of facial parameters. These can be based on observation or on the underlying structures that cause facial expression. The Parke model is based on both types. Parameters are classified into two classes: expression and conformation. Most important expression parameters are related to the eyes (pupil dilation, eyelid opening, direction of vision, etc.) and the mouth (jaw rotation, width of the mouth, smiling, etc.). Conformation parameters include the color of the skin, the color of the eyes, the neck dimensions, nose characteristics and so on.

Image generation in the Parke model is based on three polygonal surfaces: one for the face and two for the eyes. As shown in Fig. 9.16, the polygons do not all have the same size and shape. According to Parke, the topology provided is the result of trial-and-error. Five types of operations determine vertex positions from the parameter values:

1. Eyes are modelled by **procedural animation**.
2. The forehead, the cheek bone region, the neck and the mouth are calculated by **interpolation**.
3. The mouth is opened by **rotation**.
4. **Scaling** is used to control the relative size of facial features.
5. For controlling the corners of the mouth or the raising of the upper lip, **position offsets** are used.

Phong shading was chosen for image rendering (Fig. 9.17).

Platt and Badler [1981] have designed a model that is based on underlying facial structure. Points are simulated in the skin, the muscles and the bones by a set of three-dimensional networks.

The skin is the outside level, represented by a set of 3D points that define a surface which can be modified.

The bones represent an internal level that cannot be moved. Between both levels, muscles are groups of points with "elastic" arcs. In Fig. 9.18, when a force is applied to the point M, point B is immovable. Fig. 9.19 shows an example.

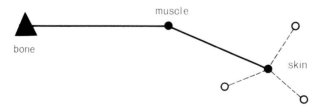

Fig. 9.18. Underlying facial structure

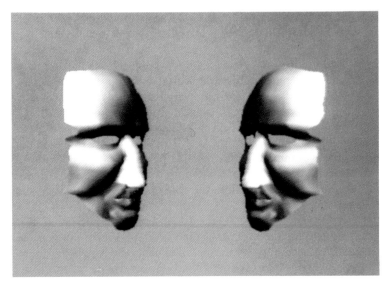

Fig. 9.19. "Two Faces" by Stephen M. Platt and Norman I. Badler, University of Pennsylvania

10. Object-oriented and Actor Languages and Systems

10.1 Classes, Modules and Processes

As indicated in chapter 6, modeled computer animation involves three main activities:

- object modeling
- motion specification and synchronization
- image rendering.

In this chapter, we study the impact of new programming languages on object modeling and motion specification and synchronization. Although, the definition of structured shaded graphical types was presented in Section 7.4 [Magnenat-Thalmann et al., 1984], research in image rendering is oriented more towards algorithm development than towards programming languages. Object modeling and motion specification and synchronization can generally be considered simultaneously, as a moving object is by definition an object that is modified during time by motion or some other transformations. As a complex scene involves several moving objects, parallelism is also important. This means that language features of interest for computer animation would include:

- tools that permit the structured definition of objects with associated operations on them
- tools that permit the definition of parallelism and quasi-parallelism
- tools that permit communication between objects.

These tools and concepts have been progressively introduced over the years. The first high-level concept for defining a complex object with its own transformations is the class concept in SIMULA-67 [Dahl and Nygaard, 1968]. SIMULA, a development of ALGOL, was initially developed for simulation. A class is composed of declarations (variables, procedures and even classes) and statements. This concept was expanded in the object-oriented languages like SMALLTALK, which will be discussed in next section. The class concept was also introduced in new programming languages like Concurrent Pascal [Brinch Hansen, 1975] and it is also the basis for the modules defined in the language MODULA-2 [Wirth, 1983].

More formally, work on data abstraction [Liskov and Zilles, 1974], [Guttag, 1977] has led to the concept of the abstract data type. This has had important implications for computer graphics, as already shown by Thalmann and Magnenat-Thalmann [1979] and Mallgren [1982].

As mentioned, objects generally move concurrently. This would suggest that the development of concepts and notations for concurrent programming, like those described by Andrews and Schneider [1983], could be important for computer animation. However, this is generally not the case, because these concepts have been designed mainly for applications in system programming, real-time programming or simulation. Frame-by-frame animation requires the presence of all actors, cameras and decor at each frame and synchronization mechanisms provided by process-oriented languages like SIMULA, CONCURRENT PASCAL or ADA are too complex for animation. However, these concepts can be very useful for real-time animation, as demonstrated by the GALATEA system [Futrelle, 1974].

Although the conventional concurrent programming approach has not had a great impact on computer animation, the object-oriented concepts introduced by Kay [1969] and Hewitt's actor theory [1971] have been very influential.

10.2 Kay's Work and SMALLTALK

The first well-known graphics system was SKETCHPAD [Sutherland, 1963]. This interactive system allowed the creation of "instances" of a basic shape, and "constraints" upon it. Based upon SKETCHPAD and SIMULA, Kay [1969] suggested that a programming system could be based on objects that send messages to each other. This idea met with great interest and two major results developed from it.

1. Kay went to Xerox Palo Alto Research Center and worked with Adele Goldberg to develop the first uniformly object-oriented language: SMALLTALK 72.
2. Projects in artificial intelligence were developed using a similar approach (see Section 10.3).

The SMALLTALK language was developed based on Kay's ideas, beginning in 1970 [Goldberg and Kay, 1976]. The latest version is SMALLTALK-80 [Goldberg and Robson, 1983], its most important concepts being:

1. Every entity is an **object**: numbers, strings, programs, compilers, etc.
2. Each object is an **instance** of a **class**.
3. Objects consist of some private memory and a set of operations.
4. Objects communicate with each other by sending messages.

A graphics system is included in SMALLTALK-80 with capabilities that are very useful for computer animation. It represents images by instances of a class **Form**. A Form has height, width and a bitmap. Animation can be displayed smoothly by using one Form as the display while the next image to be displayed is prepared in a second Form. As each image is completed, the two Forms exchange roles and the process can start again.

Basic graphical objects are defined as instances of classes Point and Rectangle. There are other display objects besides objects of the class Form. These are all defined in the class DisplayObject that contains three primary subclasses:

- DisplayMedium, which represents images that can be colored and bordered
- DisplayText, which represents textual images
- Path, that corresponds to an ordered collection of points and a Form that can be displayed at each point. The concept is very similar to the P-curves [Baecker, 1969] discussed in Section 5.6.

A conversational extensible system for the animation of shaded images, called SHAZAM, has been implemented in SMALLTALK by Baecker [1976].

10.3 Hewitt's Actor Theory

In artificial intelligence laboratories, especially those at M.I.T. and Stanford, numerous systems and languages have been developed around concepts near those of the Smalltalk school. However, research has taken a somewhat different direction, reflecting the artificial intelligence background of the researchers and the influence of LISP.

Based on his PhD thesis, Hewitt [1971] of M.I.T. first introduced the term "actor" [Hewitt et al., 1973] and this has been used in several systems designed by his team: PLANNER-73 [Greif and Hewitt, 1975], PLASMA [Hewitt and Smith, 1975].

Hewitt defined an actor as an object than can send or receive messages. All elements of a system are actors and the only activity possible in the system is the transmission of messages between them. Programming consists merely of telling the different classes of actors how to respond to the messages they receive.

There are several advantages in the Hewitt actor approach:

1. Changing a program means simply changing the responses of the actors.
2. Program complexity does not increase as programs grow.
3. It gives a natural representation of the knowledge needed for an application, and intelligence can easily be modeled as an integrated community of rather limited individuals.

Actors are defined by their behaviors. Greif and Hewitt [1975] have given the following definition of a behavior:

"A behavior is a partially ordered set of events which represent transmissions... Behaviors consist of events. An event is a four-tuple, $\langle t\ m\alpha ec\rangle$ where t is the target, m is the transmission, α is the activator, and ec is the event count of the activator α."

This approach implies programs with side-effects, parallelism and synchronization and these concepts have been formally described by Greif and Hewitt [1975] and Hewitt and Atkinson [1977].

10.4 LOGO and the DIRECTOR Actor-based Animation Language

Hewitt's actor is like a person who can receive requesting messages, send messages to other actors, and remember things. It therefore seemed to Kenneth M. Kahn to provide an ideal way of representing dynamic objects in computer animation. Kahn [1976] implemented an animation language called DIRECTOR which is based on actors.

In DIRECTOR, objects and the messages they handle are specified. In particular, an actor can be asked to do all the things that LOGO turtles can do. As the concept of the LOGO turtle is important in DIRECTOR and has also been extended to three-dimensions by Reynolds [1978, 1982] in ASAS, it will be briefly summarized here.

LOGO is a programming language that was developed at M.I.T. primarily for children [Papert, 1970]. Its most important concept is the turtle geometry which consists of polar-coordinate graphics. At the beginning of a session, the turtle (a triangle, in fact) is at the center of the screen and is invisible. The turtle appears with the command APPEAR and disappears with the command HIDE. It goes forward with the command FORWARD n and backward with the command BACKWARD n, where n is a number of steps. The commands LEFT α and RIGHT α makes the turtle turn left or right and the angle α is always calculated relative to its current orientation. For example, the following sequence of instructions draws a square of vertices $\langle\langle 0, 0 \rangle\rangle$, $\langle\langle 20, 0 \rangle\rangle$, $\langle\langle 20, 20 \rangle\rangle$, $\langle\langle 0, 20 \rangle\rangle$, $\langle\langle 0, 0 \rangle\rangle$, where $\langle\langle 0, 0 \rangle\rangle$ is the center of the screen:

> APPEAR
> REPEAT 4 [FORWARD 20 RIGHT 90]

Message passing is the mechanism of communication between two actors in DIRECTOR. The most important and the basic message-passing command is ASK. The syntax is as follows:

> ASK $\langle$actor name$\rangle$ ($\langle$message$\rangle$)

For example, ASK CORVETTE (FORWARD 10), means that a message is sent to the actor CORVETTE, and this actor is asked to go forward 10 units.

Messages begin with a key word corresponding to the action required of the actor. Among the most important key words are:

- the turtle commands: FORWARD, BACK, RIGHT, LEFT, APPEAR, HIDE, SHOW, PENUP and PENDOWN
- MAKE, that tells the actor to create a new actor and UNMAKE, that tells the actor to destroy another actor
- RECEIVE, that enables the actor to increase the set of messages it can understand
- REMEMBER and FORGET, that tell the actor to remember or forget an item, REPLACE, that tells it to replace a value and WHAT, that gives it a value.
- PLAN, that tells the actor to schedule things to do at later times.

```
TO DEFINE.FLOWER                          --LOGO command
10 ASK OBJECT(MAKE FLOWER)                --flower creation
20 ASK FLOWER(REMEMBER SIZE 10)           --flower size
30 ASK FLOWER(REMEMBER DRAW               --to draw a flower using
           USING DRAW-FLOWER)             a LOGO procedure
END


TO DEFINE .SEED
10 ASK SOMETHING(MAKE SEED)               --seed creation
20 ASK SEED (IF RECEIVE?SEED(START)       --start message and
           THEN DO.SEED.THING:?SEED)      --appropriate procedure call
END


TO DO.SEED.THING:SEED                     --procedure for handling seeds
10 LOCAL A FLOWER                         --local flower name
20 ASK FLOWER (MAKE A.FLOWER)
30 ASK A.FLOWER (APPEAR RIGHT 90)         --turtle commands
40 ASK A.FLOWER (APPEAR FORWARD
              (*100 (RANDOM)))
50 ASK A.FLOWER (APPEAR LEFT 90)
60 ASK A.FLOWER (PLAN:SHOW IN 10 TICKS)--the message ASK A.FLOWER
                                          (SHOW) will occur after
                                          A.FLOWER has received
                                          10 ticks
70 REPEAT 15 (ASK A.FLOWER                --ASK A.FLOWER (GROW 10)
           (PLAN:GROW 10 AFTER 2          will be called 15 times,
           MORE TICKS))                   2 ticks after the last
80 ASK SEED (PLAN:ASK (SEED (MAKE))       --creation of another seed that
     (START) AT THAT TIME)                must start at the same time
                                          as the last thing scheduled

90 ASK A.FLOWER (PLAN:HIDE
        AFTER 60 MORE TICKS)
END
```

Fig. 10.1. A DIRECTOR script

There are also transformation commands like GROW or conditional commands like IF. Moreover, an ASK command can be repeated several times by using REPEAT.

As an example, we present the script of a short movie, designed by Kahn [1976]:

"a garden in which seeds are born, wait, grow into flowers, create new seeds, continue growing and die."

The DIRECTOR script is shown in Fig. 10.1 with comments.

SOMETHING and OBJECT are predefined actors which are hierarchically organized. SOMETHING is at the top of the hierarchy and receives all messages that are not understood by the other actors: editing of actors, print out, creation of new actors, etc. OBJECT is an actor directly below SOMETHING and as such, inherits all of its abilities. Moreover, OBJECT can behave like a LOGO turtle. This is why, in the garden example, OBJECT is asked to create FLOWER (which does turtle-like things) and SOMETHING is asked to create SEED (which does not do turtle-like things).

For computer animation, the message-passing and matching involved are much slower than other mechanisms. However, Hewitt's concept of an actor was a significant innovation which has been influential in computer animation systems.

10.5 ASAS: The Actor/Scriptor Animation System

ASAS [Reynolds, 1978 and 1982] is a procedural programming language for animation and graphics. It was developed at the Architecture Machine Group at M.I.T. by C.W. Reynolds as a thesis project. ASAS was then integrated into the Digital Scene Simulation System of Information International Inc. The latest version, ASAS 3.0, is in fact a preprocessor for existing three-dimensional software.

ASAS was influenced by Hewitt's work and it is also a LISP-based language, from which it borrows its "parenthesized prefix notation." There are eight types of geometric objects in ASAS:

1. *vector* i.e., a 3D position

   For example: (*vector* 1 2 3)

2. *color* defined either in the RGB (red, green, blue) system or in the IHS (intensity, hue, saturation) system

   For example: (*rgb* 0.5 0.4 0.3)
   (*ihs* 0.33 0.5 1)

3. *polygon* defined by its color and a list of vertices

   For example: (*polygon* yellow a b c)

4. *solid* defined by a list of polygons

   For example: for the tetrahedron:

   (*solid* yellow
                    (*vertices:* (a 1 2 3)(b 4 5 6)
                                (c 3 2 0)(d 7 9 1))
                    (*polygon* blue a b c)
                    (*polygon* * a d b)
                    (*polygon* * a c d)
                    (*polygon* * c b d)))

5. *group* i.e., a concatenation of simpler objects

   For example: (*group* head body)

6. *point of view* (*pov*) representing the relationship between an object's local coordinate system and the external global system. The pov object is used to define the point of view of an observer (virtual camera) or of an object. A pov object is defined by four vectors: the base position vector and three vectors parallel to the local coordinate axes.

   For example: (*pov* (*vector* a b c) xvec yvec zvec)

7. *subworld* i.e., an object associated with a *pov*. A complex object can be manipulated by modifying only the *pov*.

   For example: (*subworld* (*pov* vl vx vy vz) corvette)

8. *light* composed of a position vector and a color

   For example: (*light* (*vector* 1 2 3) (*rgb* 0.33 0.5 1)).

The geometric operations are implemented as functions which produce a copy of the object on which they are applied. When these functions are used as local operators in a subworld, the effect corresponds to a three-dimensional extension of the "turtle" of the LOGO language shown in Section 10.4. Objects will be defined in such a way that their centers will be the origin of the local coordinate space. The major local operators are as follows:

grow	scale up about local center
shrink	scale down about local center
forward a	move distance a along local $+Z$ axis
backward a	move distance a along local $-Z$ axis
left α	rotate to left by angle α about local Y axis
right α	rotate to right by angle α about local Y axis
up α	rotate upward by angle α about local X axis
down α	rotate downward by angle α about local X axis
cw α	rotate clockwise by angle α about local Z axis
ccw α	rotate counter-clockwise by angle α about local Z-axis
zoom-in a	scale up of a along local Z axis
zoom-out a	scale down of a along local Z axis.

Fig. 10.2 shows the effect of the different operators. All these operators are applied to an object specified as the last parameter or, if this is omitted, to the current object defined by the operator *grasp*. For example:

(*grasp* corvette)
(*forward* 3)
(*left* (*quotient* pi 4))
(*forward* 2)
(*right* (*quotient* pi 5))
(*forward* 10)

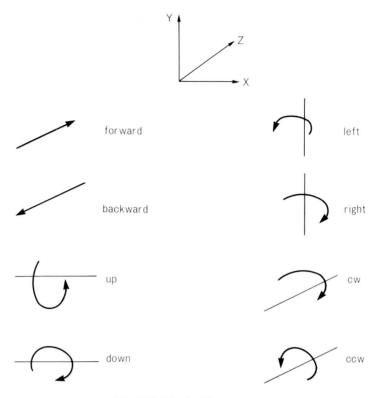

Fig. 10.2. The ASAS operators

An ASAS script (main program) generally has "animate blocks" in its main body. These are loops that automatically produce a frame at each loop step. In an animate block, objects can be made visible by the operator *see* or actors can be started and stopped at specific times with the operator *cue*.

For example, a script called transportation that starts two actors airplane (at time 10) and ship (at time 20) can be coded as:

(*script* transportation
    (*animate* (*cue* (*at* 10)
             (*start* airplane))
        (*cue* (*at* 20)
             (*start* ship))
        (*cut* 30)))

"*cut* 30" means that the animate block is exited at time 30.

An ASAS actor is, as defined by Reynolds [1982], basically a "chunk" of code that is executed once each frame. It is started by a *start* operator and stopped by a *stop* operator. It can also be displayed by the operator *see*. Fig. 10.3 shows an example of an actor which consists of an object that is rotated.

Actors can switch messages that are handled by two operators, *send* and *receive*.

```
(actor (local: (angle 0)
               (step (quo 2 runtime))
               (octa octahedron))
       (see (rotate angle y-axis octa)
       (define angle (plus angle step))))
```

Fig. 10.3. An ASAS actor

10.6 CINEMIRA: A Language Based on Actor and Camera Data Types

CINEMIRA [Thalmann and Magnenat-Thalmann, 1984] is a high-level three-dimensional computer animation language based on data abstraction. It allows the animator to write structured scripts by defining animated basic types, actor types and camera types. Static graphical objects are defined as figures and decor. Messages can be switched between actors and cameras. A director, who can also communicate with actors and cameras, assumes scene control.

Animated Basic Types

Images transformations are defined by functions depending on variables of three basic types: INTEGER, REAL and VECTOR. For example, a translation is defined by a vector translation, and a rotation by a vector (the center) and a real number (the angle). Attributes like color, intensity or source lights are also defined by parameters of these types. Viewing transformations are also based on these types. For example, a perspective projection is defined by its center, which is a vector. Animation of objects (actors) and cameras can then be based on the animation of basic parameters.

A good way of defining animation of these parameters is to introduce **animated basic types**. This concept is a generalization of the Newton concept defined in ASAS (see Section 10.5). Each variable of an animated basic type—INTEGER, REAL and VECTOR—can itself be animated. An animated type is defined by giving the starting and ending values of the number or the vector, the starting and ending times, and a function or law which describes how the value varies with time. During the specified interval, variables of animated basic types are automatically updated to the next value according to the function. For example, suppose we wish to define a vector that starts at time 10 and moves with a constant speed $\langle\langle 3, 0, 0\rangle\rangle$ from the point $\langle\langle 0, 10, 4\rangle\rangle$ and stops at time 13. This is expressed as follows:

type TVEC = *animated* VECTOR;
        val $\langle\langle 0, 10, 4\rangle\rangle$ .. UNLIMITED;

time 10..13;
law $\langle\langle 0, 10, 4\rangle\rangle + \langle\langle 3, 0, 0\rangle\rangle * (CLOCK\text{-}10)$
end;
var VEC:TVEC;

As the end position and the ending time are redundant values, they are not both required. It is possible to use UNLIMITED to avoid specifying a value.

Of course, starting and ending values of the number or vector, and starting and ending times have to be defined either by calculation or by direct input. This is why expressions can be defined using both the *val* and *time* specifications. Formal parameters can be defined in an animated basic type. These parameters must be value parameters and they can be used in *val*, *time* and *law* expressions. For example:

type TVEC = *animated* VECTOR (STARTTIME, ENDTIME:REAL;
                                         (STARTVAL, SPEED:VECTOR);
              val STARTVAL..UNLIMITED;
              time STARTTIME..ENDTIME;
              law STARTVAL + SPEED * (CLOCK-STARTTIME)
              end;

Expressions in the law can also involve "CLOCK" that is the current time and "CURVAL" that is the current value of the animated basic variable.

type TVEC = *animated* VECTOR (DELTA:VECTOR);
              $\vdots$
              law CURVAL + DELTA
              end;

Initialization of the animated basic variables is performed by the *init* statement. It is at this stage that values of the parameters are given, as shown:

init VEC $(10, 13, \langle\langle 0, 10, 4\rangle\rangle, \langle\langle 3, 0, 0\rangle\rangle)$

Animated basic variables can be used wherever a variable of the same basic type would be used. This feature is very powerful. For example, a point can be moved along a line and a sphere S can be rotated around this point, as shown in Fig. 10.4. This can be described by a single rotation where the center is an animated vector, and the angle an animated real number.

type TVEC   = *animated* VECTOR (...)
                     (* as defined previously *)
      TREAL = *animated* REAL (STARTTIME, ENDTIME:REAL);
              val 0..UNLIMITED;
              time STARTTIME..ENDTIME;
              law CURVAL * 1.2
              end;
      TREAL = *animated* REAL (STARTTIME, ENDTIME:REAL);
              val 0..UNLIMITED;
              time STARTTIME..ENDTIME;

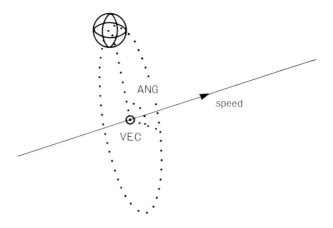

Fig. 10.4. A motion

$$law \ (CURVAL + PI/20) \ mod \ (2*PI)$$
$$end;$$
var VEC:TVEC;
    ANG:TREAL;
    S:SPHERE;
    $\vdots$

init VEC(10, 13, $\langle\langle 0, 10, 4\rangle\rangle$ $\langle\langle 3, 0, 0\rangle\rangle$);
init ANG(10, 13);
    $\vdots$

ROTATION (S, VEC, ANG, S)

Actor Data Types

An *actor* type is an animated abstract graphical data type. The syntax is very similar to the figure syntax of MIRA shown in Section 6.3, except that the life-time limits of the actor have to be specified. Animated basic types and variables can be defined within an *actor* type. *Actor* types can only be defined in a script. The syntax of an actor type is as follows:

⟨actor type⟩ ::= *actor* ⟨formal parameter list⟩; ⟨time interval⟩;
⟨actor block⟩

An actor can be constructed using *figures* that can be manipulated. The actor block can contain any declaration except *actor* and *camera* types, and any MIRA-3D statement. However, the viewing procedures cannot be invoked, because it is not the role of an actor to manipulate visual parameters. The time interval specifies when the actor exists. If the actor type BALL is defined as:

type BALL = *actor* (TINIT:REAL);
            time TINIT .. 20;
            ...

actors of BALL type will be on the scene between the time TINIT and 20.

As in the case of animated variables, actor variables are initialized by the *init* statement. For example, two differents variables of BALL type can be initialized:

var BALL1, BALL2 : BALL;

   ⋮

   init BALL1 (10);
   init BALL2 (12);

It is also possible to use an actor type as another PASCAL type. For example, we can define: *var* BALLS: *array* [1 .. 10] *of* BALL;

We now give an example of an actor type: we define an actor that is a stone (of icosahedric shape) that falls from a position P until it arrives at the level 0 (Y = 0); for example, a water surface. The *actor* type stone is defined as follows:

STONE = *actor* (P : VECTOR; TINIT, TSTART : REAL);
                time TINIT .. UNLIMITED;
                type TVEC = *animated* VECTOR;
                    val P .. ⟨⟨P . X, 0, P . Z⟩⟩;
                    time TSTART .. ⟨⟨P . X, 0, P . Z⟩⟩;
                    law P − 0.5 ∗ 9.81 ∗ SQR (CLOCK-TSTART)
                    end;
                var VEC: TVEC;
                    ICOSA : ICOSAHEDRON;
                begin
                    init VEC;
                    create ICOSA (VEC, CFA, DIR);
                    include ICOSA
                end;

A variable ROCK of STONE type is animated by the following sequence:

init ROCK (⟨⟨10, 8, 20⟩⟩, 10, 12);
...

This means that the *actor* ROCK exists from time 10, but starts moving at time 12.

In many cases, it is difficult to decide in advance when an *actor* must start moving. In our example, suppose that the stone has to begin moving when a person (another *actor*) drops it. This can be performed by removing the TSTART parameter in the STONE *actor* and replacing the lower time limit TSTART in the TVEC type by SIGNAL:

STONE = *actor* (P : VECTOR; TINIT : REAL);
                time TINIT .. UNLIMITED;
                type TVEC = *animated* VECTOR;
                    val P .. ⟨⟨P . X, 0, P . Z⟩⟩;
                    time SIGNAL .. UNLIMITED;
                    law P-0.5 ∗ 9.81 ∗ SQR (CLOCK-SIGNAL)
                    end;

> *begin*
>   …
> *end*;

The animation sequence is as follows:

> *init* PERSON (…);
> *init* ROCK (⟪10, 8, 20⟫, 10);

PERSON is a variable of *actor* type, which must contain a *start* ROCK statement at the right time.

Similarly, we may start a new actor WAVES, consisting of circular waves that begin as a stone hits the water by rewriting the STONE *actor* type as:

> *begin*
>   *init* VEC;
>   *create* ICOSA (VEC, CFA, DIR);
>   *include* ICOSA;
>   *if* VEC . Y = 0 *then start* WAVES
> *end*;

More generally, a *start* A statement has the immediate effect of replacing all lower SIGNAL time limits of the actor A by the current runtime. It can make the *actor* appear and/or start the motion of animated variables declared within the *actor* type. Similarly, a *stop* B statement has the immediate effect of replacing all higher SIGNAL time limits of the *actor* B by the current time. It can make the *actor* disappear and/or stop the motion of animated variables declared within the *actor* type.

Camera Data Types

A *camera* type is also an animated abstract type. Its syntax is exactly the same as that of an *actor* type, replacing *actor* with *camera* keywords. Time limits have the same meaning as for an *actor*. Animated basic types and variables can be defined within a camera type, but no *actor* or other *camera* types can be used. As expected, *camera* type can only be defined in a *script*. The statements cannot manipulate figures and actors because this is not the role of a camera. The goal of a *camera* type is to define the values of the visual parameters and how they vary with time. Typically, statements in a *camera* type are viewing procedure calls. These can be those of the GSPC Core System. Their parameters can, of course, be animated variables, as shown:

> *type* TCAM = *camera* (TINIT, TEND : REAL);
>   *time* TINIT .. TEND;
>   *type* TVEC = *animated* VECTOR (VSTART,
>   VSTEP : VECTOR);
>   *val* VSTART .. UNLIMITED;
>   *time* TINIT .. TEND;
>   *law* CURVAL + VSTEP
>   *end*;

```
var V1, V2: TVEC;
begin
    init V1 (⟨⟨0, 0, 1⟩⟩, ⟨⟨0, 0.1, 0⟩⟩);
    init V2 (⟨⟨20, 25, −20⟩⟩
             ⟨⟨0, 1, −0.5⟩⟩);
    VIEWPORT (⟨⟨0, 0⟩⟩, ⟨⟨1, 1⟩⟩);
    WINDOW (⟨⟨−20, −5⟩⟩, ⟨⟨20, 35⟩⟩);
    PLANENORMAL (V1);
    PERSPECTIV (V2);
end;
```

Some viewing procedures other than the GSPC procedures have also been predefined:

PARACAMERA (EYE, INTEREST, ZOOM)
PERCAMERA (EYE, INTEREST, ZOOM)

These two procedures allow the user to easily define visual parameters for parallel and perspective projections by giving the position of the eye, an interest point and a zoom value.

Rectangular and polygonal clippings can also be specified in a camera type, by using the procedures CLIPINT, CLIPEXT, POLCLIPINT and POLCLIPEXT. It is also possible to clear or color a rectangular or polygonal area. These capabilities make possible special effects similar to those created with optical printers.

To illustrate, suppose that we have two cameras, CAM1 and CAM2. Figs. 10.5a and 10.5b show the views picked up by both cameras. If both are running at the same time, we obtain the effect shown in Fig. 10.5c. If we would like to obtain the situation presented in Fig. 10.5d, we can use the following code:

```
type TCAM1 = camera (EYE, INTEREST: VECTOR);
            time 0 .. UNLIMITED;
            begin
                PERCAMERA (EYE, INTEREST, 1);
                CLIPINT (⟨⟨0.25, 0.25⟩⟩, ⟨⟨0.75, 0.75⟩⟩);
            end;
     TCAM2 = camera (EYE, INTEREST: VECTOR);
            time 0 .. UNLIMITED;
            begin
                PERCAMERA (EYE, INTEREST, 1);
                VIEWPORT (⟨⟨0.25, 0.25⟩⟩, ⟨⟨0.75, 0.75⟩⟩)
            end;
     var CAM1: TCAM1;
         CAM2: TCAM2;
            :
            :
     init CAM1 (EYE1, INTEREST1);
     init CAM2 (EYE2, INTEREST2);
```

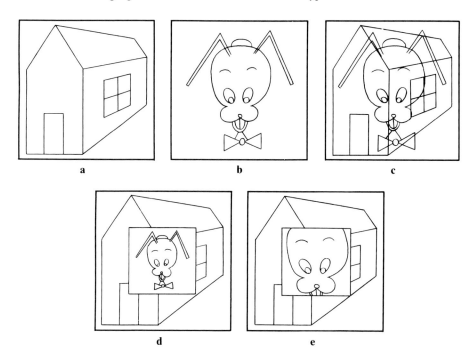

Fig. 10.5. Effects of two cameras

To obtain the situation presented in Fig. 10.5e, we have to replace the VIEWPORT call in the TCAM2 *camera* type by a CLIPEXT call. In addition, suppose we would like the size of the picture taken by the CAM2 camera to vary from the complete screen to the screen's center point, starting at time TSTART and with a speed SPD. This can be done by rewriting the TCAM1 and TCAM2 types as:

```
type TVEC = animated VECTOR (V1, V2, SP:VECTOR; TSTART:REAL);
           val V1..V2;
           time TSTART..UNLIMITED;
           law V1 + SP*(CLOCK-TSTART)
           end;
     TCAM1 = camera (EYE, INTEREST, SPD:VECTOR, TSTART:REAL);
           time 0..UNLIMITED;
           var VA, VB:TVEC;
           begin
               init VA (《《0,0》》, 《《0.5,0.5》》, SPD, TSTART);
               init VB (《《1,1》》, 《《0.5,0.5》》, -SPD, TSTART);
               PERCAMERA (EYE, INTEREST, 1);
               CLIPINT (VA, VB)
           end;
```

TCAM2 = *camera* (EYE, INTEREST, SPD:VECTOR; TSTART:REAL);
       time 0..UNLIMITED;
       var VA, VB:TVEC;
       begin
         init VA ($\langle\langle\langle 0,0\rangle\rangle\rangle$, $\langle\langle 0.5, 0.5\rangle\rangle$, SPD, TSTART);
         init VB ($\langle\langle\langle 1,1\rangle\rangle\rangle$, $\langle\langle 0.5, 0.5\rangle\rangle$, $-$SPD, TSTART);
         PERCAMERA (EYE, INTEREST, 1);
         CLIPEXT (VA, VB)
       end;

CAM1 and CAM2 variables have to be initialized with the same starting time. *Camera* types can be used just like other PASCAL types. For example,

             var CAM:*array* [1..3] *of* TCAM2;

The *start* and *stop* statements can also be applied to *camera* variables.

Scripts

A CINEMIRA *script* is a subprogram dedicated to computer animation. A program can invoke several scripts, but only one at a time. A script is under the control of a **director** which is normally not apparent, but can communicate with other entities of the system by messages. Actor and cameras can also exchange messages.
A script has the following syntax:

    ⟨script declaration⟩::= *script* ⟨script identifier⟩
    ⟨formal parameter list⟩; ⟨script block⟩;

A script has a name that is an identifier and can have parameters like a procedure.
    A script block is composed of declarations (constants, types, variables and subprograms), statements and *scenes*. The syntax of a script block is as follows:

    ⟨script block⟩::= ⟨declaration part⟩ *begin* ⟨statement⟩
    {;⟨statement⟩} * ⟨scene⟩ {;⟨scene⟩} * *end*;

The declaration part can include all declarations allowed in MIRA-3D, animated basic types, *figure* types, *actor* types, *camera* types and message variables.
    A script is a sequence of scenes. The scenes can be preceded by a sequence of statements to initialize objects that are common to several scenes.
Each scene has the following syntax:

    ⟨scene⟩::= *scene* ⟨scene identifier⟩; ⟨statement⟩;
    {⟨statement⟩;} * ⟨shoot statement⟩ *end* ⟨scene identifier⟩

The scene has a name and consists of a sequence of statements that serve mainly to initialize actors, cameras and decor. The decor is a collection of graphical objects that do not move or change during the entire scene. In CINEMIRA, a decor is defined by the statement *decor* ⟨figure list⟩ where the figure list is an enumeration of figure variables. For example:

create HOUSE(...);
create SKY;
create SUN(...);
decor HOUSE, SKY, SUN;

The *shoot* statement performs the shooting phase, during which decor, actors and cameras are automatically placed. The shoot statement can take a very simple form:

shoot until ⟨expression⟩

where the expression is the upper time limit of the scene in seconds. The lower limit is the upper limit of the previous scene (0 at the beginning).

Each scene can have initializations and must have a *shoot* statement. *Actors, cameras, decor* and animated basic variables can be activated for several scenes or parts of scenes. In this case, they have to be initialized before the first scene and not within one.

Special effects like fade-in, fade-out, and cross dissolves are only possible by overlapping scenes. This can be done by declaring an overlap of the next scene in the *shoot* statement and by specifying the overlap time, as shown:

scene ONE:
⋮

shoot until 20 *overlap* 3
end ONE;
scene TWO;
⋮

We give an example where scene ONE begins to disappear 2 seconds before the end and scene TWO appears simultaneously. The visual effect is shown in Fig. 10.6. The CINEMIRA code is presented in Fig. 10.7.

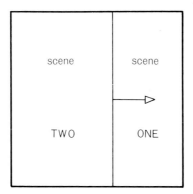

Fig. 10.6. Wipe effect

```
    type
       TREAL = animated REAL(R1,R2,TSTART:REAL);
                 val R1..R2;
                 time TSTART..UNLIMITED;
                 law R1+0.01*(CLOCK-TSTART)
              end;


       TCAM1 = camera(EYE,INTEREST:VECTOR; TWIPE:REAL);
              time 0..UNLIMITED;
              var R:TREAL;

              begin
                 init R(0,1,TWIPE);
                 PERCAMERA(EYE,INTEREST,1);
                 CLIPEXT(<< R,0 >>, << 1,1 >>)
              end;

       TCAM2 = camera(EYE,INTEREST:VECTOR; TWIPE:REAL);
              time 0..UNLIMITED;
              var R:TREAL;
              begin
                 init R(0,1,TWIPE);
                 PERCAMERA(EYE,INTEREST,1);
                 CLIPINT(<< R,0 >>, << 1,1 >>)
              end;

    var
       CAM1:TCAM1;
       CAM2:TCAM2;
       ...
    begin
       init CAM1(EYE1,INTEREST1,18);
       init CAM2(EYE2,INTEREST2,18);

       scene ONE;
       ...actor and decor initializations
          shoot until 20 overlap 2
       end ONE;

       scene TWO;
       ...actor and decor initializations
          shoot until 35
       end TWO;
    end.
```

Fig. 10.7. CINEMIRA code

10.7 MIRANIM: An Extensible Director-oriented 3D Animation System

Although there are problems in computer-aided animation, various animator-oriented systems have been developed that work. They can be used by non computer-expert artists. In modelled animation, the problem is more complex and always centers around the question: programming language or animator-oriented system? The production of three-dimensional computer-animated films using a graphical programming language is time-consuming. For example, it took 14 months to produce the 13-minute film *Dream Flight* [Thalmann et al., 1982], although we used structured programming with the MIRA-3D language [Magnenat-Thalmann, Thalmann, 1983] based on high-level graphical types. [Magnenat-Thalmann and Thalmann, 1983c].

Moreover, such an approach implies that animators also have to be programmers. User-friendly interactive systems can have the great advantage of being dedicated to artists, but they impose limits on creativity and fail to exploit all the possibilities of a computer. Special effects like the ones shown in Fig. 10.8 are difficult to produce without programming. Apart from three-dimensional key frame animation systems like BBOOP or MUTAN [Fortin et al., 1983], discussed in Sections 4.8 and 5.9, there are not many examples of artist-oriented 3D systems except ANTS, presented in Section 4.6. Some of the spectacular effects in *TRON*, for instance, were produced by Information International Inc. using ASAS, a typical programming language used for computer animation.

We came to the conclusion that artists who do not know how to program a computer (they are in the majority) have to use an artist-oriented system. That system must offer the possibility of making most scenes of a computer-animated film. It must provide facilities for controlling main actor motions, virtual cameras and lighting. In the case of very complex motions, procedural models can be programmed by a programmer, but it is essential that the control of this procedural model be given to the animator in the interactive system. This means that the new motion must be added to the system, which must therefore be extensible. We have designed and implemented such a system (called MIRANIM), composed of an animator-oriented system called ANIMEDIT and an animation sublanguage called CINEMIRA-2 [Magnenat-Thalmann, et al., 1985].

The Animator-Oriented System ANIMEDIT
With the ANIMEDIT system, the animator can specify a complete script without any programming. He or she can create actors with their motions and transformations as well as virtual cameras with their motions and characteristics. Backgrounds can also be built interactively. Multiple light sources can be defined and moved around at will. Eight modes are defined in the system, each with specific commands.

1. **Variable mode**
   This mode allows the animator to create constants and animated variables. Such variables, which drive the motion of actors, cameras and lights, are defined by evolution laws describing how their values change over time.

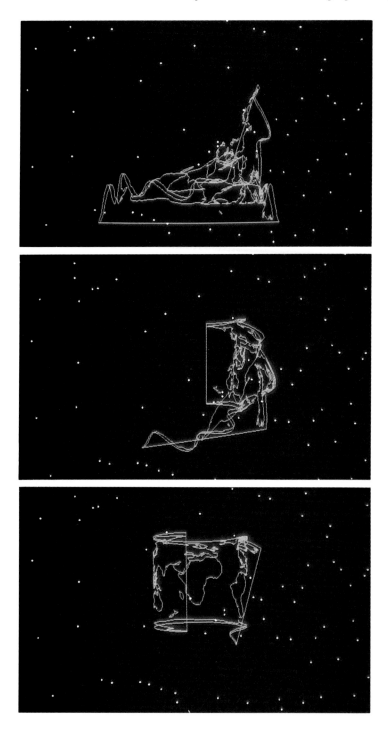

Fig. 10.8. Formation of the earth (from *Dream Flight*)

Among the available laws are the Catmull laws and the main physical motions. To define a point PT that turns from time 0 to time 10 with a circular motion around an axis passing through the vector $\langle 8, 4, 0 \rangle$ and the plane normal vector $\langle 0, 0, 1 \rangle$, with an angular velocity of 1 rd/sec and angular acceleration of 0 rd/sec^2, we type:

VEC, PT, A, 0, 0, 0	– defines point PT as a vector with an initial value.
LAW, MYLAW, MVTCIRC, 8, 4, 0, 0, 0, 1, 1, 0	– defines the law MYLAW as a specific circular motion.
EVOLUTION, PT, MYLAW, 0, 10	– associates the law with the point from time 0 to time 10.

2. **Object mode**

This mode offers the same possibilities for creating objects as a limited three-dimensional graphics editor. In fact, basic objects must be built outside the animation system. But they can be modified in the object mode by rotations, translations, scaling and coloring. For example, if we wish to use objects such as a car which is an actor and mountains which form part of the background, or decor, the objects are read from a file and they can then be colored or translated.

READ, CAR, CARFILE	– creates a car
READ, MOUNT1, MOUNTFILE	– creates a mountain
COPY, MOUNT1, MOUNT2	– duplicates the mountain
MOVE, MOUNT2, 5, 15, 20	– translates the second mountain
COLOR, CAR, 0.33, 0.5, 1	– colors the car red.

3. **Decor mode**

This mode allows the animator to build up a decor with objects and to view it. For example, to build a decor with a house and two mountains:

DECOR, MYDECOR, HOUSE, MOUNT1, MOUNT2

4. **Actor mode**

This mode is the most important one. The animator defines actors (animated objects) and then gives a list of transformations which have to be applied to each. At present, 16 kinds of transformations are available, including rotation, sizing, translation, shears, torsion, traction, flexion, stochastic transformation and color changing. The parameters of a transformation may be animated variables; the latter are also generally used to specify time dependence. For example, in a rotation, the angle can be an animated real number and the direction of the axis can be an animated vector.

The number of transformations associated with an actor is not limited and the transformations are driven by the animated variables. For example, suppose the following transformations are to be performed on a tree:

i)   changing the size
ii) flexion (or bending)
iii) changing the color from green to red

This can be performed by the following commands:

ACTOR, TREE, TREEOBJ   – defines the actor tree with the object
                                TREEOBJ as basis
SIZE, TREE, V   – V is an animated vector which defines
                                how the size changes
FLEXION, TREE, V1, V2, V3, V4 – V1, V2, V3 and V4 are flexion
                                parameters
COLOR, TREE, VC   – VC is an animated vector which
                                changes from the HLS value of green
                                to the HLS value of red according to a
                                law.

5. **Camera mode**

In this mode, the animator can define one or several virtual cameras. Each
camera has an eye point and an interest point, which can be animated vectors.
Moreover, clipping, spin, viewpoint and zoom can be specified for a camera
as well as animation. The eye point or the interest point of a camera can also
follow the motion of a specific actor. By using several cameras at the same
time, special effects like wipes can easily be achieved.

For example, it is possible to use MYCAMERA as a constant eye point and
to have an animated interest point moving along a circle. We also include the
use of a varying zoom. The camera will be defined as:

CAMERA, MYCAMERA, EYE, PT – PT is the interest point defined pre-
                             viously in the variable mode.
ZOOM, MYCAMERA, VALZOOM   – VALZOOM is an animated real
                             variable.

6. **Light mode**

In this mode, the animator can define one or several light sources and their
motion(s). For example, two moving lights can be defined by:

LIGHT, SOURCE1, POS1
LIGHT, SOURCE2, POS2 (POS1 and POS2 are two animated vectors)

7. **Animation mode**

This mode belongs to the director's mode; starting time and duration of actors,
cameras and decor are decided here. Shooting and playback are also activated
in this mode.

ACT, CAR, 0, 10, 0   – the car is at the beginning and transfor-
                          mations begin at the same time
ACT, TREE, 0, 100, 5   – the tree is at the beginning but transfor-
                          mations start only at time 5
DEC, MYDECOR, 0, 100   – the same decor is used all the time
CAM, MYCAMERA, 0, 100   – the same camera is used all the time

LIGHT, SOURCE1, 0, 100
LIGHT, SOURCE2, 0, 100   – two light sources are moving all the time
SPEED, 24   – the number of images per second is 24
SHOOT, 0, 100   – the shooting time is from 0 to 100.

8. **Control mode**
   This mode allows the animator to enter other modes, to save or retrieve actors, cameras, decors or to obtain a list of the script under the form of an "abstract table" of all variables, laws, actors, transformations, cameras, lights and so on.

The CINEMIRA-2 Sublanguage
Based on our experience with the CINEMIRA language and actor and camera data types [Thalmann and Magnenat-Thalmann, 1983], we have designed a sublanguage called CINEMIRA-2, less complex than CINEMIRA. This sublanguage is limited to the programming of entities to be used by ANIMEDIT; it is not possible to write a program in CINEMIRA-2. What is innovative about this approach is that an entity programmed in CINEMIRA-2 is directly accessible to ANIMEDIT. For example, suppose an animator would like to introduce a transformation EXPLOSION in a scene where an actor CAR is running, crashes and is destroyed by an explosion. The animator would like to control the EXPLOSION by parameters like the speed of the car V and the distance from an obstacle D. We assume that the animator does not know how to program. He or she asks a programmer to implement a transformation EXPLOSION (V, D). With this done, the animator can define in the actor mode:

EXPLOSION, CAR, V, D

where V is an animated vector and D an animated real variable. Fig. 10.9 shows an explosion.

Apart from actor transformations, CINEMIRA-2 allows the programming of six kinds of entities:

– animation blocks
– laws
– transformations
– objects
– subactors
– cameras.

Commands in ANIMEDIT give the animator access to these entities. These commands have parameters corresponding to the parameters of the entities defined in CINEMIRA-2.

– VECTOR
– REAL
– OBJ for graphical objects
– ACT for actors
– CAM for cameras.

An animation block is a subprogram executed at each frame. For instance:

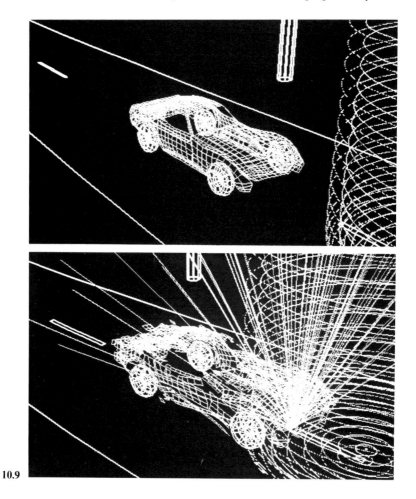

10.9

```
block BALL (CENTER : VECTOR);
var SPH : SPHERE;
begin
    create SPH (CENTER, 3); draw SPH
end;
```

The animator can activate a block in the editor by calling the command BLOCK and then choosing the parameters, as shown:

BLOCK, BALL, 10, 5, CENTER – where 10 is the activation time, 5 the duration time and CENTER an animated vector.

Laws can be defined in a similar way to functions in PASCAL. However, the function type is necessarily REAL or VECTOR and these laws are functions of time (CLOCK). For example:

Fig. 10.9. Explosion of a Corvette (four frames from NIRVANA. © N. Magnenat-Thalmann and D. Thalmann 1983)

law MVTACC (SPDINIT, ACC: VECTOR): VECTOR;
begin
    MVTACC := 0.5 * ACC * SQR (CLOCK) − SPDINIT * CLOCK
end

These laws can then be used by the animator with the editor command **LAW**.

Procedural objects can be defined in the form of graphical types, as already shown in Sections 6.3 and 7.4, and they can be modeled either as line-drawing objects or as three-dimensional shaded objects.

In the editor, the animator can create procedural objects and, of course, he or she can choose any parameter desired by the command **PROJECT**. For instance:

PROBJECT, BOX1, BOX, V1, V2, V3, V4, COL − BOX is the type defined in Section 7.4.

The object mode allows the modification of procedural objects as well as other objects introduced interactively or by digitalization. For example:

COLOR, BOX1, H, L, S

Subactors can either be treated as parts of an actor in the editor or as complete actors. Synchronization between actors and subactors is assured by parameters, which can themselves be animated variables. For example, we can define in the editor, an actor CAR with a velocity V. The car possesses 4 wheels which are subactors. These wheels have a rotation speed dependig on the speed of the car. The wheels are implemented in CINEMIRA-2 in the form:

type WHEEL = *subactor* (CENTER, V: VECTOR)
     begin
      ⋮
     end;

In the editor, the CAR with animated wheels is created as:

ACTOR, CAR, CARFILE
TRANSLATION, CAR, A, POSITION
SUBACTOR, WHEEL1, WHEEL, POINT1, SPEED
SUBACTOR, WHEEL2, WHEEL, POINT2, SPEED
SUBACTOR, WHEEL3, WHEEL, POINT3, SPEED
SUBACTOR, WHEEL4, WHEEL, POINT4, SPEED
HIERARCHY, CAR, WHEEL1, WHEEL2, WHEEL3, WHEEL4

Cameras are generally defined in the editor with numerous facilities to produce special effects like those provided by optical printers. However, it is also possible for an animator to define procedural cameras.

In this case, cameras are defined as entities of camera type. For instance:

type TCAM = *camera* (P: VECTOR);
     begin
      if NORME (P) < LIMIT
       then PERCAMERA (P, INT, ZOOM, SPIN)
       else PARCAMERA (F(P), INT, ZOOM, SPIN)
     end;

A camera of the TCAM type can be activated in the editor by the command:

PROCAM, CAM1, TCAM, POINT – where POINT is an animated vector.

Other specifications (e.g., SPIN, CAM1) can be defined for such a camera.

Implementation

ANIMEDIT is a 12000-line source program written in MIRA-SHADING (Magnenat-Thalmann et al., 1984b), a structured language that enables the programmer to specify, manipulate and animate three-dimensional shaded objects using high-level graphical types. (MIRA-SHADING was briefly presented in Section 7.4.)

Like MIRA-SHADING, CINEMIRA-2 was implemented by developing a preprocessor written in ISO PASCAL. This preprocessor produces standard PASCAL modules and a specification feil. To extend ANIMEDIT with new entities, programmed in CINEMIRA-2, the following steps have to be taken:

- precompile new entities
- compile PASCAL output
- link output with ANIMEDIT relocatable code.

At runtime, access to the new entities by ANIMEDIT is performed by checking the specification file produced by the CINEMIRA-2 preprocessor. Fig. 10.10 shows the complete organization of this process.

ANIMEDIT and CINEMIRA-2 have been implemented on a VAX 11/780 with various terminals. Shaded images are produced with an AED 767 terminal.

Examples of Scripts

1. A person visits a gallery which contains several paintings.

VA⟩	VECTOR, VISITOR, C, 75, 50, −100	− defines a constant vector VISITOR.
VA⟩	VECTOR, INTEREST, A, 300, 50, 150	− defines an animated vector INTEREST.
VA⟩	LAW, PAN, 8, 75, 50, −100, 0, 10, 0, −0.2, 0	− defines a pan law.
VA⟩	EVOLUTION, INTEREST, PAN, 0, 30	− applies the law to INTEREST.
VA⟩	REAL, ZOOMR, C, 0.7	− defines a real constant.
OB⟩	READ, WALLS, FILE	− reads objects.
	⋮	
DE⟩	BUILD, GALLERY, WALLS, PAINT1, ...	− builds the decor GALLERY with walls, ceiling and paintings.
CA⟩	CAMERA, CAM, VISITOR, INTEREST	− defines a camera with the view-point VISITOR and the interest point INTEREST.
CA⟩	ZOOM, CAM, ZOOMR	− adds a constant ZOOM to the camera.
AN⟩	DECOR, GALLERY, 0, 30	− activates the decor GALLERY.

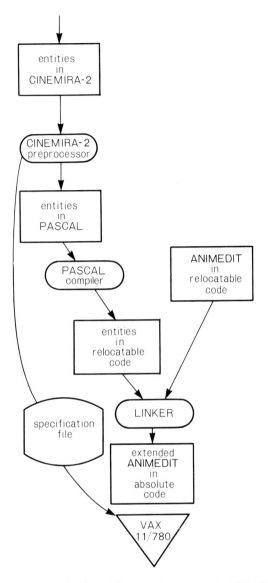

Fig. 10.10. Organization of the extension process in MIRANIM

AN⟩   CAMERA, CAM, 0, 30, 0   – activates the
                                                  camera CAM.
AN⟩   SHOOT, 0, 30   – shoots 30 seconds

Fig. 10.11 shows a frame.

2. Four letters M, I, R and A come from different directions to build the title
   MIRA. Then the letters are triplicated.

VA⟩   VECTOR, MOTION1, A, 1875, 750, 500, −150, 0, 0   − defines three animated vectors.

VA⟩   VECTOR, MOTION2, A, 1875, 750, 500, −150, 0, 0

VA⟩   VECTOR, MOTION3, A, 1875, 750, 500, −150, 0, 0

VA⟩   LAW, UNIFORM, 2, 3, 3, 3   − defines a uniform law.

VA⟩   LAW, FARE, 6, 0.25   − defines an oscillation.

VA⟩   EVOLUTION, MOTION1, UNIFORM, 0, 5   − applies the uniform law to MOTION1.

VA⟩   EVOLUTION, MOTION2, FARE, 0, 4   − applies the FARE

VA⟩   EVOLUTION, MOTION3, FARE, 0, 4   − law to MOTION2 and MOTION3.

      etc.

VA⟩   VECTOR, EYE, C, 0, 0, −400   − defines a constant vector EYE.

Fig. 10.11. A frame of "Visit of a Gallery" (Designers: S. Lafrance, F. Marceau. © N. Magnenat-Thalmann and D. Thalmann 1984)

VA⟩	VECTOR, INTEREST, C, 0, 0, 10000	– defines a constant vector INTEREST.
OB⟩	READ, LETM, FILE	
	⋮	
AC⟩	ACTOR, LETM1, LETM	– defines the letter M as an actor.
AC⟩	TRANSLATION, LETM1, A, MOTION1	– applies a translation to this actor with the motion MOTION1.
	⋮	
AC⟩	TRANSLATION, LETM2, A, MOTION2	
AC⟩	TRANSLATION, LETM3, A, MOTION3	
	⋮	
CA⟩	CAMERA, CAM, EYE, INTEREST	– defines a camera.
AN⟩	ACTOR, LETM1, 0, 11, 0	– activates the actors.
AN⟩	ACTOR, LETM2, 6, 4, 6	
AN⟩	ACTOR, LETM3, 6, 4, 6	
	⋮	
AN⟩	CAMERA, CAM, 0, 11, 0	– activates the camera.
AN⟩	SHOOT, 0, 11	– shoots 11 seconds

11. Case Studies

11.1 Decor with Bridges and Houses

In computer animated films, bridges and houses are impressive objects that take a long time to produce. In this section we present two tools for creating these objects more easily. The first one is a BRIDGE graphical type [Thalmann et al., 1982] and the second is a user-oriented system for drawing house facades.

Bridges

Bridges are difficult architectural constructions to define using parameters. They are very dependent on factors that resist easy description, such as landscapes, building materials, building techniques, and the imagination of architects and engineers. A procedure for drawing any bridge would require more than 100 parameters. The graphics technique presented here allows the user to draw a great number of bridges, although not all. In particular, the following types of bridges cannot be represented by using our method: curved bridges, bascule bridges, swing bridges, corniche viaducts, masonry bridges, wooden bridges and cable-stayed bridges. If these types are excluded, about 90 per cent of bridges can be drawn using our system.

Elements of a bridge can be classified into four groups:

1. Road: as a bridge is used to pass over an obstacle, the road is the major element; the other parts are required to support the road.
2. Superstructure: this is generally the set of elements that support the road but are not between the road and the ground.
3. Piers: elements used to support the road by linking it to the ground with pillars and columns.
4. Parapets: a parapet is a protective wall at the side of the bridge; it is used especially by pedestrians.

Bridges are created in our system as graphical variables. These variables are of the type BRIDGE defined as:

type BRIDGE = *figure* (ROAD:ROADTYPE; PIER:PIERTYPE;
                          SUPER:SUPERTYPE; PARAPET:PARATYPE;
                          ORIENTATION:REAL)

where the first four parameters correspond to the four elements of a bridge and
ORIENTATION defines the orientation of the bridge by rotating this around the
y-axis.

The road is composed of an unlimited sequence of rectangles. The characteristics are defined by the following type definition:

type ROADTYPE = *record*
                    HEIGHT, WIDTH, LENGTH:REAL;
                    NBJOINTS:INTEGER
        end

HEIGHT, WIDTH and LENGTH are the three dimensions of the road.
NBJOINS is the number of joints along the road; these are represented by
transversal and equidistant line segments.

Piers are composed using a complex system of basic figures such as cylinders,
cones, parallelepipeds, circles, parabolic arcs and line segments. Piers are defined
using the following type:

type PIERTYPE = *record*
                    KIND:PIERKIND; PIERFIG:FIG;
                    D, H, P, Q:REAL; NB, NGP, NDP:INTEGER
        end

KIND defines the kind of pier that is used. There are eight possible values for
the KIND field:

type PIERKIND = (NONE, ARCH, DOUBLETRIMMER,
                        TIMBERPRIER,
                        DOUBLEPIER, HAMMERPIER,
                        PIERCANTILEVER, TOWER)

These values are defined as follows:

- NONE corresponds to no piers.
- ARCH covers the case of an arched bridge. In this case, D is the distance
  between two columns and H the height of a conical pier.
- DOUBLETRIMMER represents double piers with trimmers. Here, the trimmers are half-spheres of radius H and D is the distance between two trimmer
  centres. The piers are conical.
- TIMBERPIER represents bridges with a succession of NB timber piers across
  the width of the bridges. D is then the distance between two piers and H the
  height of a pier. Piers are conical with a parallelepiped support in the upper
  section.
- DOUBLEPIER corresponds to the previous case with NB = 2, because there
  are two piers in the width of the bridge. However, the piers are cylindrical and
  there is no support.
- HAMMERPIER provides a representation of hammer piers. The fields D and
  H have the same meanings as in TIMBERPIER. The lower part of the pier is a
  truncated cone; the support (upper parts) has two subparts (P and Q), which
  have the same height in this case.

- PIERCANTILEVER represents cantilever bridges.
- TOWER corresponds to the case of suspension bridges.

In all cases, PIERFIG is the director of the piers, NDP is the number of pier sections that have to be drawn and NGP allows the user to control the number of generators in a pier (for example, every point of the director, every two points...).

Superstructures are defined using the following hierarchical structure:

type SUPERTYPE = *record*
                         KIND:SUPERKIND; SUPERMOTIF:FIG;
                         NSECTION:INTEGER; L1, L2:REAL;
                         CENTERMOTIF:FIG;
                         CENTERNSECTION:INTEGER
                    end

KIND defines the kind of superstructure that is used. There are six values that are possible for the KIND field:

type SUPERKIND = (SIMPLE, RIGHTLATTICE, TWOPEAKS,
                    CANTILEVER,
                    STEELARCH, SUSPENSION)

Apart from the simple superstructure, in all cases NSECTION is the number of sections in the bridge. The detail of a section is given by SUPERMOTIF which can be any figure. The various fields are explained below.

- SIMPLE applies to a bridge with no real superstructure.
- RIGHTLATTICE corresponds to a traditional lattice bridge; L1 is then the height of a section.
- TWOPEAKS corresponds to a lattice bridge with two peaks.
- CANTILEVER represents cantilever bridges; this implies that the kind of pier is set to PIERCANTILEVER. The number of sections in the center can be chosen using the parameter CENTERSECTION and the motif is given by CENTERMOTIF.
- STEELARCH corresponds to a steel-arch bridge for which L1 determines the ratio of the arch length to the road.
- SUSPENSION, corresponding to a suspension bridge, implies that the kind of pier must be TOWER.

Parapets can be built on each side of the bridge road. The characteristics of a parapet are given by the following type:

type PARATYPE = *record*
                       NSUPPORT:INTEGER;
                       HEIGHT:REAL
                  end

NSUPPORT is the number of equidistant supports between the parapet and the road (except at both ends). If NSUPPORT is negative, no parapet is created, otherwise HEIGHT is the parapet height relative to the road.

Fig. 11.1 shows different bridges created with the BRIDGE graphical type.

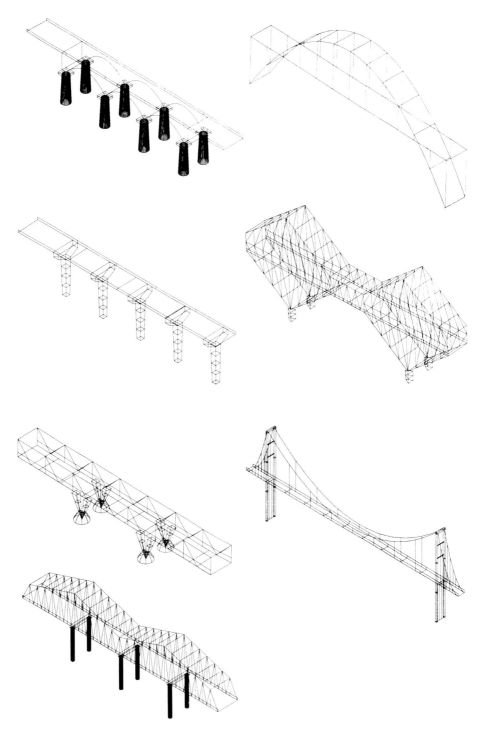

Fig. 11.1. Bridges produced as MIRA graphical types by D. Thalmann, D. Ouimet and C. Roy

An Architectural System

This interactive system allows the user to create house façades. The components can be gradually included by using commands and menus. First, the user chooses the shape of the house and the type of facing required (e.g., brick, cement, shingle, stone). Then, doors and windows must be selected. Menus containing approximately 20 models are available and the user can choose the size and complexity of the doors and windows. Other components can be added, such as garage doors and chimneys. Fig. 11.2 and Fig. 11.3 show two house façades created with this system.

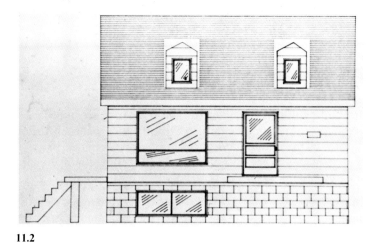

11.2

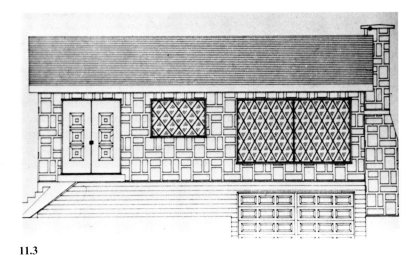

11.3

Figs. 11.2 –3. House façades (MIRA software)

11.2 Computer Animation of a Robotic Arm

SEER (Système d'Emulation d'Environnement Robotique) is an interactive graphics program that allows the user to study the motion of a robotic arm and to produce computer animated film sequences. The robotic arm studied is the one used in our computer science laboratory, i.e., a SHART-ARMS 6E. The system runs in two modes: In the "visual" mode, the different arm motions are shown at their initial and final positions without any interpolation between them. In the "animation" mode, sequences of small moves are produced that correspond to a sequence of frames. For each frame, a signal is sent to a camera to take a picture. There are 17 commands in SEER, classified into four groups:

1. **Environment description commands**
   These allow the user to create and delete different entities in the system. Several robotic arms can be created in a SEER session, characterized by the coordinates of the base and a direction. Arms and objects that they manipulate can be deleted by a specific command.

2. **Arm manipulation commands**
   These are compatible with the real robotic arm. An arm can be moved or reset to the initial position. Commands also allow the user to modify the orientation and aperture of the manipulator. Motions can be specified in absolute or in relative coordinates. Since the final goal is the production of animated films, a motion speed in mm/sec has to be given.

3. **Program control commands**
   With these, the user can obtain a list of the different commands, a report on the status of the different entities of the system (positions, speeds, angles), or he or she can send the commands from a file instead of the terminal. A frame can also be copied onto a file, and, of course, the user can terminate the program. A powerful command allows the user to modify the visual parameters: eye position, interest point, perspective and camera speed; these can simulate pan and travelling.

4. **Film shooting commands**
   A command tells the system to enter the animation mode. The camera speed can be chosen in frames/sec and it is also possible to simulate a delay to allow the real camera to take a picture. In this mode, interpolations are computed depending on the speed of motion and the camera speed.

All information about the entities of the system (robotic arms, spheres and cubes) is stored in a linear list. For spheres the position of the center and the height of the object are stored; cubes additionally require orientation data. For a robotic arm, the system needs the position of the center of the base, the initial arm angle, the position of the center of the manipulator, the orientations, aperture and speed of the manipulator and six rotation angles for the different articulations.

At the graphical level, robotic arms are structured in abstract graphical data types that are composed of six parts: the base, the arm, the forearm, the support, the manipulator and the jaw.

Two pictures of robotic arms produced by SEER are shown in Fig. 11.4 and 11.5.

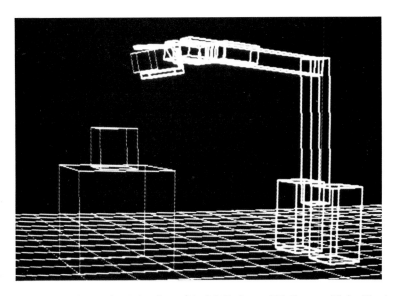

Fig. 11.4. A robotic arm (MIRA software) by M. Feeley and F. Gagnon, Univ. Montreal

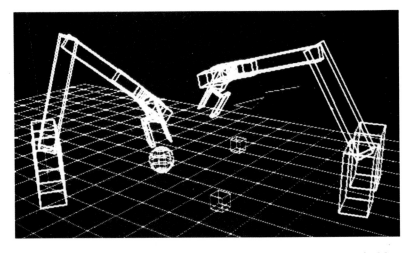

Fig. 11.5. Two robotic arms (MIRA software) by M. Feeley and F. Gagnon, Univ. Montreal

11.3 An Example of the Design of a Camera Path

One of the most spectacular but relatively simple effects in modeled animation is the viewing of a beautiful object using an appropriate camera motion. The object is completely static or its position is not changed during the animation process.

A pleasing camera motion has been shown (by experience) to be composed of two steps:

1. **A linear approach** during a time APPTIME controlled by the Catmull acceleration-deceleration law

2. **A circular or spiral movement** of 360 degrees with an optional elevation during a time CURTIME.

Using a system like MIRANIM, described in Section 10.7, the scene can be easily produced by the following ANIMEDIT commands:

VA⟩ VEC, EYE, A, O, YEYE, −DAPP – defines an animated vector EYE.
VA⟩ VEC, INT, C, O, O, O – defines a constant vector INT.
VA⟩ LAW, CAMLAW, DEFLAW – defines a law CAMLAW.
VA⟩ EVOLUTION, EYE, CAMLAW – applies the law to EYE.
CA⟩ CAMERA, MYCAM, EYE, INT – defines a camera with EYE and INT.

The heart of the solution to this problem is in the programming of the law for the variable EYE. This can be done in the CINEMIRA-2 language. Before presenting the law, we need to understand how to implement the desired path. For this, consider the curves in Fig. 11.6. Part a of the figure shows the projection of the path in the XZ plane. Parts b and c give two different possibilities for varying the height Y during rotation around the center of the object.

The path is separated into three parts:

1. A linear path from the point $E1 = \langle\langle 0, YEYE, -DAPP\rangle\rangle$ to the point $E2 = \langle\langle 0, YEYE, -DTRANS\rangle\rangle$. The length of the path is of course DAPP-DTRANS, and the time is assumed to be TAPP seconds. As we use the acceleration-deceleration law, the eye position at any time T is given by:

$$EYE := \langle\langle 0, YEYE, ZEYE\rangle\rangle \qquad (11.1)$$

where $ZEYE = LAW\,(4, DAPP - DTRANS, T/TAPP) - DAPP$

2. A transition path between the linear and the spiral path. We assume a circular arc with center

$$C = \langle\langle XC, YEYE, -DTRANS\rangle\rangle$$

It can be shown that the position of the eye during the transition path is:

$$EYE = \langle\langle R1 * (1 - COS(\beta)), YEYE, -DTRANS + R1 * SIN(\beta)\rangle\rangle \qquad (11.2)$$

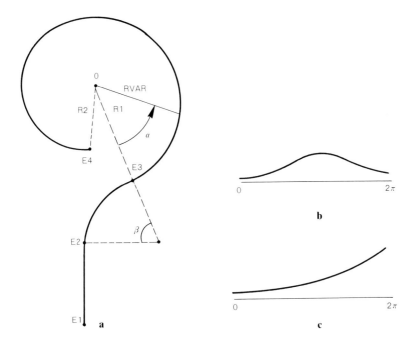

Fig. 11.6. A camera path

where β varies uniformly from 0 to βmax. Of course, the continuity condition is verified:

$$\beta = 0 \quad \text{EYE} = \langle\!\langle 0, \text{YEYE}, -\text{DTRANS}\rangle\!\rangle = \text{EYE2} \qquad (11.3)$$

3. The spiral path is obtained by a variation of the angle α from $\frac{\pi}{2} - \beta$max to 2π. Assume that the variation in angle and the variation in radius from R1 to R2 are linear with time. Then the EYE position is given by:

$$\text{EYE} = \langle\!\langle \text{RVAR} * \text{SIN}(\alpha), \text{YVAREYE}, -\text{RVAR} * \text{COS}(\alpha)\rangle\!\rangle \qquad (11.4)$$

RVAR is given by $R1 - (R1 - R2) * \text{FRACT}$

where FRACT is the time fraction between 0 and 1 and YVAREYE is the function that gives the height of the eye during the spiral path. For example, the functions corresponding to Fig. 11.6b and 11.6c are (see Section 5.4):

$$\text{YVAREYE} = 2 * \text{YMAX} * (1 + \text{COS}(-\pi + \text{FRACT} * 2 * \pi))/2 \quad \text{and}$$

$$\text{YVAREYE} = \text{YMAX} * (1 - \text{COS}(\pi * \text{FRACT}/2)) \qquad (11.5)$$

Fig. 11.7 presents the listing of the complete law for the motion of this virtual camera.

```
law DEFLAW:VECTOR;


(*DAPP,DTAPP,DIST,DTRANS,TTRANS,R1,R2,YEYE and YMAX are global
variables,CLOCK is a predefined function in CINEMIRA-2*)


var
    FRACT,ALPHA,BETA,YVAREYE,RVAR:REAL;
begin
    FRACT := (CLOCK-DTAPP)/DIST;
    if CLOCK <= DTAPP then (* linear approach *)
        DEFLAW := <<0,YEYE,LAWC(4,DAPP-DTRANS,CLOCK/DTAPP)-DAPP>>
    else
        if FRACT <= TTRANS then
            begin (* transition *)
                BETA := 4*PI*FRACT;
                YEYE := 2*YMAX*(1+COS(BETA/2-PI))/2;
                DEFLAW := <<R1*(1-COS(BETA)),YEYE,-DTRANS+R1*SIN(BETA)>>
            end
        else
            begin (* spiral *)
                ALPHA := 2*PI*FRACT;
                YVAREYE := 2*YMAX*(1+COS(ALPHA-PI))/2;
                FRACT := (FRACT-TTRANS)/(1-TTRANS);
                RVAR := R1-(R1-R2)*FRACT;
                DEFLAW := <<RVAR*SIN(ALPHA),YVAREYE,-RVAR*COS(ALPHA)>>
            end
end;
```

Fig. 11.7. The camera motion law

11.4 A Scene with a Shaded Corvette

In this section, we shall show how a Corvette can be digitized, reconstructed, shaded and animated. As this is an irregular object, a digitizing tablet must be used, as indicated in Section 6.3. However, as our model must be three-dimensional, we use a 3D reconstruction program we have developed. A grid is drawn on the Corvette and pictures of the car are taken from several different angles, chosen in such a way as to eliminate any perspective effect. Intersection points are then numbered so that the points have the same number on different photographs. Fig. 11.8 and Fig. 11.9 show two of these photographs. Points are then digitized and the 3D interactive reconstruction program is used to obtain the three-dimensional model, checking that the user digitizes each point on at least two different photographs.

The reconstruction process is then, in fact, a calculation based on the knowledge of two coordinates of a point on one photograph (for example X and Y) and two coordinates on a second photograph (for example Y and Z). It is thus possible to rebuild the points in space.

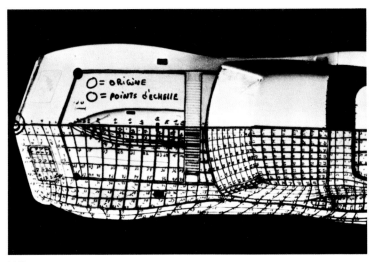

11.8

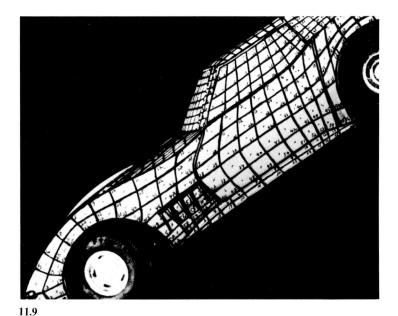

11.9

Figs. 11.8–9. A Corvette to digitize

```
begin
   WRITELN('3D RCONSTRUCTION PROGRAM');
   WRITELN('TURN ON THE DIGITIZER');
   WRITELN('TYPE SPACE TO CONTINUE');
   READ(CH);
   INITTABPOINTS;
   SPECPHOTOS; (*determination of photograph specifications *)
   repeat
      repeat
         WRITELN; WRITELN;
         WRITELN('COMMAND LIST:');
         WRITELN('(1) ENTER THE POINTS');
         WRITELN('(2) LIST THE POINTS');
         WRITELN('(3) WRITE THE POINTS TO A FILE');
         WRITELN('(4) READ POINTS FROM A FILE');
         WRITELN('(5) REDEFINE THE POINTS');
         WRITELN('(6) START AGAIN');
         WRITELN('(7) TERMINATE THE SESSION');
         WRITELN;
         WRITELN('COMMAND:');
         READLN; READ(CH)
      until CH in ['1'..'7'];
      if CH < '7' then
         case CH of
            '1': ENTERPOINTS;
            '2': LISTPOINTS;
            '3': WRITEPOINTS;
            '4': READPOINTS;
            '5': REDEFINEPOINTS;
            '6': SPECPHOTOS
         end;
      if SECURITY and (CH='7') then
      begin
         WRITELN('NOTICE:YOU DONT''T HAVE SAVED THE POINTS');
         WRITELN('DO YOU WANT TO TERMINATE THE SESSION? (Y/N)');
         YESORNO(OK);
         if not OK then CH:=' '
      end
   until CH='7';
   WRITELN; WRITELN('BYE')
end.
```

Fig. 11.10. The 3D reconstruction program (excerpts)

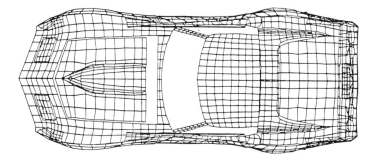

Fig. 11.11. The reconstructed Corvette

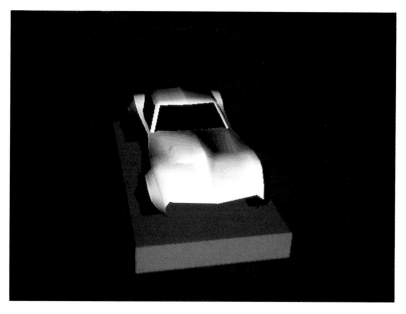

Fig. 11.12. The shaded Corvette (Designers: N. Chourot and L. Langlois. © N. Magnenat-Thalmann and D. Thalmann)

In order to shade the car, polygons must be defined from the digitized points. This step is also performed in the reconstruction program, of which Fig. 11.10 shows an excerpt. Fig. 11.11 shows the reconstructed Corvette. Shading can be applied by using a model like the Phong model [1975], described in Chapter 7. We merely have to specify the direction of light and the color of the light source.

One problem may arise because of the type of terminal used. For example, for an AED 767, which can display only 256 colors at the same time, a look-up table has to be specified. The problem is in the choice of the colors: In the case of a white car, about 50 or 60 intensity levels of white are required. Fig. 11.12 shows an example of the shaded Corvette. As an example of animation, suppose that a wire-frame Corvette without wheels comes down into the picture, falls onto its wheels, and then becomes shaded. Virtual camera motion is used in capturing the motion of the Corvette. The car then turns back into a wire-frame, rises and disappears. Fig. 11.13 shows an excerpt of the corresponding script developed with the ANIMEDIT animation editor.

```
VA    VEC INT,C,0,25,0
VA    VEC EYE,A,200,60,-200
VA    LAW EYELAW,MVTCIRC,75,25,-75,0,10,0,-1.26,0
VA    EVOLUTION EYE,EYELAW,0,5
VA    VEC DOWN,A,0,150,0,0,25,0
VA    LAW DOWNLAW,CATMULL,1,1,1
VA    VEC EYEFIX,C,200,60,-200
VA    VEC SOURCE,A,200,400,-200
VA    LAW SOURCELAW,MVTCIRC,0,0,0,0,10,0,-1.26,0
VA    EVOLUTION SOURCE,SOURCELAW,0,5
VA    VEC INTENS,C,0.8,0.8,0.8
VA    VEC DIFFUS,C,0.2,0.2,0.2
VA    REAL ANGROT,C,6.81


   ... object and decor creation


AC    ACTOR,FLYINGCAR,CAR
AC    TRANSLATION,FLYINGCAR,DOWN
AC    ROTATION,FLYINGCAR,DOWN,ANGROT


CA    CAMERA,CAMFIX,EYEFIX,INT
CA    CAMERA,CAMMOV,EYE,INT


LI    DIFFUSION,DIFFUS
LI    SOURCE,LIGHT,SOURCE,INT
LI    SPECTRUM,LIGHT,INTENS


AN    ACTOR,FLYINGCAR,0,4.99,0
AN    CAMERA,CAMFIX,0,4.99,0
AN    CAMERA,CAMMOV,5,5,0
AN    SOURCE,LIGHT,5,5,5
AN    DIFFUSION,5,10,5
```

Fig. 11.13. Excerpts of a ANIMEDIT script

11.5 Fireworks

Fireworks are interesting phenomenon to model. An interactive system for this was implemented during a graduate course in Computer Animation Techniques.

In this system, the most important commands control the rockets. The first one defines a rocket by its number, velocity and two angles: one for rotation in the plane XZ and one for elevation with respect to the plane XZ. The commands EXPLOSION and DISPERSION control the explosion and dispersion of particles. These two commands also have specific parameters. For an explosion with dispersion, the number of exploded fragments as well as their shape and color must be specified. For the dispersion, the radius, duration and minimal velocity for the explosion must be determined.

An explosion can be a primary explosion, or a fragment may be considered to be rocket. This means that for each fragment a secondary explosion may occur. This can be controlled by commands for secondary explosions and dispersion.

The trajectory of a rocket is determined by applying the following general equation for projectiles:

$$r = r_0 + v_0*(t - t_0) + 0.5*g*(t - t_0)^2 \tag{11.6}$$

where r is the position of the projectile at time t; r_0 is the position of the projectile at the initial time t_0 and v_0 is the initial speed.

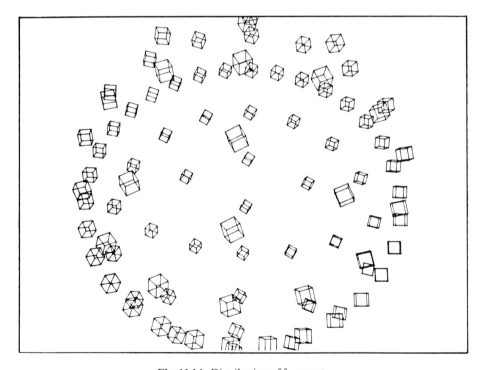

Fig. 11.14. Distribution of fragments

v_0 is, in fact, obtained by the velocity v_0 multiplied by a unitary vector computed using the two angles given in the command that creates the rockets.

For dispersion the process was simplified because the different fragments have to be distributed over a sphere. This is a very complex problem with no analytical solution. It was decided to limit the number of fragments to 6, 18, 42 or 90, because for these numbers, the method is rather simple. The sphere is separated into different levels and a scan is applied to these levels, using a polar representation of the position of a fragment. The extreme levels have only one fragment, the following levels have four; the number of fragments is doubled relative to the preceding levels until we obtain the maximum number of fragments at the central level. The necessary deceleration is calculated using the dispersion radius, the given time duration and the minimal velocity.

Secondary explosions take place immediately after the time duration assigned to the primary one. At the end of an explosion, the fragments are simple projectiles that fall with gravity.

Fig. 11.14 shows the distribution of fragments on a sphere and Fig. 11.15 gives an example of fireworks generated with this system.

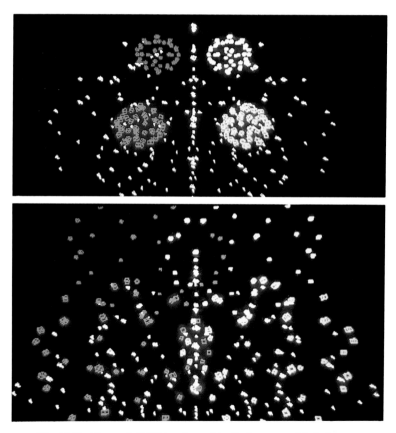

Fig. 11.15. Firework (MIRA software) by R. Burton and S. Lafrance

12. A Case Study: *Dream Flight*

12.1 Why *Dream Flight*?

Computer animation is currently developing very quickly because of its usefulness for advertising purposes. The three giants (NBC, CBS and ABC) of American television often use this technique to present their logos or to augment their programs. At the same time, film studios in Hollywood have become interested in computer animation because of the spectacular effects that can be created.

However, in 1979 at SIGGRAPH, during a twenty-four hour retrospective of the best computer graphics and videotapes of the past ten years, we saw only one animated fiction film (*Hunger*, by Peter Foldes of the National Film Board of Canada). The interesting point about this film was that its production technique was adapted to the film community rather than scientists. But the film was in two dimensions, and we believed that there were still no widely known fictional 3D animated films made by computer. For these reasons, we set out to produce one. The film was called *Dream Flight* [Thalmann et al., 1982] and was directed by both authors and P. Bergeron, research assistant at the Business School of Montreal.

The film was a great success. It won first prize at the Computer Graphics '82 Film Festival in London and was shown at various Computer Graphics Film Festivals: SIGGRAPH '83 in Detroit, InterGraphics '83 in Tokyo, Graphics Interface '83 in Edmonton. *Dream Flight* was also selected in traditional animation festivals: "Journées Internationales 83 d'Animation" in Annecy (France), "Festival des Films du Monde" in Montreal (Canada) and "Solothurner Film-tage" in Solothurn (Switzerland). It was also nominated at the Yorkton Festival in Canada. Moreover, *Dream Flight* was shown (in whole or in part) on various TV channels in Canada, the U.S., France, Switzerland and the United Kingdom.

The projection time of the film is about 13 minutes. The hardware used consists of the CDC Cyber of the University of Montreal, a TEKTRONIX 4027 color terminal and a GRADICON digitizer. Images were shot using an electronic signal connected to the ring of the terminal. All the software was written in MIRA-3D, including the animation system, the graphics editors and the digitizing programs.

In the next sections, we present the scenario of the film followed by discussions of three specific scenes and how they were directed. The last section presents an

overview of the organization of a scene. Fig. 12.1 shows the different stages of the
production of a film scene.

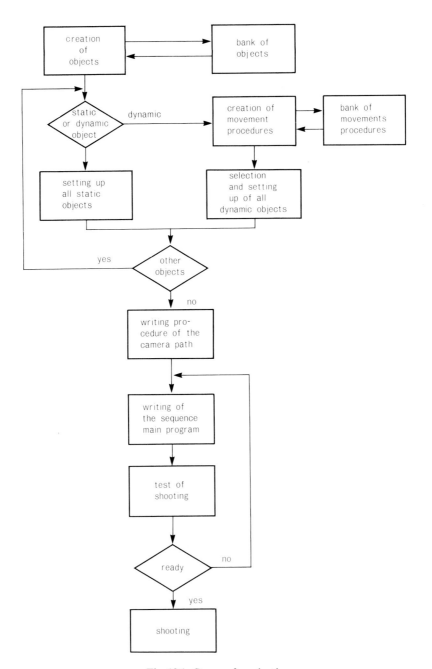

Fig. 12.1. Stages of production

12.2 Scenario and Storyboard

Dream Flight is a fictional film with a simple scenario. A futuristic version of *The Little Prince*, it begins with the opening line, "Once upon a time, a small being lived on a distant planet. He was lonely and dreamed of seeing new world."

It is night. Hipi is sad, and throws stones into a small pond in the middle of a forest. A bird flying over the pond arouses in Hipi a desire to be free.

Inspired by the bird, Hipi flies towards new horizons—flying through space, travelling past strange objects towards Earth. He takes us through Europe, past the Eiffel Tower, and plunges into the Atlantic among yellow fish and seaweed, until a violent storm illuminates the surface of the water.

Then he arrives in New York. We see the Statue of Liberty, the streets of Manhattan, the city constructed entirely in glass. Hipi stops in the middle of Central Park where four human beings appear before him. After a minute of hesitation, Hipi extends his hand as a sign of friendship. One of the men advances his arm but stops and turns away suddenly. Frustrated, Hipi becomes very angry. Everything explodes. Rocks fall on New York, and the city collapses with the sound of thunder and a flash of lightning.

The towers of the World Trade Center emerge from a small pond. Hipi, sitting by the side of the pond, throws a pebble into the water, as at the beginning of the film, and the towers disappear.

Hipi's voyage was a dream, transformed into a nightmare by human rejection. The rocks that fell on New York were thrown by Hipi, who saw the entire scene in the pond. The bird passes again, and Hipi flies towards the horizon.

After devising a scenario, the next step was to establish the storyboard. For *Dream Flight*, the storyboard consisted of about 100 sketches with associated information. Fig. 12.2 shows an excerpt of the storyboard.

12.3 Decor Creation

A decor can be considered a list of static objects. These objects can be built up using one of the three methods described in Section 6.3. In *Dream Flight*, various decors are used: trees, buildings, a bridge, the Statue of Liberty. We examine here how these four kinds of static objects were created.

Trees
Trees are defined by the position and the height of the main trunk. Branches are only present in the upper two thirds of the trunk and their length is considered constant. The lower, primary branches are oriented in the four major directions. Other branches are uniformly distributed in the vertical direction, but are randomly distributed around the trunk. The angle of the branch relative to the ground is dependent on the height of the branch.

Trees are described by three-dimensional graphical types:

type TREE = *figure* (*var* BRANCHES: TEXT; NBRANCHES: INTEGER;
                    POSITION: VECTOR; HEIGHT, LENGTH: REAL);

where BRANCHES is a file of kinds of branches, NBRANCHES is the number of

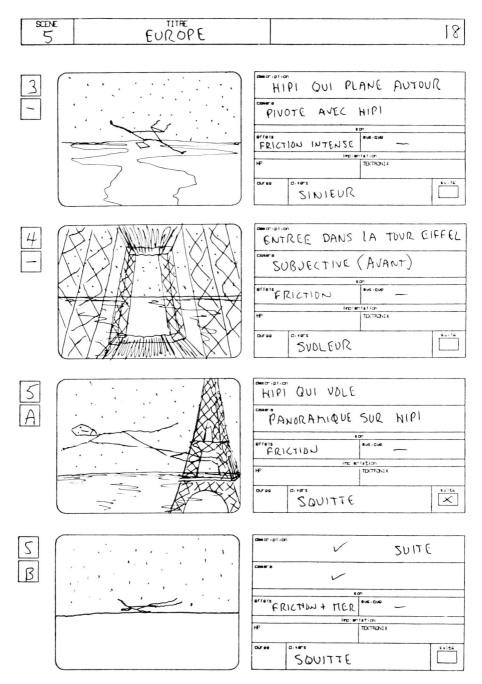

Fig. 12.2. Excerpts of the storyboard of *Dream Flight* (Directors: P. Bergeron, N. Magnenat-Thalmann, D. Thalmann)

branches, POSITION is the position of the trunk, HEIGHT is the height of the trunk and LENGTH the length of the branches.

A forest can be defined by the following declaration:

$$var \ FOREST : array \ [1 .. NBTREES] \ of \ TREE$$

Fig. 12.3 shows a frame of *Dream Flight* with the forest.

The Verrazzano-Narrows Bridge and the Eiffel Tower
This bridge (Fig. 12.4) and the Eiffel Tower were produced by digitizing one part and by building the object by programming. In Section 11.1, a more systematic

Fig. 12.3. Sitting in the forest

Fig. 12.4. The Verrazano-Narrows Bridge

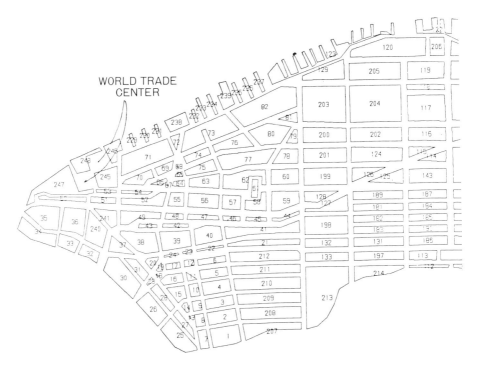

Fig. 12.5. Manhattan map

Fig. 12.6. Arrival in New York

Fig. 12.7. Base of the Statue of Liberty

way of building bridges is described. Manhattan was built by digitizing a map, shown in Fig. 12.5.

Of course, the map is not precise; in fact, each polygon represents several blocks. A height is associated with each polygon in a file. A program rebuilt the city by using the digitized map file and the height file. Fig. 12.6 shows an example.

The Statue of Liberty
This complex object was separated into two parts: the base, which was partly digitized and then rebuilt by programming using symmetry operations (Fig. 12.7), and the statue itself, which was digitized with a method similar to that described in Section 6.3:

1. Interesting points were detected on the 3D object.
2. Four orthogonal pictures were taken of the object. It is important to maximize the distance betwen the object and the camera and to use a telephoto lens. The error caused by perspective is then partially corrected.
   In fact, the object was situated on a turntable that allowed the angle of the object to be changed depending on the orientation of the camera.
3. An appropriate coordinates system was drawn for each of the four pictures.
4. Each point was identified by a number. Points had to be identified in at least two pictures to compute the X, Y and Z coordinates of each point.
5. After placing the four pictures on the digitizer, the user marked points that determined the boundaries of the four pictures and those that identified the coordinates systems.

Fig. 12.8. Six views of the Statue of Liberty

6. For each point, two different positions were successively marked.
7. Connections between the points were identified with numbers. This defined the points' strokes.

Figure 12.8 shows six different views of the Statue of Liberty (including the head, which was digitized using the same method). The torch was not built according to this principle.

12.4 Actors and Dynamic Objects in the Forest

In the first scene, Hipi is sitting in a forest at night, throwing stones into a small pond. He sees a bird in flight and imagines that he, too, is flying. This scene involves dynamic objects like Hipi and the bird. It also involves several static objects: trees, the pond, the horizon and the spherical sky with stars.

Although our hero Hipi is not human, we decided to represent him using human movement techniques. We used a method where body movements are described by rotation only, as suggested by N.I. Badler [1978]. Hipi is composed of 32 segments and 15 joints and dependent vertices.

Figure 12.9 shows a graph of human movements, which follow the following rules:

1. The arrival nodes are dependent on the departure nodes.
2. Each node represents a join and/or a single vertex.
3. Loops are represented by cycles.

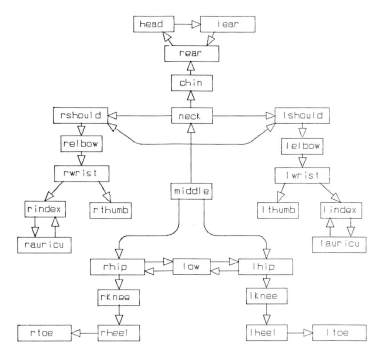

Fig. 12.9. Graph of "human" movement

A bird is represented by an abstract graphical type:

type BIRD = *figure* (FRAME:INTEGER; H:HALFBODY; W:WING;
            C, D:VECTOR);

where H is the right halfbody, W the right wing, C the rotation center of the right
wing and D the direction of that rotation. As the right wing always starts in the
maximal vertical position, it is only necessary to determine the angle of rotation
downwards. This angle depends on the frame. For this we used a rotation with the
Catmull acceleration/deceleration law.

Fig. 12.10 shows an excerpt of the code which is executed when a variable of
BIRD type is created. In this code, CYCLE is the number of frames required to
make one wing flap up and down; FRAME is the current frame number; BETA is
the rotation angle of the wing; ANGLEMAX is the maximum angle and FRAC
the phase fraction. For example, a bird is created and drawn according to the
following sequence:

procedure DRAWBIRD (FRAME:INTEGER);
var FIRSTBIRD:BIRD;
begin
    create FIRSTBIRD (FRAME, RIGHTBODY, RIGHTWING, C, D);
    TRANSLATION (FIRSTBIRD, ⟨⟨0, 0, FRAME * BIRDSTEP⟩⟩,
                FIRSTBIRD);

> *draw* FIRSTBIRD;
> *delete* FIRSTBIRD;
end;

The parameters in the *create* statement correspond to the parameters in the definition of the BIRD type.

The BIRD type contains a parameter which is the frame number. This is a way of implementing actors in a language which does not provide actor data types. This was the case in the film *Dream Flight* that was developed using the MIRA-3D language. However, we can imagine how a BIRD actor type could be defined, using the syntactic construction introduced in Section 10.6. An excerpt from that code is shown in Fig. 12.11.

Instead of the procedure DRAWBIRD, an actor bird need only be initialized by the statement:

$$\textit{init } \text{FIRSTBIRD (H, W, C, D, 10, 16)}$$

The bird is started at time 10 and stopped at time 16. Animation frames are produced automatically and the bird can be synchronized with other actors.

```
type
   BIRD = figure(FRAME:INTEGER; H:HALFBODY; W:WING; C,D:VECTOR);
         const
              ACCDEC = 4;
         var
              RELATIVE:0..CYCLE;
              FRACTION,BETA:REAL;
              W2:WING;
              RIGHTPART,LEFTPART:FIG;
         begin
              RELATIVE := FRAME mod CYCLE;
              if RELATIVE > CYCLE div 2 then
                  RELATIVE := CYCLE-RELATIVE;
              FRACTION := (RELATIVE*2)/CYCLE;
              BETA := LAW(ACCDEC,ANGLEMAX,FRACTION);
              ROTATION(W,C,BETA,D,W2);
              UNION(H,W2,RIGHTPART);
              delete H,W2;
              SYMYZ(RIGHTPART,LEFTPART);
              include RIGHTPART,LEFTPART
         end;
```

Fig. 12.10. The BIRD type

```
type
   BIRD = actor(H:HALFBODY; W:WING; C,D:VECTOR; T1,T2:REAL);
         time T1..T2;
         type
            ANG = animated REAL;
                     val 0..ANGLEMAX;
                     time T1..T2;
                     law ACCDEC(...)
                  end;

            POS = animated VECTOR;
                     val ORIGIN..UNLIMITED;
                     time T1..T2;
                     law BIRDSTEP*BIRDSPEED
                  end;

         var
            TRANS:POS;
            BETA:ANG;
            W2:WING;
            RIGHTPART,LEFTPART:FIG;
         begin
            init TRANS;
            init BETA;
            ROTATION(W,C,BETA,D,W2);
            UNION(H,W2,RIGHTPART);
            TRANSLATION(RIGHTPART,TRANS,RIGHTPART);
            delete H,W2;
            SYMYZ(RIGHTPART,LEFTPART);
            include RIGHTPART,LEFTPART
         end;
```

Fig. 12.11. The BIRD actor type

12.5 Seascape

This scene shows a rough sea with heavy clouds and a thunderstorm (Fig. 12.12).

Sea and Waves
The sea is basically represented by a series of parallel lines perpendicular to the eye direction. This gives a better appearance than a grid representation. Waves are simulated by the application of an image transformation called WAVE. The transformation call can be described as:

$$\text{WAVE (SEA, NOR, DIR, INT, CYC, PHA, SEA)}$$

SEA is the graphical representation of the sea before and after image transformation processing.

A wave is characterized by five parameters:

1. **the normal vector to the sea NOR:** This is usually $\langle 0, 1, 0 \rangle$ but it can be modified.
2. **the wave direction DIR:** This is usually parallel to the plane XZ, which means that $\text{DIR}_Y = 0$.
3. **the wave intensity INT:** this gives the wave height.
4. **the wave cycle CYC:** This is defined as a fraction of intensity $1/\text{INT}$, multiplied by a factor (e.g., 0.2).
5. **the wave phase PHA:** This is the wave displacement per second which is related to the intensity.

The wave transformation is obtained by applying to each point the T matrix defined as:

Fig. 12.12. A thunderstorm

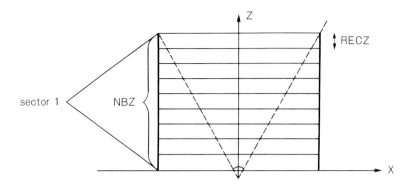

Fig. 12.13. The infinite "decor" concept

$$T = \begin{bmatrix} DIR_X & DIR_Y & DIR_Z \\ NOR_X & NOR_Y & NOR_Z \\ DNR_X & DNR_Y & DNR_Z \end{bmatrix}$$

where DNR is computed as the cross product of vectors DIR and NOR.
The following function is applied:

$$V_X := V_X$$
$$V_Y := V_Y + INT * SIN(V_X * CYC + PHA)$$
$$V_Z := V_Z$$

After the inverse transformation, points return to their original system. During the thunderstorm, the sea is represented by a grid and white color is used.

Clouds

Nine kinds of clouds have been digitized and are displayed using the infinite "decor" concept.

This technique works as follows: the synthetic camera moves forward (for example, in the direction $\langle 0, 0, 1 \rangle$).

During the movement, graphical elements are added to the background and elements behind the synthetic camera are deleted. The scene is divided into sectors that include NBZ rectangles of length RECZ. The method is presented visually in Fig. 12.13. If NBREC is the number of rectangles that the virtual camera has passed and CURR is the number of rectangles inside the sector, the following code describes the technique:

```
if CURR ≠ PREV then
begin
   NTIMES := CURR − PREV;
   if NTIMES < 0 then NTIMES := NTIMES + NBZ; (*NEW SECTOR*)
   for I := NTIMES downto 1 do
      begin (*find the lowest Z position*)
      POSZ := (NBREC + NBZ − I + 1) * RECZ;
```

CURRENT := CURR − I + 1;
if CURRENT < 0 *then* CURRENT := CURRENT + NBZ;
delete TABLE [CURRENT]; (*delete elements behind the camera*)
update TABLE with POSZ
end;
  PREV := CURR (*update the previous rectangle number*)
end;

Lightning
Each lightning flash is defined by the start frame STRT, which is related to the start frame of the thunderstorm THUNDSTRT. The duration of the flash LNG is defined in terms of frames and varies between 3 (0.125 sec) and 15 frames (0.625). The location of the flash is defined by POS. Lightning flashes have been digitized; there are four different shapes.

The main branch of the flash is displayed during the entire LNG period. Auxiliary branches are gradually displayed to make the thunderstorm appear more realistic.

12.6 Undersea Scene

This scene shows seaweed waving under the sea. Fish move between the weeds (Fig. 12.14).

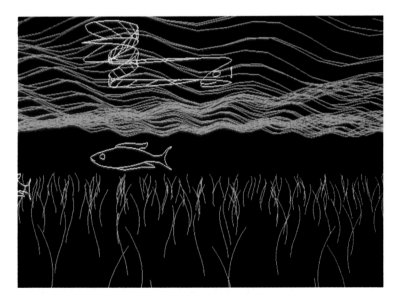

Fig. 12.14. Under sea

Seaweed

Weeds are initialized as a sequence of ten segment lines. They are displayed using the same infinite decor concept used for clouds. The array that represents a sector is defined as:

TALGUE = *array* [0 .. NB2M1] *of record*
                                        DEBX, POSZ:REAL;
                                        LINE: *packed array* [1 .. NBX]
                                                    of 1 .. 4
                                        end

POSZ is the Z position of the weed line, DEBX is the left-most X position and LINE is the array of weed numbers. The weed is curved by an image transformation that modifies the basic shape. Each point of the weed is rotated around the Z axis passing through the origin. If all points are rotated with the same angle (ANGROT), the transformation can be illustrated by the following code:

```
TEMP := RELATIVE_FRAME_NUMBER mod CYCLE;
if TEMP > CYCLE/2 then TEMP := CYCLE-TEMP;
ANGLE := −ANGROT * (1 − COS(TEMP*2*/CYCLE))/2
```

CYCLE is the number of frames required to complete the rotation and ANGLE is the angle value for a given frame number, as shown in Fig. 12.15.

If the different weed points are rotated at different angles, the first assignment statement in the above code must be replaced by the following:

```
TEMP := (RELATIVE_FRAME_NUMBER
          + ROUND(OLDFIG.Y * CST))
      mod CYCLE;
```

where OLDFIG.Y is the Y component of the weed point and CST is a constant depending on the weed height. Thus, the computed value ANGLE varies, depending on the Y position in the weed as shown in Fig. 12.16.

Fish

Three kinds of fish have been chosen for the undersea scene: a flatfish (FLATFIG), a sun fish (SUNFIG) and an eel (SNAKEFIG).

To define the path and the direction of each fish, we first assume that the eye is fixed and all fishes start their movement at the same frame number. The code corresponding to fish movement is then as follows:

```
READ(FILEF, FRAMEDEP, FRAMEDURATION);
```
(∗read from a file the departure frame number and the duration of movement in frame∗)

```
READ(FILEF, POSDEP, POSARR);
```
(∗read from the file the departure position and arrival position of the fish∗)

```
POSARR.Y := POSDEB.Y;
```
(∗set the Y component of the arrival position to the Y component of the departure position∗)

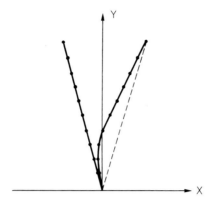

Fig. 12.15. Weed movement (with constant angle)

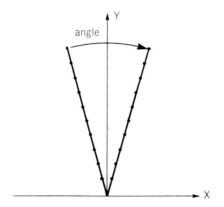

Fig. 12.16. Weed movement (with angle dependant on Y)

RELPOS:= POSARR − POSDEP;
(∗compute a relative position∗)

POSDEP.Z:= POSDEP.Z + FRAMEDEP ∗ STEP;
(∗update the departure position to take into account the departure frame number∗)

RELPOS.Z:= RELPOS.Z + FRAMEDURATION ∗ STEP;
(∗update the relative position, because the synthetic camera also moves forward∗)

ANGLE:= ARCCOS (‖ ≪0, − RELPOS.Z, RELPOS.Y≫ ‖ / ‖ RELPOS ‖);
(∗compute the rotation angle of the fish in such a way that it is parallel to its path∗)

if (RELPOS.Z < 0) and (ANGLE < π) *then*
    ANGLE:= 2 ∗ π − ANGLE;

Before displaying the fishes, an oscillation is applied to their bodies. This oscillation is computed along the Z axis using the following expression:

$$Z := AMPLI * SIN(2 * \pi * X/CYCLE)$$

where AMPLI and CYCLE is dependent on the kind of fish:

FLATFIG, SUNFIG: AMPLI = 5 and CYCLE = 100
SNAKEFIG: AMPLI = 40 and CYCLE = 150

12.7 The Organization of a Scene and Shooting

Each scene is programmed with the common skeleton shown in Fig. 12.17. (We will not discuss the display priority problems associated with colors.) To check whether a sequence is ready to be filmed, it has to be examined before the shooting. However, it is useless to look at each frame. It is necessary, then, to choose a check step. For example, if a step of 24 frames is chosen, a scene can be visualized by only looking at one frame per shooting second.

The viewing procedure and the procedures for displaying dynamic objects must be programmed specifically, as these depend on the frame number. We shall first give an example of camera movement within a film sequence:

1. The camera moves from position 1 (EYE1) to position 2 (EYE2) in 100 frames. The interest point (INT1) is fixed.
2. At position 2, the camera performs a circular movement during 150 frames while panning from INT1 to INT2.
2. The camera stops its circular movement (EYE3) when the view is above the object (INT2). It stays fixed during 24 frames.
4. The camera zooms (3-fold magnification) on to the upper part of the object in 200 frames.

The vectors EYE1, EYE2, EYE3, INT1 and INT2 and the value 3 for the zoom have been chosen using an interactive system, developed to specify camera movements. Table 12.1 shows a schematic table of the camera movements. The viewing procedure which simulates this movement is shown in Fig. 12.18.

Table 12.1. Schematic table of the camera movements

Number	Length	Previous frame	Movement type
1	100 (LNG1)	0	tilt
2	150 (LNG2)	100 (FRAME1)	circular movement pan
3	24 (LNG3)	250 (FRAME2)	fixed
4	200 (LNG4)	274 (FRAME3)	zoom

```
begin
    READLN(FIRSTFRAME,FINALFRAME,STEP);
    INITMOVIE('SCENETITLE',FIRSTFRAME,FINALFRAME);

    (* initializations of static and dynamic objects *)

    INITOBJ1;
    INITOBJ2;
     ...
    INITOBJN;

    (* main animation loop *)

    FRAME := FIRSTFRAME;
    while FRAME < = FINALFRAME do
    begin
        VISUAL(FRAME,EYE,INTEREST,ZOOM);
        CINECAMERA(EYE,INTEREST,ZOOM);

        (* draw the static objects *)

        draw OBJECT1,OBJECT2,...,OBJECTM;

        (* draw the dynamic objects *)

        DRAWOBJ1(FRAME);
        DRAWOBJ2(FRAME);
         ...
        DRAWOBJN(FRAME);

        FRAME := FRAME+STEP;

        (* signal to the physical camera;
           display the number of the next frame *)

        TAKEPICTURE
    end
end.
```

Fig. 12.17. Skeleton of a scene

```
procedure VISUAL(FRAME:INTEGER; var EYE,INTEREST:VECTOR;
                        var ZOOM:REAL);
const DECELER = 3;
begin
   if FRAME <= FRAME1 then
   begin
      FRACTION := FRAME/LNG1;
      EYE := TILT(EYE1,EYE2,FRACTION);
      INTEREST := INT1;
      ZOOM := 100
   end
   else
      if FRAME <= FRAME2 then
      begin
         FRACTION := (FRAME-FRAME1)/LNG2;
         EYE := REVOLUTION(EYE2,INT1,FRACTION);
         INTEREST := PAN(INT1,INT2,FRACTION);
         ZOOM := 100
      end
      else
         if FRAME <= FRAME3 then
         begin
            EYE := EYE3;
            INTEREST := INT2;
            ZOOM := 100
         end
         else
         begin
            FRACTION := (FRAME-FRAME3)/LNG4;
            EYE := EYE3;
            INTEREST := INT2;

            (* exponential zoom *)

            ZOOM := 100-LAW(DECELER,0.66,FRACTION)
         end
end;
```

Fig. 12.18. Viewing procedure

It can be easily seen that it is possible to have direct access to any camera position inside a sequence. Moreover, this method of coding is similar to the conventional method that is used by animators to code their camera movements. Our example is very simple because it only uses tilt movements and revolutions or pan functions. But this method can also be applied with very complex mathematical functions for the eye or the interest point position.

When the procedure VISUAL (described in Fig. 12.18) has returned the values EYE, INTEREST and ZOOM, the procedure CINECAMERA is called to position the virtual camera. Static and dynamics objects are created and drawn at this stage. For dynamic objects, the frame number is a required parameter. As shown in Section 12.4 for example, a bird is created and drawn according the following sequence:

```
procedure DRAWBIRD (FRAME:INTEGER);
var FIRSTBIRD:BIRD;
begin
  create FIRSTBIRD (FRAME, RIGHTBODY, RIGHTWING, C, D);
  TRANSLATION (FIRSTBIRD, ⟨⟨0, 0, FRAME * BIRDSTEP⟩⟩,
  FIRSTBIRD);
  draw FIRSTBIRD;
  delete FIRSTBIRD;
end;
```

The program shown in Fig. 12.17 is very simple. However, one problem with it is that **all** objects are drawn without reference to the position of the camera. Moreover, some objects are not to be present in the scene until later in the sequence. As in conventional movies, it would be easier to consider only the objects which are in front of the camera; it would also require less memory space, as only useful objects would be present. That approach is quite similar to the overlay technqiue in an operating system. Experience has shown that it is preferable to handle this process manually rather that to use sophisticated algorithms. Fig. 12.19 presents the principles of such a technique. STATE is an array of frame numbers where a decision can be taken and FIRSTIME is a boolean array to test whether this is the first encounter with this state. The shooting test is performed by assigning to STEP a value greater than 1.

When there are different states in the program, a constraint is applied to STEP. The value of STEP must be less than the least difference between two states. This avoids drawing an object which has not previously been created.

```
FRAME := FIRSTFRAME;
while FRAME <= FINALFRAME do
begin
    VISUAL(FRAME,EYE,INTEREST,ZOOM);
    CINECAMERA(EYE,INTEREST,ZOOM);
    if FRAME <= STATE[1] then;
    begin
        if FIRSTTIME[1] then
        begin
            FIRSTTIME[1] := FALSE;
            INITOBJ1;
            INITOBJ2;
            INITOBJ3
        end
        else
            if FRAME <= STATE[2] then
            begin
                if FIRSTTIME[2] then
                begin
                    FIRSTTIME[2] := FALSE;
                    delete OBJECT2;
                    INITOBJ4
                end;
                draw OBJECT1;
                DRAWOBJ3(FRAME);
                DRAWOBJ4(FRAME-STATE[1])
            end
            else
                if FRAME <= STATE[3] then
                begin
                    if FIRSTTIME[3] then
                    begin
                        FIRSTTIME[3] := FALSE;
                        delete OBJECT1;
                        delete OBJECT3;
                        INITOBJ5
                    end
                    else
                        ...
    FRAME := FRAME+STEP;
    TAKEPICTURE
end;
```

Fig. 12.19. Overlay technique for the frames

References

Titles that are preceded with an asterisk (*) are not referred to in the text.

*Ackland B, Weste N (1980) Real time animation playback on a frame store display system. *Proc. SIGGRAPH '80, Computer Graphics*, 14(3):182–188

Akima H (1970) A new method of interpolation and smooth curve fitting based on local procedures. *Journal of the ACM*, 17(4):589–602

Alexander S, Huggins WH (1967) *User's manual on PMACRO*. John Hopkins University

Andrews GR, Schneider FB (1983) Concepts and notations for concurrent programming. *ACM Computing Surveys*, 15(1):3–43

Appel A (1967) The notion of quantitative invisibility and the machine rendering of solids. *Proc. ACM National Conf.*, pp 387–393

Appel A (1968) Some techniques for shading machine rendering of solids. *SJCC, AFIPS*, 32:37–45

*Armbrust R (1983) The simulation of space. *Computer Pictures*, 1(1):24–27

Atherton P, Weiler K, Greenberg D (1978) Polygon shadow generation. *Proc. SIGGRAPH '78, Computer Graphics*, 12(3):275–281

*Badler NI (1975) *Temporal scene analysis: conceptual descriptions of objects movements* (Ph.D. Dissertation). University of Toronto

Badler NI (1982) Human body models and animation. *IEEE Computer Graphics and Applications*, 2(9):6–7

Badler NI, Morris MA (1982) Modellig flexible articulated objects. *Proc. Computer Graphics '82*, Online Conf. pp 305–314

Badler NI, O'Rourke J, Kaufman B (1980) Special problems in human movement simulation. *Proc. SIGGRAPH '80*, Computer Graphics, 14(3):189–197

Badler NI, O'Rourke J, Toltzis (1979) A spherical representation of a human body for visualizing movement. *Proc. IEEE, vol 67*, 10:1397–1403

Badler NI, Smoliar SW (1979) Digital representations of human movement. *Computing Surveys*, 11(1):19–38

*Baecker RM (1969) *Interactive computer-mediated animation* (Ph.D. Dissertation). MIT, Project Mac-Tr-61

Baecker RM (1969b) Picture-driven animation. *Proc. Spring Joint Computer Conference*, AFIPS Press, 34:273–288

*Baecker R (1970) Current issues in interactive computer-mediated animation. *Proc. 9th Annual Meeting UAIDE*, pp 273–288

Baecker RM (1976) A conversational extensible system for the animation of shaded images. *Proc. SIGGRAPH '76. Computer Graphics*, 10(2): 32–39

Ballard DH (1981) Strip trees, a hierarchical representation for curves. *Communications of the ACM*, 24(5): 310–321

Barr AM (1981) Superquadrics and angle-preserving transformations. IEEE *Computer Graphics and Applications*, 1(1): 11–23

Barsky BA (1985) *Computer graphics and geometric modelling using beta-splines.* Springer, Tokyo Berlin Heidelberg New York

Barsky BA (1981) *The bets-spline: a local representation based on shape parameters and fundamental geometric measures* (Ph.D. Thesis) University of Utah

Batson RM, Edwards E, Eliason EM (1975) Computer generated shaded relief images. *Journal of Research U.S. Geological*, 3(4): 401–408

*Begley S (1982) The creative computers. *Newsweek*, July 12, pp44–47

Bezier PE (1972) *Numerical control—mathematics and applications.* John Wiley, London

Blinn J (1977) Models of light reflection for computer synthesized pictures. *Proc. SIGGRAPH '77*, 11(2): 192–198

Blinn JF (1978) Simulation of wrinkled surfaces. *Proc. SIGGRAPH '77, Computer Graphics*, 12(3): 286–292

Blinn JF (1982) A generalization of algebraic surface drawing. *ACM Transactions on Graphics*, 1(3): 235–256

Blinn JF (1982b) Light reflection functions for simulation of clouds and dusty surfaces. *Proc. SIGGRAPH '82, Computer Graphics*, 16(3): 21–29

Blinn JF, Newell ME (1976) Texture and reflection in computer generated images. *Communications of the ACM*, 19(10): 542–547

Bloomenthal J (1983) Edge inference with applications to anti-aliasing. *Proc. SIGGRAPH '83, Computer Graphics*, 17(3): 157–162

Blum R (1979) Representing three-dimensional objects in your computer. *BYTE*, May Issue, pp14–29

*Booth S, Kochanek DH, Wein M (1983) Computers animate film and video. *IEEE spectrum*, pp44–51

Booth KS, MacKay S (1982) Techniques for frame buffer animation. *Proc. Graphics Interface '82*, pp213–219

*Borrell J (1981) The magic of computer animation. *Computer Graphics World*, 10: 25–33

Bosche C (1967) Computer generated random dot images. *Design and Planning*, 2: 87–92

Bouknight WJ, Kelley K (1970) An algorithm for producing half-tone computer graphics presentations with shadows and moveable light sources. *SJCC*, AFIPS, 36: 1–10

Brinch Hansen P (1975) The programming language concurrent PASCAL. *IEEE Transactions on Software Engineering*, SE-1, 2: 199–206

*Burtnyk N, Pulfer JK, Wein M (1971) Computer graphics and film animation. *INFOR*, pp1–11

Burtnyk N, Wein M (1971) Computer-generated key-frame animation. *Journal of*

Society for Motion Picture and Television Engineers, 80:149–153

Burtnyk N, Wein M (1971b) A computer animation system for the animator. *Proc. UAIDE 10th Annual Meeting*, pp3–5 to 3–24

Burtnyk N, Wein M (1974) Towards a computer animating production tool. *Proceedings Eurocomp Congress*, Online, Brunel, England, pp174–185

Burtnyk N, Wein M (1976) Interactive skeleton techniques for enhancing motion dynamics in key frame animation. *Comm. ACM*, vol 19, 10:564–569

*Buxton W (1982) Computer assisted filmmaking. *American Cinematographer*, vol 63(8)

Calvert TW, Chapman J (1978) Notation of movement with computer assistance. *Proc. ACM Annual Conf.*, 2:731–736

Calvert TW, Chapman J, Patla A (1980) The integration of subjective and objective data in animation of human movement. *Proc. SIGGRAPH '80, Computer Graphics*, 14(3):198–203

Calvert TW, Chapman J, Patla A (1982) Aspects of the kinematic simulation of human movement. *IEEE Computer Graphics and Applications*, 2(9):41–50

Calvert TW, Chapman J, Patla A (1982b) The simulation of human movement. *Proc. Graphics Interface '82*, pp227–234

Carlson WE (1982) An algorithm and data structure for 3D object synthesis using surface patch intersections. *Proc. SIGGRAPH '82, Computer Graphics*, 16(3):255–263

*Carr JW, et al. (1970) Interactive movie making. *Proceedings 9th UAIDE Annual Meeting*, pp381–397

Catmull E (1972) A system for computer generated movies. *Proc. ACM Annual Conference*, pp422–431

Catmull E (1974) *A subdivision algorithm for computer display of curved surfaces* (Ph.D. Thesis). Computer Science Department, University of Utah

Catmull E (1975) Computer display of curved surfaces. *Proc. IEEE Conf. on Computer Graphics, Pattern Recognition and Data Structures*, also in: *Tutorial on Interactive Computer Graphics*, IEEE Press, pp309–315

Catmull E (1978) A hidden-surface algorithm with anti-aliasing. *Proc. SIGGRAPH '78, Computer Graphics*, 12(3):6–11

Catmull E (1978b) The problems of computer-assisted animation. *Computer Graphics*, 12(3):348–353

Catmull E (1979) New frontiers in computer animation. *American Cinematographer*, October Issue

CGW (1982) Digital paint systems survey. *Computer Graphics World*, 5(4):62–65

*Christopher R (1982) Digital animation does dallas. *Videography*, February Issue, pp37–42

*Chuang R, Entis G (1983) 3D shaded computer animation—step by step. *IEEE Computer Graphics and Applications*, 3(9):18–25

Citron J, Whitney J (1968) CAMP computer assisted movie production. *FJCC, AFIPS Conference Proceedings*, 33(2):1299–1305

Clark JH (1976) Hierarchical geometric models for visible surface algorithms. *Communications of the ACM*, 19(10):547–554

Cook RL, Torrance KE (1982) A reflection model for computer graphics. *ACM Trans. Graphics*, 1(1):7–24

Coons SA (1964) *Surfaces for computer-aided design of space figures.* MIT, ESL 9442-M-139

Coons SA (1974) Surface patches and B-spline curves. In: Barnhill, Riesenfeld (eds), *Computer Aided Geometric Design*, Academic Press

Crow FC (1977) The aliasing problem in computer-generated shaded images. *Communications of the ACM*, 20(11):799–805

Crow FC (1977b) Shadow algorithms for computer graphics. *Proc. SIGGRAPH '77, Computer Graphics*, 11(2):242–248

Crow FC (1978) Shaded computer graphics in the entertainment industry. *Computer*, IEEE Press, 11(3):11–23

Crow FC (1978b) The use of grayscale for improved raster display of vectors and characters. *Proc. SIGGRAPH '78, Computer Graphics*, 12(3):1–5

Crow FC (1981) A comparison of anti-aliasing techniques. *IEEE Computer Graphics and Applications*, 1(1):40–48

Csuri C (1970) Real-time film animation. *Proc. 9th UAIDE Annual Meeting*, pp289–305

Csuri C (1974) Real-time computer animation. *Proc. IFIP Congress '74*, North-Holland, pp707–711

*Csuri C (1974) Computer graphics and art. *Proc. IEEE*, 62(4):503–515

Csuri C (1975) Computer animation. *Proc. SIGGRAPH '75*, pp92–101

Csuri C, Hackathorn R, Parent R, Carlson W, Howard M (1979) Towards an interactive high visual complexity animation system. *Proc. SIGGRAPH '79, Computer Graphics*, 13(2):289–299

*Csuri C, Shaffer J (1968) Art, computers and mathematics. *Proc. Fall Joint Computer Conf*, AFIPS, pp1293–1298

Dahl M, Nygaard K (1968) *The SIMULA 67 common base language.* Norwegian Computing Centre

DeFanti T (1976) The digital component of the circle graphics habitat. *Proc. National Computer Conference '76*, pp195–203

DeFanti T (1980) Language control structures for easy electronic visualization. *BYTE*, November Issue, pp90–106

Dietrich F (1983) A micro computer system for real-time animation. *The Artist Designer and Computer Graphics*, Tutorial SIGGRAPH '83, 18:43–47

Dooley M (1982) Anthropometric modeling programs—a survey. *IEEE Computer Graphics and Applications*, 2(9):17–25

*Duncan W Jr (1982) Computer Animation at information international. *Tutorial notes on 3D Computer Animation*, SIGGRAPH '82

Dungan W, Stenger A, Sutty G (1978) Texture tile considerations for raster graphics. *Proc. SIGGRAPH '78, Computer Graphics*, 12(3):130–134

*Duff DS (1976) *Simulation and animation* (M.Sc. Thesis). Computer Science Department, University of Toronto

Duff T (1979) Smoothly shaded renderings of polyhedral objects on raster displays. *Proc. SIGGRAPH '79, Computer Graphics*, 13(2):270–275

Duff T (1983) Computer graphics in the biggest box office hit: *return of the jedi*. *Proc. Computer Graphics '83*, Online Conf., pp283–289

Encarnacao J (1970) Survey of and new solutions for the hidden-line problem. *Proc. GC Symp. Delft.*

Eshkol N, Wachmann A (1958) *Movement notation.* Weidenfeld and Nicolson, London

Evans SM (1976) *User's guide for the programs of combiman.* Report AMRLTR-76-117, University of Dayton, Ohio

Feibush EA, Levoy M, Cook RL (1980) Synthetic Texturing Using Digital Filters. *Proc. SIGGRAPH '80, Computer Graphics,* 14(3):294–301

* Feiner S, Salesin D, Banchoff T (1982) Dial: a diagrammatic animation language. *IEEE Computer Graphics and Applications,* 2(9):43–54

* Ferderber S (1983) The commercial production designer. *Millimeter,* February Issue, pp52–66

* Fetter WA (1964) *Computer graphics in communication,* McGraw-Hill, New York

Fetter WA (1981) Wide angle displays for tactical situations. *Proc. US Army Third Computer Graphics Workshop,* pp99–103

Fetter WA (1982) A progression of human figures simulated by computer graphics. *IEEE Computer Graphics and Applications,* 2(9):9–13

Fiume E, Fournier A, Rudolph L (1983) A parallel scan conversion algorithm with anti-aliasing for a general-purpose ultracomputer. *Proc. SIGGRAPH '83, Computer Graphics,* 17(3):141–150

* Foley JD, Van Dam A (1982) *Fundamentals of interactive computer graphics,* Addison-Wesley

Fortin D, Lamy JF, Thalmann D (1983) A multiple track animator system. *Proc. SIGGRAPH/SIGART Interdisciplinary Workshop on Motion: Representation and Perception,* Toronto, pp180–186

Fournier A, Fussell D, Carpenter L (1982) Computer rendering of stochastic models. *Communications of the ACM,* 25(6):371–384

* Fox, Waite (1982) Computer animation with color registers. *BYTE,* pp194–214

* Friesen DP (1969) A professional animator looks at computer animation. *Proceedings 8th UAIDE Annual Meeting,* pp187–194

Fuchs H, Barros J (1979) Efficient generation of smooth line drawings on video displays. *Proc. SIGGRAPH '79, Computer Graphics,* 13(2):260–269

Futrelle RP (1974) GALATEA: Interactive graphics for the analysis of moving images. *Proc. Information Processing 74,* North Holland, pp712–715

Galimberti R, Montanari U (1969) An algorithm for hidden-line elimination. *Comm. ACM,* 12(4):206

* Geschwind DM (1982) The NOVA opering: a case study in digital computer animation. *Proc. Computer Graphics '82,* Online Conf., pp325–335

Goldberg A, Kay A (1976) *SMALLTALK-72 instruction manual.* Palo Alto, California, XEROX PARC

Goldberg A, Robson D (1983) *SMALLTALK-80, the language and its implementation.* Addison-Wesley

* Goldstein RA (1971) A system for computer animation of 3-D objects. *Proceedings 10th UAIDE Annual Meeting,* pp3–128 to 3–139

Goldstein RA, Nagel R (1971) 3-D visual simulation. *Simulation,* pp25–31

* Goss T (1983) Animation and the new machine. *Print,* March/April Issue, pp57–64

Gouraud H (1971) Continuous shading of curve surfaces. *IEEE Transactions on*

Computers, vol C-20, 6:623–629

*Green M (1981) A system for designing and animating objects with curved surfaces. *Proc. Canadian Man-Computer Communications Society '81*, pp377–384

*Greenberg D, Marcus A, Schmidt AH, Gorter V (1982) *The computer image*. Addison-Wesley

Greif I, Hewitt C (1975) Actor semantics of PLANNER-73. *Proc. ACM SIGPLAN SIGACT Conf.*, pp67–77

Gupta S, Sproull R (1981) Filtering edges for gray-scale displays. *Proc. SIGGRAPH '81, Computer Graphics*, 15(3):1–5

Guttag J (1977) Abstract data types and the development of data structures. *Communications of the ACM*, 20(6):396–404

Hackathorn R (1977) ANIMA II:A 3-D color animation system. *Proc. SIGGRAPH '77, Computer Graphics*, 11(2):54–64

Hackathorn R, Parent R, Marshall B, Howard M (1981) An interactive microcomputer based 3-D animation system. *Proc. Canadian Man-Computer Communications Society Conference '81*, pp181–191

*Haflinger DJ, Ressler PC (1971) Animation with IGS. *Proceedings 10th UAIDE Annual Meeting*, pp3–227 to 3–234

Halas J, Manvell R (1968) *The technique of film animation*. Hastings House, New York

*Halas J (ed) (1974) *Computer animation*. Hastings House, New York

Hall RA, Greenberg DP (1983) A testbed for realistic image synthesis. *IEEE Computer Graphics and Applications*, 3(8):11–20

Hanrahan P (1983) Ray tracing algebraic surfaces. *Proc. SIGGRAPH '83, Computer Graphics*, 17(3):83–90

Herbison-Evans D (1978) NUDES 2: a numeric utility displaying ellipsoid solids, version 2. *Proc. SIGGRAPH '78, Computer Graphics*, 12(3):354–356

Herbison-Evans D (1980) Rapid raster ellipsoid shading. *Computer Graphics*, 13(4):355–361

Herbison-Evans D (1982) Real-time animation of human figure drawings with hidden-lines omitted. *IEEE Computer Graphics and Applications*, 2(9):27–33

*Herbison-Evans D (1983) Caterpillar and the inaccurate solutions of cubic and quartic equations. *Australian Computer Science Comm.*, 5(1):80–90

*Herbison-Evans D (1983b) Manipulating ellipsoids in animation. *Computer Graphics World*, 7:78–82

*Herbison-Evans D (1983c) Hidden arcs of interpenetrating and obscuring ellipsoids. *The Australian Journal*, 15(2):65–68

Hewitt C (1971) *Description and theoretical analysis (using schemata) of PLANNER: a language for proving theorems and manipulating models for a robot* (Ph.D. Dissertation). MIT

Hewitt C, Atkinson R (1977) Parallelism and synchronization in actor systems. *Proc. ACM Symposium on Principles of Programming Languages*

Hewitt C, Bishop P, Steiger R (1973) A universal modular actor formalism for artificial intelligence. *Proc. Intern. Joint Conf. on Artificial Intelligence*, pp235–245

Hewitt C, Smith B (1975) Towards a programming apprentice. *IEEE Transactions on Software Engineering*, SE-1, 1:26–45

Honey FJ (1971) Artist oriented computer animation. *Journal of Society of Motion Picture and Television Engineers*, 80(3):154

Honey FJ (1971) Computer animated episodes by single axis rotations. *Proc. 10th UAIDE Annual Meeting*, pp3–120 to 3–226

*Hopgood FRA (1969) GROATS: a graphic output system for atlas using the 4020. *Proceedings 9th UAIDE Annual Meeting*, pp401–410

*Hubschman H, Zucker SW (1982) Frame-to-frame coherence and the hidden surface computation: constraints for a convex world. *ACM Trans. on Graphics*, 1(2):129–162

*Huggins WH, Entwisle DR (1969) Computer animation for the academic community. *SJCC, AFIPS Conference Proceedings*, Vol 34, p623

*Hunter GM (1977) Computer animation survey. *Comput. and Graphics*, Pergamon Press, 2:225–229

*Hurn B (1981) Computer animation for industrial training. *Computer Graphics World*, 10:65–68

*Iversen WR (1982) Processor animates 3-D surface images. *Electronics*, pp149–150

Judice JN, Jarvis JF, Ninke W (1974) Using ordered dither to display continuous tone pictures on an AC plasma panel. *Proc. Society for Information Display*, pp161–169

Julesz B (1966) *Computers, patterns and depth Perception*. Bell Laboratories Record, 44(8):261–267

Kahn KM (1976) *An actor-based computer animation language*. MIT AI Working Paper No 120

Kajiya JT (1982) Ray tracing parametric patches. *Proc. SIGGRAPH'82, Computer Graphics*, 16(3):245–254

Kajiya JT (1983) New techniques for ray tracing procedurally defined objects. *Proc. SIGGRAPH '83, Computer Graphics*, 17(3):91–99

*Kallis SA (1971) Computer animation techniques. *Journal of the SMPTE*, 80(3):145–148

*Kawaguchi Y (1981) *Digital image* (in Japanese). ASCII Publishing

Kay A (1969) *The reactive engine* (Ph.D. Thesis). University of Utah

Kay DS, Greenberg D (1979) Transparency for computer synthesized images. *Proc. SIGGRAPH '79, Computer Graphics*, 13(2):158–164

*Kinnucan P (1982) Solid modelers make the scene. *High Technology*, Vol 2, 4:38–44

Kitching A (1973) Computer animation-some new ANTICS. *Br. Kinematography Sound Television J.*, 55(12):372–386

Knowlton KC (1964) A computer technique for producing animated movies. *Proc. SJCC AFIPS Conference*, 25:67–87

Knowlton KC (1965) Computer-produced movies. *Science*, 150:1116–1120

*Knowlton K (1968) Computer-animated movies. *Emerging Concepts in Computer Graphics*, Benjamin, New York, pp243–370

Knowlton KC (1970) EXPLOR-A generator of images. *Proc. 9th UAIDE Annual Meeting*, pp543–583

*Knowlton K (1972) Collaborations with artists: a programmer's reflections.

Proc. IFIP Working Conf. on Graphic Languages, North-Holland, pp399–418

Knowlton K, Cherry L (1977) Atoms, a 3D opaque molecule system. *Comput. Chem.*, 1(3):161–166

Korein J, Badler N (1983) Temporal anti-aliasing in computer generated animation. *Proc. SIGGRAPH '83, Computer Graphics*, 17(3):377–388

Laban R (1966) *Choreutics*. Ullman L (ed) MacDonald and Evans, London

Lane JM, Carpenter LC, Whitted T, Blinn JF: Scan line methods for displaying parametrically defined surfaces. *Communications of the ACM*, 23(1):23–34

*Lansdown RJ (1982) Computer aided animation: a concise review. *Proc. Computer Graphics '82*, Online Conf., pp279–290

*Lansdown J (1983) The economics of computer-aided animation. *Proc. Computer Graphics '83*, Online Conf., pp267–275

*Laybourne K (1979) *The animation book*. Crown

*Levine SR (1975) Computer animation at lawrence livermore laboratory. *Proc. SIGGRAPH '75*, pp81–84

*Levitan EL (1977) *Electronic imaging techniques*. Van Nostrand

*Levoy M (1977) A color animation system based on the multiplane technique. *Proc. SIGGRAPH '77, Computer Graphics*, 11(2):65–71

*Lewell J (1981) The computer pointings of David Em. *Business Screen*, October Issue, pp38–40

*Lewell J (1983) The pioneers: John Whitney Sr. *Computer Pictures*, 1(3):22–24

Liardet M (1978) PICAX-polyhedron input to the computer using an axonometric drawing. *Proc. Intern. Conf. on Interactive Techniques in Computer-aided Design*, IEEE Press

*Lieberman LI (1971) Compufilms: a computer animation process. *Simulation*, 16(1):33–36

Lipscomb JS (1981) Reversed apparent movement and erratic motion with many refreshes per update. *Computer Graphics*, 14(4):113–118

Liskov B, Zilles S (1974) Programming with abstract data types. *Proc. SIGPLAN Symposium on Very High Level Languages*, pp50–59

Magnenat-Thalmann N, Chourot N, Thalmann D (1984) Color gradation, shading and texture using a limited terminal. *Computer Graphics Forum, the EUROGRAPHICS journal*, March Issue

Magnenat-Thalmann N, Thalmann D, Fortin M (1985) MIRANIM: An Extensible Director-Oriented System for the Animation of Realistic Images, *IEEE Computer Graphics and Applications*, March Issue

Magnenat-Thalmann N, Thalmann D, Fortin M, Langlois L (1984b) MIRASHADING: a language for the synthesis and the animation of realistic images. *Frontiers in Computer Graphics*, Springer, Tokyo Berlin Heidelberg New York, pp101–113

Magnenat-Thalmann N, Thalmann D, Larouche A, Lorrain L (1982) GRAFEDIT: an interactive general-purpose graphics editor. *Computers and Graphics*, Pergamon Press, 6(1):41–46

Magnenat-Thalmann N, Larouche A, Thalmann D (1983) An interactive and user-oriented three-dimensional graphics editor. *Proc. Graphics Interface '83*, pp39–46

Magnenat-Thalmann N, Thalmann D (1981) A graphical PASCAL extension based on graphical types. *Software Practice and Experience*, 11(1):53–62

Magnenat-Thalmann N, Thalmann D (1983) MIRA-3D: A three-dimensional graphical extension of PASCAL. *Software-Practice and Experience*, 13:797–808

* Magnenat-Thalmann N, Thalmann D (1983b) 3D computer animation films using a programming language and interactive systems. *Proc. Computer Graphics '83*, Online Conf., pp247–257

Magnenat-Thalmann N, Thalmann D (1983c) The use of 3D high-level graphical types in the MIRA animation system. *IEEE Computer Graphics and Applications*, 3(9):9–16

Magnenat-Thalmann N, Thalmann D (1984) CINEMIRA: a 3D computer animation language based on actor and camera data types. Technical Report, University of Montreal

Magnenat-Thalmann N, Thalmann D (1984b) 3D shaded director-oriented computer animation. *Proc. Graphics Interface '84*, Ottawa

Mallgren WR (1982) Formal specification of graphic data types. *ACM Transactions on Programming Languages and Systems*, 4(4):687–710

Mandelbrot BB (1975) Stochastic models for the earth's relief, the shape and fractal dimension of coastlines, and the number area rule for islands. *Proc. National Acad-Sc. USA*, 72(10):2825–2828

Mandelbrot BB (1977) *Fractals: form, chance and dimension.* Freeman, San Francisco

Mandelbrot BB (1982) *The fractal geometry of nature.* Freeman, San Francisco

Mandelbrot BB, Van Ness JW (1968) Fractional brownian motions, fractional noises and applications. *SIAM Review*, 10(4):422–437

Marshall R, Wilson R, Carlson W (1980) Procedure models for generating three-dimensional terrain. *Proc. SIGGRAPH '80, Computer Graphics*, 14(4):154–159

Max NL (1979) Atom LLL:—atoms with shading and highlights. *Computer Graphics*, 13(2):165–173

* Max N, Blunden J (1980) Optical printing in computer animation. *Proc. SIGGRAPH '80, Computer Graphics*, 14(3):171–177

* McCarthy M (1982) Animation's new protege. *Video Systems*, pp40–46

Mezei L, Zivian A (1971) ARTA: an interactive animation system. *Proc. Information Processing 71*, North-Holland, pp429–434.

* Miskowich D (1982) Digital technology and motion pictures. *Computer Graphics World*, 7:50–62

* Mittelman P (1983) Computer graphics at MAGI. *Proc. Computer Graphics '83*, Online Conf., pp291–301

Miura T, Iwata J, Tsuda J (1967) An application of hybrid curve generation—cartoon animation by electronic computers. *Proc. Spring Joint Computer Conference*, p141

* Mudur SP, Singh JH (1978) A notation for computer animation. *IEEE Trans. on Systems, Man and Cybernetics*, SMC-8(4):308–311

* Myers AJ (1976) A digital video information storage and retrieval system. *Proc. SIGGRAPH '76, Computer Graphics*, 10(2):45–50

* Negroponte N, Pangaro P (1976) Experiments with computer animation. *Computer Graphics*, 10(2):40–44

Newell ME, Newell RG, Sancha TL (1972) A new approach to the shaded picture problem. *Proc. ACM National Conf.*, pp443

*Newman WM, Sproull RF (1973) *Principles of interactive computer graphics.* McGraw-Hill

Nishita T, Nakamae E (1974) An algorithm for half-toned representation of three-dimensional objects. *Information Processing Society of Japan*, vol 14

Nolan J, Yarbrough L (1968) An on-line computer drawing and animation system. *Proceedings IFIP Congress 1968*, North-Holland, Amsterdam, p605

Noll AM (1965) Stereographic projections by digital computers. *Computers and Automation*, 14:32–34

*Noll AM (1965b) Computer generated three-dimensional movies. *Computers and Automation*, November Issue, p20

Noll AM (1967)Computers and the visual arts. *Design and Planning*, 2:65–80

Norton A (1982) Generation and display of geometric fractals in 3-D. *Proc. SIGGRAPH '82, Computer Graphics*, 16(3):61–67

*Odgers CR (1982) Criteria for choosing a camera for use in a video digitizing system. *Tutorial notes on Computer Animation, SIGGRAPH '82*, pp108–119

*Odgers CR (1983) Fundamentals of video recording for computer animation. *Tutorial notes on Computer Animation SIGGRAPH '83*, pp175–186

Oppenheim AV, Schafer RW (1975) *Digital signal processing.* Prentice-Hall, Englewood Cliffs

O'Rourke J, Badler NI (1979) Decomposition of three-dimensional objects into spheres. *IEEE Transactions on Pattern Analysis and Machine Intelligence*, RAMI-1:295–306

Papert S (1970) Teaching children thinking. *Proc. IFIP World Conference on Computer Education*, New York, ppI/73–I/78

Parke FI (1972) Animation of faces. *Proceedings ACM Annual Conference* vol 1

*Parke FI (1975) A model for human faces that allows speech synchronized Animation. *Computers and Graphics*, Pergamon Press, 1(1):1–4

*Parke FI (1980) Adaptation of scan and slit-scan techniques to computer animation. *Proc. SIGGRAPH '80, Computer Graphics*, 14(3):178–181

Parke FI (1982) Parameterized models for facial animation. *IEEE Computer Graphics and Applications*, 2(9):61–68

*Patterson R (1982) The making of *Tron*. *American Cinematographer*, vol 63(8)

Phong BT (1975) Illumination for computer generated pictures. *Communications of the ACM*, 18(6):311–317

Piller E (1980) Real-time raster scan unit with improved picture quality. *Computer Graphics*, 14(1–2):35–38

Platt S, Badler N (1981) Animating facial expressions. *Proc. SIGGRAPH '81, Computer Graphics*, 15(3):245–252

Porter T (1978) Spherical shading. *Proc. SIGGRAPH '78, Computer Graphics*, 12(3):282–285

*Potel MJ (1977) Real-time playback in animation systems. *Proc. SIGGRAPH '77, Computer Graphics*, 11(2):72–77

Potmesil M, Chakravarty I (1982) Synthetic Image Generation with a Lens and Aperture Camera Model. *ACM Transactions on Graphics*, 1(2):85–108

Potmesil M, Chakravarty I (1983) Modeling motion blur in computer-generated images. *Proc. SIGGRAPH '83, Computer Graphics*, 17(3):389–399

Potter TE, Willmert KD (1975) Three-dimensional human display model. *Computer Graphics*, 9(1):102–110

*Potts J (1983) Animating the indescribable. *Government Data Systems*, May/ June Issue, pp10–13

Reeves WT (1980) *Quantitative representations of complex dynamic shape for motion analysis* (Ph.D. Thesis). Computer Science Department, University of Toronto.

Reeves WT (1981) Inbetweening for computer animation utilizing moving point constraints. *Proc. SIGGRAPH '81*, ACM, pp263–269

Reeves WT (1983) Particle systems—a technique for modeling a class of fuzzy objects. *Proc. SIGGRAPH '1983, Computer Graphics*, 17(3):359–376

*Ressler SP (1982) An object editor for a real time animation processor. *Proc. of Graphics Interface '82*, pp221–226

Reynolds CW (1978) *Computer animation in the world of actors and scripts* (SM Thesis). Architecture Machine Group, MIT

Reynolds CW (1982) Computer animation with scripts and actors. *Proc. SIGGRAPH '82, Computer Graphics*, 16(3):289–296

Riesenfeld RF, Cohen E, Fish RD, Thomas SW, Cobb ES, Barsky BA, Schweizer DL, Lane JM (1981) Using the oslo algorithm as a basis for CAD/CAM geometric modelling. *Proc. NCGA '81*, National Computer Graphics Association, pp345–356

Roth SD (1982) Ray casting for modeling solids. *Computer Graphics and Image Processing*, 18:109–144

Rubin S, Whitted T (1980) A three-dimensional representation for fast rendering of complex scenes. *Proc. SIGGRAPH'80, Computer Graphics*, 14(3):110–116

*Russett R, Starr C (1976) *Experimental animation*. Van Nostrand Reinhold, New York

Schachter BJ (1980) Long crested wave models. *Computer Graphics and Image Processing*, 12:187–201

Schachter BJ (1980b) Real time display of texture. *Proc. 5th International Conference on Pattern Recognition*, pp789–791

Schachter BJ (1981) Computer image generation for flight simulation. *IEEE Computer Graphics and Applications*, 1(4):29–68

Schachter BJ (1983) Generation of special effects. in *Computer Image Generation*, John Wiley, New York, pp155–172

*Schneegans C, Poulard S (1972) FILOMENE-FILEMON, un système complexe pour la production de films d'animation sur ordinateurs. *Proc. CIPS '72*, pp212,301–212,329

Schmacker RA, Brand B, Gilliland M, Sharp W (1969) *Study for applying computer-generated images to visual simulation*. AFHRL-TR-69-14, US Air Force Human Resources Lab.

Schweitzer D (1983) Artificial texturing: an aid to surface visualization. *Proc. SIGGRAPH '83, Computer Graphics*, 17(3):23–29

Schweizer D, Cobb ES (1982) Scanline rendering of parametric surfaces. *Proc. SIGGRAPH '82, Computer Graphics*, 16(3):265–271

Shoup RG (1973) Some quantization effects in digitally generated Pictures. *Proc. Society for Information Display Intern. Symposium*, p58

Shoup RG (1979) Colour table animation. *Proc. SIGGRAPH '79, Computer Graphics*, 13(2):8–13

* Shoup RG (1979) SUPERPAINT: the digital animator. *Datamation*, May Issue, pp150–156

Sinden FW (1967) Synthetic cinematography. *Perspective 7*, 4:279–289

Smith AR (1979) Tint fill. *Proc. SIGGRAPH '79, Computer Graphics*, 13(2):276–283

Smith AR (1978) *PAINT.* Technical Memo No 7, NYIT

Smoliar SW, Tracton W (1978) A lexical analysis of labanotation with an associated data structure. *Proc. ACM Annual Conf.* 2:727–730

Smoliar SW, Weber L (1977) Using the computer for a semantic representation of labanotation. *Computing and the Humanities*, Univ. Waterloo Press, pp253–261

* Sorensen P (1981) Computer imaging—an apple for the dreamsmiths. *Cinefex 6*, October Issue

* Sorensen P (1982) Tronic imagery. *Cinefex 8*, Apris Issue

* Sorensen P (1983) Movies, computers and the future. *American Cinematographer*, January Issue

* Spina L (1982) Paint-by-pixels: computer power comcs to TV artists. *Millimeter Magazine*, vol 10, No 2

Stern G (1979) Softcel: an application of raster scan graphics to conventional cel animation. *Proc. SIGGRAPH '79, Computer Graphics*, 13(3):284–288.

Stern G (1983) Bboop: a system for 3D key frame figure animation. *SIGGRAPH '83 tutorial*, pp240–243

* Stevenson R (1973) *The animated film.* AS Barnes, New York

Sutherland I (1963) *SKETCHPAD: a man-machine graphical communication system* (Ph.D. Thesis). MIT

Sutherland IE, Sproull RF, Schumacker RA (1974) A characterization of ten hidden-surface algorithms. *Computing Surveys*, 6(1):1–55

Szabo NS (1978) Digital image anomalies: static and dynamic. *Proc. Symposium Society of Photo-Optical Instrumentation Engineers*, vol 162: Visual Simulation and Realism, pp11–15

Talbot PA, Carr III JW, Coulter RC Jr, Hwang RC (1971) Animator: an on-line two-dimensional film animation system. *Communications of the ACM*, 14(4):251–259

* Taylor R (1983) Designing for the feature film. *Tutorial notes on the Artist/Designer and Computer Graphics, SIGGRAPH '83*, pp31

Thalmann D, Magnenat-Thalmann N (1979) Design and implementation of abstract graphical data types. *Proc. 3rd Intern. Computer Software and Applications Conf. (COMPSAC '79)*, Chicago, IEEE Press, pp519–524

Thalmann D, Magnenat-Thalmann N (1983) Actor and camera data types in computer animation. *Proc. Graphics Interface '83*, pp203–210

Thalmann D, Magnenat-Thalmann N, Bergeron P (1982) *Dream flight:* a fictional film produced by 3D computer animation. *Proc. Computer Graphics '82*, Online Conf., pp353–368

Thalmann D, Ouimet D, Roy C (1982b) Drawing bridges by computer. *Computer-aided Design*, IPC Press, 14(4):195–200

*Thornton R (1983) Computer assisted animation at NYIT. *Proc. Computer Graphics '83*, Online Conf., pp277–282

Torrance KE, Sparrow EM (1967), Theory for off-specular reflection from roughened surfaces. *J. Opt. Soc. Am.*, 57(9):1105–1114

Turkowski K (1982) Anti-aliasing through the use of coordinate transformations. *ACM Transactions on Graphics*, 1(3):215–234

Walker RJ (1950) *Algebraic curves*. Springer, Berlin Heidelberg New York (Reprint 1980)

*Wallace BA (1981) Merging and transformation of raster images for cartoon animation. *Proc. SIGGRAPH '81, Computer Graphics*, 15(3):253–262

*Warn DR (1983) Lighting controls for synthetic images. *Proc. SIGGRAPH '83, Computer Graphics*, 17(3):13–21

Warnock J (1969) *A hidden-surface algorithm for computer-generated half-tone pictures*, Univ. Utah Comp. Sc. Dep., TR4-15, NTIS AD-753 671

Watkins GS (1970) *A real-time visible surface algorithm*. Univ. Utah Comp. Sc. Dep., UTEC-CSc-70-101, NTIS AD-762004

Weber L, Smoliar SW, Badler NI (1978) An architecture for the simulation of human movement. *Proc. ACM National Conference*, pp737–745

Weiler K, Atherton P (1977) Hidden surface removal using polygon area sorting. *Proc. SIGGRAPH '77, Computer Graphics*, 11(2):214–222

*Wein M, Burtnyk N (1972) A computer facility for film animation and music. *Proc. CIPS '72*, pp212, 201–212, 205

*Wein M, Burtnyk N (1976) Computer animation. In: *Encyclopedia of Computer Science and Technology*, vol.5, Marcel Dekker, pp397–436

*Weiner DD, Anderson SE (1968) A computer animation movie language for educational motion pictures. *Proc. FJCC*, pp1318

*Weinstock N (1983) New technologies for the realization of ideas. *Millimeter*, February Issue, pp71–76

*Whitney JH (1971) A computer art for the video picture wall. *Proceedings IFIP Congress 1971*, North-Holland, Amsterdam, pp1382–1386

*Whitney J (1980) *Digital harmony*.Peterborough, NH: Byte Books, McGraw-Hill

Whitted T (1980) An improved illusmination model for shaded display. *Communications of the ACM*, 23(6):343–349

Whitted T (1983) Anti-aliased line drawing using brush extrusion. *Proc. SIGGRAPH '83, Computer Graphics*, 17(3):151–156

*Williams L (1978) Casting curved shadows on curved surfaces. *Proc. SIGGRAPH '78, Computer Graphics*, 12(3):270–274

*Williams L (1983) Overview of 3D animation. *Tutorial notes on Computer Animation SIGGRAPH '83*, pp212–219

*Willmert KD (1978) Graphic display of human motion. *Proc. ACM '78 Conf.*, pp715–719

Wirth N (1983) *Programming in MODULA-2*, 2nd edition. Springer, Berlin Heidelberg New York Tokyo

Withrow C (1970) *A dynamic model for computer-aided choreography.* Computer Science Department, University of Utah, No 70–103

Wylie C, Romney GW, Evans DC, Erdahl AC (1967) Halftone perspective drawings by computer. *Proc. FJCC*, pp49–58

*Zajac EE (1965) Computer animation: a new scientific and educational tool. *J. SMPTE* 74, 1006–1008

Zajac EE (1966) Film animation by computer. *New Scientist 29*, pp346–349

*Zeltzer D Csuri C (1981) Goal-directed movement simulation. *Proc. Canadian Man-Computer Communications Society '81*, pp271–280

Zeltzer D (1982) Motor control techniques for figure animation. *IEEE Computer Graphics and Applications*, 2(9):53–59

*Zeltzer D (1982b) Representation of complex animated figures. *Proc. Graphics Interface '82*, pp205–211

*Zeltzer D (1983) Knowledge-based animation. *Proc. SIGGRAPH/SIGART Workshop on Motion*, pp187–192

*Zimmerlin R, Stanley J, Stone W (1978) A sensor simulation and animation system. *Proc. SIGGRAPH '78, Computer Graphics*, 12(3):105–110

Appendix A: Computer Animation Organizations and Teams

This list is not exhaustive; as people in computer animation often move, it may not be completely up to date.

Aurora systems	D. Patton, L. Zimmermann, L. Mars, C. Kozak
Bell Labs	T. Whitted, S.M. Rubin, D. Weimer, M. Potmesil
Bo Gehring Associates	B. Gehring, W. Dungan, J. Alles, K. Colonna
Cornell University	D. Greenberg, K.J.Weiler
Cranston-Csuri Productions	C. Csuri, M. Collery, D. Stredney, W. Carlson, H. Ho, J. Berton
Digital Effects	J. Rosebush, J.M. Kleiser, M. Lindquist, A. Green
Digital Productions	J. Whitney Jr, M. Browne
Hiroshima University	E. Nakamae
Images Transfert	M. Francois
Lawrence Livermore Labs	N. Max, C. Upson, P. Weidhaas, M. Gerhardt
Lucasfilm Ltd	E. Catmull, R. Cook, L. Carpenter, B. Reeves, A.R. Smith, T. Duff
MAGI Synthavision	P.S. Mittelman
MIT	A. Lippman
NASA Jet Propulsion Lab	J.F. Blinn, D. Em, R. Wolff
New York Institute of Technology	F.I. Parke, G. Stern, L. Williams, P. Xander D. Lundin, R. McDermott, N. Greene
NHK	M. Yoshinari
Nippon Electronics College	Y. Kawaguchi
Ohio State University	C. Csuri, D. Zeltzer, R. Conley, S. Van Baerle
Omnibus Computer Graphics	J.C. Penney
Pacific Data Images	G. Entis, R. Chuang
Real Time Design Inc.	C. Giloth, J. Veeder
Robert Abel and Associates	B. Kovaks, D. Herigstad, K. Mirman, C. Buchinski, C. Anderson, R. Davis

System Simulation	T. Pritchett, J. Lansdowne
UCLA	J. Whitney Sr
University of Illinois	T. DeFanti, F. Dietrich
University of Montreal/HEC	N. Magnenat-Thalmann, D. Thalmann
University of Pennsylvania	N.I. Badler

Appendix B: Computer Animation Systems and Languages

The authors and year correspond to the bibliographic references.

ANIMA	C. Csuri, 1975 Ohio State University	3D Real-time system
ANIMA II	R.J. Hackathorn, 1977 Ohio State University	3D shaded system
ANIMATOR	P.A. Talbot et al., 1971 University of Pennsylvania	2D system
ANTTS	C. Csuri et al., 1979 Ohio State University	3D shaded system
ANTICS	A. Kitching, 1973	
ASAS	C. Reynolds, 1982 Triple I	3D actor language
ARTA	L. Mezei and A. Zivian, 1971 University of Toronto	2D system
ATOMLL	N. Max, 1979 Lawrence Livermore Labs	3D atoms
BBOOP	G. Stern and L. Williams, 1983 NYIT	3D key-frame system
BEFLIX	K. Knowlton, 1964 Bell Labs	2D language
CAESAR	F.J. Honey, 1971 Computer Image Corporation	analog system
CAFE	J. Nolan and L. Yarbrough, 1969	
CAMP	J. Citron and J. Whitney, 1968 UCLA	Computer-assisted production system
CINEMIRA	N. Magnenat-Thalmann and D. Thalmann 1984, University of Montreal/HEC	3D actor language
DIRECTOR	K.M. Kahn, 1976 MIT	2D actor language
EXPLOR	K. Knowlton, 1970 Bell Labs	2D language

GAS	G. Stern, 1978 University of Utah	key-frame system
GENESYS	R. Baecker, 1969 MIT	interactive, P-curves
GRASS	T. DeFanti, 1976 University of Illinois	Real Time system
MIRA	N. Magnenat-Thalmann and D. Thalmann 1981, University of Montreal/HEC	graphics language
MIRANIM	D. Thalmann and N. Magnenat-Thalmann 1985, University of Montreal/HEC	Extensible 3D actor system
MOP	E. Catmull, 1972 University of Utah	3D shaded system
MSGEN	N. Burtnyk and M. Wein, 1971 National Research Council Canada	key-frame system
MUTAN	D. Fortin et al., 1983 University of Montreal	3D key-frame system
PAINT	A.R. Smith, 1978 NYIT	2D paint system
SCANIMATE	F.J. Honey, 1971 Computer Image Corporation	analog system
SHAZAM	R. Baecker, 1976 University of Toronto	2D shaded system
SKELETON	D. Zeltzer, 1982 Ohio State University	3D human motion
SOFTCEL	G. Stern, 1979 NYIT	2D Computer-aided animation system
SYNTHAVISION	P. Mittelman et al. MAGI	3D software
TWEEN	E. Catmull, 1978 NYIT	2D key-frame system
VIDEOCEL	Computer Creations	
VISIONS	J. Rosebush et al. Digital Effects	3D software

Appendix C: Computer-generated Films

1961
TWO-GYRO GRAVITY-GRADIENT ATTITUDE CONTROL SYSTEM
  E.E. Zajak, 4 min.

1962
AND-HANDS
  S. Van Der Beek, Univ. Texas, 2 min.

1964
A COMPUTER TECHNIQUE FOR THE PRODUCTION OF
  ANIMATED MOVIES
  K. Knowlton, Bell Labs, 17 min.
POEMFIELD
  S. Van Der Beek, K. Knowlton, Bell Labs, 5 min.

1966
L6: BELL TELEPHONE LABORATORIES LOW-LEVEL LINKED
  LIST LANGUAGE
  K. Knowlton, Bell Labs, 16 min.
AN EXAMPLE OF L6 PROGRAMMING
  K. Knowlton, Bell Labs, 32 min.
FORCE, MASS AND MOTION
  F.W. Sinden, 10 min.
SST COCKPIT VISIBILITY SIMULATION
  W. Fetter, 8 min.
LAPIS
  J. Whitney, L.A. Studio, 10 min.

1967
MAN AND HIS WORLD
  S. Van Der Beek and K. Knowlton, 1 min.
DYNAMIC FIELD DISTRIBUTIONS IN GUNN-EFFECT DEVICES
  D.E. McCumber, 12 min.

STUDIES WITH RANDOM TEXTURE
  B. Julesz and C. Bosche, 4 min.

1968
POEMFIELD 2
  S. Van Der Beek and K. Knowlton, 8 min.
EXPERIMENTS IN MOTION GRAPHICS
  J. Whitney and J. Citron, 12 min.
PER-MU-TA-TIONS
  J. Whitney and J. Citron, 7 min.
4-DIMENSIONAL HYPERCUBE
  A.M. Noll, 3 min.
4-D HYPERMOVIE
  A.M. Noll, 5 min.
COMPUTER-GENERATED BALLET
  A.M. Noll, 3 min.
SIMULATED BASILAR MEMBRANE MOTION
  R.C. Lummis and A.M. Noll, 5 min.
A PAIR OF PARADOXES
  R.N. Shepard and E.E. Zajak, 2 min.
BINARY BIT PATTERNS
  M. Whitney and J. Whitney, 3 min.
MEASURE FOR MEASURE
  NYIT, 14 min.

1969
TRANSFORMS
  S. Van Der Beek and R. Baecker, 4 min
SORCERER'S APPRENTICE
  W. Fetter, 4 min.
THE SECOND MAN
  W. Fetter, 10 min.
GENESYS
  R. Baecker, E. Martin and L. Smith, MIT, 25 min.
STRUCTURE OF PROTEINS
  J. de Rosnay, D. Barry, 9 min.
DYNAMICS SYMBOLS
  W. Huggins and P. Beck, 3 min.

1970
UFO'S
  K. Knowlton and L. Schwartz, Bell Labs, 3 min.
PIXILLATION
  K. Knowlton and L. Schwartz, Bell Labs, 4 min.
A RELATIVISTIC RIDE
  J. Schwartz and E. Taylor, 4 min.

REAL TIME
  Ohio State University, 10 min.
INTEGRATION OVER A SOLID OF REVOLUTION
  S. Anderson
THE GAME OF CHESS
  S. Anderson, 10 min.
MATRIX
  J. Whitney and J. Citron, 6 min.

1971
ART FROM COMPUTERS
  L. Mezei, 8 min.
MATRIX II
  J. Whitney and J. Citron, 6 min.
PATCHWORK 71
  K. Wilson, 30 min.
CAESAR
  Computer Image Corp.,
METADATA
  P. Foldes, National Film Board Canada, 9 min.
NRC SAMPLER
  National Research Council Canada, 9 min.
SPACE SHUTTLE FLIGHT SIMULATION
  LBJ Space Center, 6 min.
OLYMPIAD
  K. Knowlton and L. Schwartz, Bell Labs, 3 min.

1972
ABSTRACTIONS ON A BEDSHEET
  B. Etra, 7 min.
VIEW OF THE ROAD
  W. Fetter, 10 min.
SPACE FILLING CURVES
  N. Max, 25 min.
1984
  General Electric, 25 min.
MATRIX III
  J. Whitney and J. Citron, 7 min.
AFFINITIES
  L. Schwartz and K. Knowlton, 4 min.
ENIGM
  L. Schwartz and K. Knowlton, 4 min.
GOOGOLPLEX
  L. Schwartz and K. Knowlton, 5 min.
APOTHEOSIS
  L. Schwartz and K. Knowlton, 4 min.

MUTATIONS
  L. Schwartz and K. Knowlton, 7 min.
I HAD AN IDEA
  G. Demos, 10 min.
PHOSPHENES
  F. Foster and R. Speer, 5 min.
MORNING ELEVATOR
  A. Layzer and J. Miller, 4 min.
MAN-COMPUTER SYNERGISTICS
  J.B. Schneider et al., 23 min.
CGI FOR REAL-TIME VISUAL SIMULATION
  General Electric, 11 min.
GRASS
  T. DeFanti, Ohio State University, 10 min.
ROBOTICS
  R. MacGhee, Ohio State University, 7 min.
HAND/FACE
  E. Catmull, Univ. Utah, 5 min.
FLEXIPEDE
  T. Pritchett, Atlas Lab., 1 min.

1973
JEKYLLUM
  J. Baudot and C. Schneegans, Univ. Montreal, 4 min.
IKE'S WOMEN-TINA
  J. Biehl and J. Aken, 3 min.
SONG OF URANUS
  B. George and R. Siegel, 4 min.
COYOTE AND SKUNK
  Computer Image Corp., 7 min.
ALGOL THE DEMON STAR
  M.L. Meeks and S. Martin, 7 min.
SIRIUS AND THE THE WHITE DWART
  M.L. Meeks and S. Martin, 8 min.
THE MOTION OF STARS
  M.L. Meeks and S. Martin, 8 min.
PAPILLONS
  L. Schwartz and K. Knowlton, 4 min.
INNOCENCE
  L. Schwartz and K. Knowlton, 2 min.
THE GAME OF LIFE
  S. Anderson, 12 min.
REGULAR HOMOTOPICS IN THE PLANE
  N. Max, 29 min.
HARMONIC PHASORS II
  W. Huggins, 17 min.

LIMITED VISIBILITY LANDINGS
   General Electric, 4 min.
METAMORPHOSIS
   K. Knowlton and L. Schwartz, 10 min.

1974
FIRST FIG
   L. Cuba and G. Imhoff, 6 min.
HUNGER
   P. Foldes, National Film Board Canada, 12 min.
THE TAINTED SKY
   K. Wilson, 8 min.
RON HAYS MUSIC-IMAGE PRESENTATION
   R. Hays, 50 min.
SHAPES
   G. Demos, 7 min.
ABC
   C. Playfair et al., 2 min.
PLANETARY MOTION AND KEPLER'S LAWS
   M.L. Meeks and S. Martin, 9 min.
STAR CLUSTERS
   M.L. Meeks and S. Martin, 7 min.
TALKING FACE
   F.I. Parke, Univ. Utah, 5 min.
ANIMATION COURSE FILM
   University of Utah, 15 min.

1975
THREE VIEWS OF WATER
   D. Sandin, 6 min.
THE ANTICS SHOWREEL
   A. Kitching and C. Emmett, 5 min.
MS MUFFETT
   L. Katz, B. Etra and L. Etra, 3 min.

1976
THE PRISM SHOWREEL
   Imperial College, 4 min.
NCC/GRASS POOP TAPE
   D. Sandin, T. DeFanti and P. Morton, 15 min.
NYIT SAMPLERS
   NYIT, 10 min.
YIN HSIEN
   M. Whitney, L.A. Studio, 9 min.
TURNING A SPHERE INSIDE OUT
   N. Max, 23 min.

WIPEPOEM
  P. Scala, Syracuse Univ., 6 min.
SCOPE II
  P. Scala, Syracuse Univ., 5 min.

1977

*CELL DIVISION IN THE CARTILAGE PLATE DURING BONE
  GROWTH*
  N. Kembler, Univ. London, 7 min.
THE INTERACTION OF D+ +HD
  K. Birkinshaw, Univ. London, 7 min.
THE STAR WARS COMPUTER ANIMATION
  L. Cuba, Univ. Illinois, 10 min.
ANIMA II
  Ohio State Univ., 20 min.
VISULINK
  Advanced Products Operations, 4 min.
NEW DEVELOPMENTS IN DAY/NIGHT CGI
  Evans and Sutherland, 7 min.
FINITE ELEMENTS
  A. Kitching and C. Emmett, Atlas lab, 10 min.
TAYLOR POLYNOMIALS
  J. Gilbert and J. Richmond, BBC, 3 min.

1978

SPACE SHUTTLE FLIGHT SIMULATION
  R. Weinberg and J. Smith, LBJ Space Center, 7 min.
LIMIT SURFACES AND SPACE FILLING CURVES
  N. Max, Topology Films Project, 10 min.
CHEMICAL CONFORMATION
  T. Pritchett, P. Chandler and B. Whatley, Atlas Lab, 3 min.
DRIVING THROUGH A JUNCTION
  G. Lupton, CAD Centre, 1 min.
WIRE TREES WITH 4 VECTORS
  Univ. Illinois, 4 min.
REFERENCE CARRIER
  P. Morton, Univ. Illinois, 2 min.
LOOP CYCLE
  P. Morton and J. Veeder, Univ. Illinois, 2 min.
DATA BURSTS: THIRD MOVE+
  Univ. Illinois, 3 min.
SPIRAL 3
  T. DeFanti et al., Univ. Illinois, 10 min.
CRYSTAL GROWTH
  K. Knowlton, G. Gilmer and M. Shugard, Bell Labs, 10 min.

1979

EUCLIDEAN ILLUSIONS
  S. Van Der Beek and R. Weinberg, NASA, 11 min.
VOYAGER 1 ENCOUNTERS JUPITER
  J. Blinn and C.E. Kohlhase, 3 min.
VOYAGER 2 ENCOUNTERS JUPITER
  J. Blinn and C.E. Kohlhase, 6 min.
PIONEER 11 SATURN ENCOUNTER
  J. Blinn et al., 2 min.
THEMES TV TITLE SEQUENCE
  T. Pritchett, Atlas Lab, 1 min.
THE ALIEN
  J. Lansdown, Systems Simulation, 2 min.
THE STRUCTURE AND FUNCTION OF HAEMOGLOBIN
  D. Clarke, Univ. London, 5 min.
VAPOR TRAILS
  S. Pettigrew, 5 min.
CASE WESTERN SAMPLER
  F.I. Parke, Case Western Univ., 5 min.
BAOBAB
  K. Knowlton and E. Ghent, 20 min.
VISUAL LEARNING
  T. Linehan and C. Csuri, Ohio State Univ., 8 min.
SUNSTONE
  E. Emshwiller, NYIT, 3 min.
TOPES
  Bell Labs
NEWSHOLE
  University of Toronto
VIDEOCEL
  Computer Creations Inc.

1980

INFORMATION INTERNATIONAL DEMO REEL
  Information International Inc.
DNA WITH ETHIDIUM
  N. Max, Lawrence Livermore Lab
THE COMPLEAT ANGLER
  T. Whitted, Bell Labs
PEAK
  N. Snitly

1981

DOXORUBICIN/DNA
  N. Max, Lawrence Livermore Lab
DIGITAL EFFECTS DEMO REEL
  Digital Effects Inc.

MAGI/SYNTHAVISION DEMO REEL
  MAGI Inc.
SPATIAL DATA MANAGEMENT SYSTEM
  C. Herot et al.
PANTOMATION
  T. DeWitt et al.
ARTIFACTS
  The Vasulkas
CTS FLIGHT SIMULATOR
  Evans and Sutherland
TIME RIDER
  JVC Japan
IMAGINATION
  Acme Cartoon Company Inc.
VIDSIZER
  D. Franzblau
ZGRASS PAINT DEMO
  C. Giloth, Real Time Design Inc.
ABEL DEMO REEL
  W. Kovacs et al., Robert Abel and associates
*OIIIO STATE COMPUTER GRAPHICS RESEARCH GROUP TERRAIN
  MODEL*
  C. Csuri et al., Ohio State University
COMPUTER-ASSISTED DANCE NOTATION
  T. Calvert et al., Simon Fraser University
THE GRIP-75 MAN-MACHINE INTERFACE
  Computer Science Department, University of North Carolina
ARABESQUE
  J. Whitney, UCLA, 5 min.
ABEL SAMPLER
  Robert Abel and associates, 5 min.
SUBWAY
  Digital Effects, 4 min.
SORTING OUT SORTING
  R. Baecker and D. Sherman, University of Toronto, 30 min.

1982
EVANS AND SUTHERLAND DEMO '82
  Evans and Sutherland
CARLA'S ISLAND
  N. Max, Lawrence Livermore Lab
ZGRASS DEMO
  Real Time Design Inc.
ABEL '82 DEMO
  Robert Abel and Associates

GALILEO
  J. Blinn et al., Jet Propulsion Lab., NASA
DISSPLA ANIMATION
  ISSCO
TRIPLE-I DIGITAL SCENE SIMULATION REEL
  Information International Inc.
ACME CARTOON COMPANY SAMPLES '82
  ACME Company
CLOCK
  R. Balabuck, 1 min.
TRON (partial)
  Walt Disney Productions
  Animation by Robert Abel and Associates, Digital Effects,
  Information International Inc., MAGI/Synthavision
STAR TERK II (partial)
  Paramount Pictures
  Animation by Lucasfilm Ltd
DIGITAL EFFECTS '82 DEMO REEL
  Digital Effects, 7 min.
FOUR SEASONS OF JAPAN
  M. Yoshinari, NHK, 5 min.
EXPO '85
  M. Yoshinari, NHK, 30 sec.
CUCUMBER ST UDIOS DEMO REEL
  Cucumber studios
T-POT AND FACES
  S. Colson
DIGITAL PICTURES DEMO REEL
  Digital Pictures
VIDEO GRAPHICS DEMO
  Molinaire
IMATIQUE SHOWREEL
  Image West
NOVA OPENING
  D. Geschwind, NYIT
ILLUSION 2
  C. Stanbury
MAGI/SYNTHAVISION SHOWREEL
  MAGI/Synthavision
DILEMNA
  J. Halas
SYMMETRY TEST 11A
  P.A. Newell, 4 min.
GRUNMAN NON-EDGE CIG
  Grunman Aerospace, 4 min.
HUMANONON
  M. Francois, 4 min.

VOL LIBRE
  L. Carpenter, Lucasfilm, 2 min.
DREAM FLIGHT
  P. Bergeron, N. Magnenat-Thalmann and D. Thalmann
  Hautes Etudes Commerciales et Université de Montréal, 13 min.
THE CUBE CUBE
  M. Gerhard, Lawrence Livermore Lab, 2 min.
SPACE OPERATIONS SIMULATOR
  P. Galicki, 8 min.
DANCING IMAGES
  A.R. Marion, Atari Research, 18 min.

1983

GROWTH MYSTERIOUS GALAXY
  Osaka University, 5 min.
COMPUTER CREATION DEMO TAPE
  Computer Creation Inc., 8 min.
NIPPON UNIVAC KAISHA DEMO REEL
  Nippon Univac Kaisha Ltd., 3 min.
UNIVERSITY OF NORTH CAROLINA 1983 SAMPLER
  University of North Carolina, 5 min.
INTERIOR LIGHT AND SHADOW
  Hiroshima University, 5 min.
JULIA
  H.O. Peitgen, 1 min.
RETURN OF THE JEDI (partial)
  Lucasfilm Ltd, 6 min.
ACT III
  VCA Teletronics, 6 min.
CRANSTON/CSURI PRODUCTIONS DEMO REEL
  Cranston/Csuri Productions Inc., 8 min.
COMPOSITE NEWS
  N. Burson, 8 min.
LASER PRESENTATION
  S. Heminover, 7 min.
MOVIE MAKER DEMO TAPE
  Interactive Picture Systems, 4 min.
CALYPSO CAMEO
  V. Sorenson and T. DeWitt, 2 min.
PACIFIC DATA IMAGES DEMO REEL
  Pacific Data Images Inc., 4 min.
INERTIAL CONFINEMENT FUSION
  N. Max, Lawrence Livermore Lab., 3 min.
RAY TRACINGS
  Raster Technologies, 1 min

ABEL AND ASSOCIATES RECENT WORK
Robert Abel and associates, 6 min.
SNOW WHITE AND THE SEVEN PIXELS
D. Em, 2 min.
NYIT CGL SAMPLER
New York Institute of Technology, 11 min.
BLINN DEMO
J. Blinn, 4 min.
TRANSLATION
R. Moran, Graphic Communications, 3 min.
MANDALA 1983
Seibu Promotional Network, 2 min.
SUZUKI GR650 "TEMPER"
R. and B. Efx, 1 min.
SUPERMAN III, LET THE GAMES BEGIN
Atari, 2 min.
MARKS AND MARKS SAMPLE REEL
Marks and Marks, 2 min.
ONLY EYES
M. Rawlings, 3 min.
BO GEHRING DEMO TAPE
Bo Gehring associates, 8 min.
OMNIBUS VIDEO DEMONSTRATION TAPE: HI LITES
Omnibus Computer Graphics, 1 min.
NUKE THE DUKE
C. Kesler, 5 min.
EXERCISES IN DIGITAL HARMONY
J. Whitney, UCLA, 7 min.
BLOOMING STARS
E. Genda, Japan, 7 min.
OUA OUA/DIGITAL DANCER
E. Tannenbaum, 7 min.
OHIO STATE UNIVERSITY SAMPLE REEL
Ohio State University, 3 min.
ORIGAMI
NHK, Japan, 5 min.
SYSTEMS SIMULATION DEMO REEL
T. Pritchett and J. Lansdown, Systems Simulation Ltd., 3 min.
PANOPTICA PREVIEWS '83
Vertigo Graphics, 20 sec.
AURORA SYSTEMS DEMO 1983
Aurora Systems, 4 min.
ECONOMARS EARTH TOURS
Lawrence Livermoore Lab., 7 min.
VERTIGO GRAPHICS DEMO TAPE
Vertigo Graphics, 3 min.

ANTI-FRICTION DRIVE
  R. Abel and associates, 4 min.
WHEN MANDRILLS RULED THE HEAVENS
  Sandia National Lab., 2 min.
DIGITAL EFFECTS DEMO REEL
  Digital Effects Inc., 7 min.
MOBILE IMAGE DEMO REEL
  Mobile Image, 5 min.
NADIA'S CRIME
  J. Gurrin, 6 min.
VIDCOLOR DEMONSTRATION
  Mobile Image, HRS Industries and Hal Roach Studios, 3 min.
MENULAY
  B. Buxton et al., 10 min.
TELIDON ANIMATION
  E. Gordon, 5 min.
TACTICAL EDGE
  Evans and Sutherland, 10 min.
NEVER BEFORE
  Robert Abel and associates
COMPUTER GRAPHICS SHOWREEL
  Ellis and Barton Productions
BMW TECHNOLOGY
  Steiner Films, Germany
NORWICH UNION-FAMILY MAN
  Lodge/Cheesman Productions, U.K.
SHARP-VOYAGE IN PERFECTION
  Sogitec Audiovisual, France
CHANNEL 4-LOOK FORWARD
  Electronic Art, U.K.
TVS-THE REAL WORK
  Moving Picture Company, U.K.
SMITHS INDUSTRIES INDUSTRIAL TITLE SEQUENCE
  Digital Productions
COLLECTION COMPOSITES
  Pearce Studios, U.K.
JAPAN COMPUTER GRAPHICS LAB DEMO
  Japan Computer Graphics Lab, 3 min.
PIXEL PLAY
  Nakajima, Japan
SPN
  Seibu Production Network
BENESH NOTATION
  Singh
SMALLTALK
  Xerox Corp.
LISA
  Apple Computers, 3 min.

SHRIOGUMI DEMO
Shirogumi, Japan, 2 min.

1984

ABEL AND ASSOCIATES DEMO
Robert Abel and associates, Holywood, 5 min.
THE AVENTURES OF ANDRE AND WALLY B.
Lucasfilm Ltd, 2 min.
BEETHOVEN'S SIXTH IN CIG
G. Gardner, Grumman Aerospace Corp., 5 min.
THE BICYCLE COMPANY
John Cavala, 1 min.
BIO-SENSOR
Osaka University, 3 min.
BROADWAY VIDEO 84 SPECIAL EFFECTS
Broadway video, 2 min.
COMPOSITE NEWS (2nd edition)
Nancy Burson, 5 min.
CRANSTON CSURI PRODUCTIONS DEMO REEL
Cranston Csuri Productions, 6 min.
THE CUBE'S TRANSFORMATION
R. Resch, 5 min.
DIGITAL EFFECTS: OUR FAVORITES
Digital Effects, 5 min.
DIGITAL FANTASY
Visible Language Workshop, 1 min.
DIGITAL PICTURES SHOW REEL
Digital Pictures Ltd, 3 min.
DREAM HOUSE
S. Pryor, 3 min.
EIDOS SHOW REEL
Eidos, 4 min.
FIRST FLIGHT
MAGI Synthavision, 4 min.
FLY LORENZ
H. Jurgens, 4 min.
GRAPHICS AT GLOBO
TV GLOBO, 7 min.
GROWTH II: MORPHOGENESIS
Y. Kawaguchi, 6 min.
I, ROBOT
Atari Inc., 2 min.
JCGL DEMO
Japan Computer Graphics Lab, 5 min.
JOBLOVE/KAY SAMPLE REEL
Joblove/Kay Inc., 2 min.

THE LAST STARFIGHTER (preview)
  Digital Productions, 3 min.
THE LAST SUPPER AT THE COMPUTER
  Eidos, 1 min.
LINK FLIGHT SIMULATION DEMO
  The Singer Company, 2 min.
MAGI DEMO REEL
  MAGI Synthavision, 6 min.
LA MAISON VOLE
  Institut National de l'Audiovisuel, 3 min.
MARTIAN MAGNOLIA
  J. Mareda, 2 min.
THE MECHANICAL UNIVERSE
  JPL Computer Graphics Lab., 7 min.
MOVIE MAKER DEMO REEL
  Interactive Picture Systems Inc., 1 min.
NYIT COMPUTER GRAPHICS LAB.
  New York Institute of Technology, 10 min.
OHIO STATE UNIVERSITY DEMO REEL
  Ohio State University, 8 min.
OMNIBUS PRESENTATION
  Omnibus Computer Graphics Inc., 3 min.
PACIFIC DATA IMAGES DEMO
  Pacific Data Images, 6 min.
PORTAL
  D. Ackerman, 5 min.
PUZZLE
  G. Lorig, 1 min.
RAY TRACING
  M. Sweeney, D. Forsey, 4 min.
SEASONS
  Videograf, 1 min.
SKIN MATRIX $
  E. Emshwiller, 7 min.
SOUND INTO GRAPHICS
  Univ. Illinois and Univ. Utah, 2 min.
STAR RIDER
  Computer Creations, 5 min.
STILL LIFE
  E. Nakamae, 5 min.
THE SUDANESE MOEBIUS BAND
  D. Asimov, 1 min.
TANTRA '84
  Ko Nakajaima, 4 min.
TERMS OF ENTRAPMENT
  Research Institute of Scripps Clinic, 2 min.

VERTIGO PRESENTATION
  Vertigo Computer Imagery Inc., 3 min.
VIDEO WALLPAPER I
  VCA Teletronics, 3 min.
VISUAL IMAGE PRESENTATION
  Acme Graphics, 3 min.
WAG THE FLAG
  Southern Software, 5 min.
WE ARE BORN OF STARS (preliminary version)
  Toyo LINKS Corporation, 1 min.
WHISPERS IN A PLANE OF LIGHT
  Viper Optics, 10 min.
WONDER WORKS
  Omnibus Computer Graphics, 30 sec.
9600 BAUDS
  H. Huitric and M. Nahas, 5 min.
MIRA '84 DEMO REEL
  N. Magnenat-Thalmann and D. Thalmann, 5 min.

Subject Index

Symbolic Computation

Managing Editors: **J. Encarnação, P. Hayes**

Computer Graphics

Editors: **K. Bø, J. D. Foley, R. Guedj, J. W. ten Hagen, F. R. A. Hopgood, M. Hosaka, M. Lucas, A. G. Requicha**

G. Enderle, K. Kansy, G. Pfaff

Computer Graphics Programming

GKS – The Graphics Standard

1984. 93 figures, some in color. XVI, 542 pages
ISBN 3-540-11525-0

Contents: Introduction to Computer Graphics Based on GKS. – The Process of Generating a Standard. – Graphics Kernel System Programming. – The GKS Environment. – Appendix 1: GKS Metafile Format. – Appendix 2: Vocabulary. – References. – Index.

The book covers computer graphics programming on the base of the Graphical Kernel System GKS. GKS is the first international standard for the functions of a computer graphics system. It offers capabilities for creation and representation of two-dimensional pictures, handling input from graphical work-stations, structuring and manipulating pictures, and for storing and retrieving them. It represents a methodological framework for the concepts of computer graphics and establishes a common understanding for computer graphics systems, methods and applications. This book gives an overview over the GKS concepts, the history of the GKS design and the various system interfaces. A significant part of the book is devoted to a detailed description of the application of GKS functions both in a Pascal and a FORTRAN-Language environment.

Springer-Verlag
Berlin
Heidelberg
New York
Tokyo

Symbolic Computation

Managing Editors:
J. Encarnação, P. Hayes

Computer Graphics

Editors: K. Bø,
J. D. Foley, R. Guedj,
J. W. ten Hagen,
F. R. A. Hopgood,
M. Hosaka, M. Lucas,
A. G. Requicha

Springer-Verlag
Berlin
Heidelberg
New York
Tokyo

J. Encarnação, E. G. Schlechtendahl

Computer Aided Design

Fundamentals and System Architectures
1983. 176 figures (12 of them in color).
IX, 348 pages. ISBN 3-540-11526-9

Contents: Introduction. – History and Basic
Components of CAD. – The Process Aspect of
CAD. – The Architecture of CAD Systems. –
Implementation Methodology. – Engineering
Methods of CAD. – CAD Application Examples.
– Trends. – Subject Index. – Author Index. –
Color Plates.

This outstanding work is a thorough introduction
to the fundamentals of CAD. Both computer
science and engineering sciences contribute to
the particular flavor of CAD. Design is interpre-
ted as an interactive process involving specification, synthesis, analysis, and evaluation, with
CAD as a tool to provide computer assistance in
all these phases.
The book is intended primarily for computer
scientists and engineers seeking to become profi-
cient in CAD. It will help them obtain the necessary expertise in designing, evaluating or implementing CAD systems and embedding them into
existing design environments. Major topics of the
book are: system architecture, components and
interfaces, the data base aspects in CAD, man-
machine communication, computer graphics for
geometrical design, drafting and data representation, the interrelationship between CAD and
numerical methods, simulation, and optimiza-
tion. Economic, ergonomic, and social aspects
are considered as well.